D1084783

CHRISTIE WHITMAN

FOR THE PEOPLE

CHRISTIE WHITMAN

A Political Biography

FOR THE PEOPLE

by SANDY McCLURE

 Prometheus Books

59 John Glenn Drive
Amherst, NewYork 14228-2197

Published 1996 by Prometheus Books

00 99 98 97 96   5 4 3 2 1

Library of Congress Cataloging-in-Publication Data

McClure, Sandy.
   Christie Whitman for the people : a political biography / Sandy McClure.
     p.   cm.
   ISBN 1–57392–014–2 (hardcover : alk. paper)
   1. Whitman, Christine. 2. Governors—New Jersey—Biography. 3. New Jersey—Politics and government—1951–   I. Title.
F140.22.W45M33   1996
974.9'043'092—dc20
[B]   95–43777
                                         CIP

Printed in the United States of America on acid-free paper

To John C. Bensinger

Contents

Preface

On November 2, 1993, I was standing on a chair above a sea of jubilant Republicans in the Princeton Marriott ballroom when Christie Whitman claimed her victory as New Jersey's first woman governor. As a reporter for the *Trentonian,* a Trenton-based newspaper where I had covered New Jersey politics for five years, I was assigned to the Christie Whitman campaign for governor from start to finish. Starting as routine campaign coverage, her race for the statehouse turned into an amazing story of personal perseverance. From Labor Day to election day, I traveled thousands of miles and wrote more than sixty stories detailing the issues and the events of the governor's race. I watched her campaign at press conferences, diners, and farmers' markets. I saw her stumble into a political hole from which many said she could never recover, and I documented her climb to victory.

After Christie Whitman was inaugurated, I continued to report on the first eighteen months of her term as governor, recording the promises she kept, and those she didn't. While writing this political biography, I interviewed the governor, members of her staff, her friends, and her family. As I pieced together her past, certain family members, who normally shy away from press coverage, opened their homes, family albums, and scrapbooks to me. This is a story about a wealthy woman from a politically prominent family—a wife, a mother, a governor—who is fulfilling the deeper promise of her heritage.

Acknowledgments

The author thanks agent Elizabeth Frost Knappman; photographers Tom Kelly and Craig Orosz; *Trentonian* editor Gale Baldwin; *The Trentonian*; Christie Whitman; Carl Golden and Ted Pilalides of the governor's office; Lib, Georgie, and Reeve Schley III; reporter Phyllis Plitch, who followed Gov. Jim Florio's campaign and coauthored the *Trentonian*'s 1993 campaign coverage; New Jersey Office of Legislative Services Library; Nancy Risque Rohrbach; Kate Beach; Ann West; Kayla Bergeron; Gretchen, Rachel, and Mansell Bensinger; and especially Barbara and Eileen McClure for their support.

1

Christie

"I'm more comfortable in this kind of clothing."
Christie Whitman (October 21, 1993)
when asked why she was campaigning for
governor of New Jersey in a pair of blue jeans.

Perched on the branch of a huge sycamore tree overlooking the Black River at Pontefract, seven-year-old Christie Temple Todd was an American version of the mischievous Madeline in Ludwig Bemelmans's famous books. Dressed in the shabbiest clothing she could find, hidden away from grown-ups, Christie was scheming, planning the havoc she might create in the days ahead.

Christie's life was a curious combination of events and circumstances. She might spend the day pestering the teachers at the Far Hills Country Day School and then ride old Stuffy bareback to her best friend Faith's nearby farm to see what mischief they could create there. Or Mother might whisk her away on another trip to hobnob with potential presidential candidates and movie stars—a delightful setting offering a whole range of opportunities for pranks that would exasperate her parents.

Christine Todd Whitman, the first woman to become governor of New

11

Jersey, was reared at Pontefract, the Todd estate and farm in Oldwick, a small town nestled in the rolling hills of northwestern New Jersey where many of the state's privileged are born and bred. Her early years were a mixture of mundane farm life and the opportunities and privileges afforded only to those with old money and political connections.

During her 1993 campaign for governor, there were signs of the amalgam of early experiences that had shaped Christie's character. The same aristocratic woman who, when asked about taxes, said "As funny as it seems, $500 is a lot [of money]," put on blue jeans, boarded a bus, and toured the state in a meet-the-people effort that sparked her come-from-behind victory.

Born in New York City on September 26, 1946, Christie was the youngest of four children born to Webster Todd, Sr., and Eleanor Schley Todd, a politically prominent Republican couple active in national politics and part of the old-money clique tucked into rural Somerset and Hunterdon counties in New Jersey. Young Christie spent most of the first thirteen years of her life at Pontefract. Far younger than her two brothers, John and Dan, and older sister, Kate, she lived, for the most part, the life of an only child until departing in 1960 for Foxcroft School in Virginia. Christie's middle name, Temple, came from Eleanor's side of the family. After Web Todd had reared his first three children with a firm hand, Eleanor convinced him to allow her to take the lead in raising Christie.

On her father's side of the family, the Todd men were construction magnates who earned their money and borrowed their *noblesse oblige* politics from the Rockefellers. The family firms built colonial Williamsburg and Rockefeller Center, two famous landmarks, for John D. Rockefeller.

Her mother's family, the Schleys, were among the first New Yorkers to settle in Somerset County, where a pocket of moderate, wealthy Republicans were drawn, forming a small circle of politically active and socially conscious families. Her grandmother, Kate Schley, and her mother, Eleanor Schley, were strong, politically active matriarchs. Whereas Webster Todd, Sr., was to become the leader of the Republican party in New Jersey in the 1960s and 1970s, keeping it alive with his own personal finances, both Kate and Eleanor Schley were political leaders in their own right, chairing the Women's State Republican Club of New Jersey and serving as delegates to the Republican National Convention. In the 1950s, a Newark newspaper said that if New Jersey were ready for a woman governor, Eleanor Todd would be on the "short list" of candidates.

Christie's sister, Kate, who was to become a top bureaucrat in George Bush's administration, was born twelve years before Christie; her brother John, who made architectural models for a living until his death in 1988, was ten years older; her other brother, Dan, who became a self-styled Montana rancher, dabbling in politics, was eight years older.

When Christie was growing up, her playground was 232 acres of fields and woodlands through which the Black River flowed. Eleanor and Webster Todd purchased the 227-year-old Pontefract, which means "broken bridge" in Latin, in 1933, and on the grounds were a three-story white mansion, tennis courts, and a swimming pool. But the Todd estate also was a working farm with a farm house and barn where a farmer employed by the Todds grew hay and oats and raised a small number of beef cattle, dairy cows, sheep, pigs, and chickens.

The setting was perfect for a tomboy who loved to spend her days roughhousing with boys, riding horses, fishing, and climbing trees. Christie was a willful, spoiled child, a homely tomboy who tested the patience of her parents and her teachers. She was, however, a free spirit, who loved the outdoors and always had a reason for her willful behavior. She loved the farm and all its creatures, including snakes and spiders. Brother Dan says her name was shortened to Christie during childhood. "I can't recall her being called anything else." The shortened version suited her tomboy personality far better than the more formal Christine.

Her best physical features were her large blue eyes and heavy eyelashes. Otherwise, she was a plain, overweight child with stick-straight hair who wore blue jeans or the scruffiest clothing that she could get away with in the privileged atmosphere in which she grew up. Christie even tried to convince her mother to take her to a barber shop where she could get a "butch," a boy's closely cropped haircut, for her straight hair to complete the tomboy image.

"I felt, oh dear, she isn't very pretty," says her godmother, Barbara Lawrence. "Her hair was straight. Her front teeth were enormous. Later, she became wonderful looking."

Mrs. Lawrence recalls Christie as a strong child, always fighting for things and never ready to accept rules. It terrified Christie to have to behave like a girl. With a soft laugh, Christie looks back forty years and says, "The thing I hated more than anything else in the world was putting on a skirt."

Christie and the other Todd children were supposed to learn all the niceties of etiquette—e.g., how to eat properly and how to be polite—at an early age because they were included in the adult activities at the Todd home. They put on their "Sunday" clothes and went to church each week at St. John's on the Mountain, a small Episcopalian chapel in Bernardsville, and later they joined the Presbyterian church in Lamington. A skirt also was required when grandmother Alice Todd, whom the children called "Ga Ga," came to visit. Alice Todd made it clear that she disapproved of Christie's unladylike behavior, particularly her roughhousing with boys.

The Todds hired Swedish nannies to help care for Christie for about a year, then a housekeeper, Marie Stewart, a black woman from South Carolina, helped with her care for approximately nine years. Christie can still recall the aroma of Marie's cooking wafting through the house. "She was one of the world's greatest cookie bakers. She had a wonderful chocolate-and-vanilla swirl cookie. And the best barbecued spareribs in the world." The family always had fresh milk, butter, and meat from the smoke house. "Mother would have a special recipe for basting the meat and smoking it," Christie remembers.

While growing up at Pontefract, Christie often played alone, looking to the horses and farm animals for companionship. Her best friend, Faith Heaton, lived on a nearby farm. But, aside from Faith, Christie preferred to play with boys. Shunning dolls, she wanted to be outdoors doing the things that were generally restricted to boys in the 1940s and 1950s. "I was not the world's most wildly popular child. I was a roughneck bully and tomboy. I tended to have a couple of good friends, and that was about it."

Christie also had a terrible temper. "I would smash things around and stomp," she admits with her eyes revealing the warmth of the memory. "Growing up on a farm with an older brother, one learns a lot of descriptive adjectives, which I would use from time to time." When Christie's sister, Kate, was sixteen years old, she would warn her friends about the four-year-old Christie by telling them, "Be aware. I have a younger sister who sits under the table and chews her hair and bites people."

More than anything else, Christie loved to ride the horses at Pontefract.

She would throw a bridle on one of the ponies and ride bareback to the Heatons, put a western saddle on one of the horses and pretend she was out west, or settle for an English saddle and go fox hunting. In addition, she spent some of her younger years cleaning out stalls because Web and Eleanor Todd demanded that their children help with the care of the riding equipment and horses.

During her early years, she saddled and rode Stuffy, a Welsh pony from South Carolina on which all the Todd children learned to ride, and she also rode his companion, a broken-down thoroughbred mare named Patty. Later, she enjoyed an old, cold-blooded dun (a dull grayish-brown horse), which her mother had discovered on the beach in Atlantic City, where it was giving rides to children. When Eleanor found out that the horse was named "Kate," she thought the dun should be a part of the family and brought it home for Christie. Later, when Christie was nineteen years old, her parents purchased Vagabond, her hunter. The boys who tried to pursue Christie quickly learned that they had competition. One would-be suitor, his ego damaged, finally wrote her a letter saying that it was obvious she cared more for her horses than she did for him.

When Christie wasn't spending her time riding, she was catching bugs, searching for snakes, or fishing in the Black River. "Dad made me practice fly fishing, which didn't interest me," Christie says, her forehead wrinkling slightly as she talks about fishing with artificial flies for bait. "I was interested in catching fish. Most of my fishing was with worms. I dug them and put them on a hook. I would fish in the river a lot, catching sunnies and catfish."

Always an athlete, in her early years she was leaping in and out of the swimming pool, climbing trees, and scaling hay piles inside the barn. As she grew older, she played tennis and golf at the Somerset Hills Country Club. While playing golf and other sports, Christie had complete confidence in her ability to compete at whatever she tried. "When everyone else was afraid of missing the ball, she would always assume she could hit it, and she did," remembers her sister, Kate.

While living in the world of the privileged and wealthy, Christie managed to spend a great deal of her time with the family of Meryl Stiles, the farmer who lived in Pontefract's tenant house and worked the farm. When she was nine, Christie hid in the hayloft with Meryl's son Eddie and smoked cigarettes. And Meryl, himself, gave her one of only two spankings she received as a child.

Meryl did most of the farm work, but sometimes Christie would help. "We all helped bale hay because he didn't have automatic balers. We had to toss them up on the back of the wagon and then load them into the hayloft. There was a time when we grew oats and did the harvesting. Every once in a while, we would pitch in to milk the cows."

From kindergarten through the eighth grade, Christie attended the Far Hills Country Day School, a small, exclusive school filled with children from wealthy families living in the area. The landed gentry of Somerset and Hunterdon counties sent their children to the school to prepare them for the exclusive boarding schools they would attend during their later years. One of Christie's classmates was Malcolm S. Forbes, Jr., the son of the New York publisher, who lived nearby.

A stubborn, difficult child, Christie frequently misbehaved at school. "I would usually get right to the edge. I just was kind of bullheaded, shall we say, doing my own thing."

At five years of age, Christie gave her kindergarten teacher the most memorable day of her career by bringing a dead duck to school. "My brother [John] had shot the duck. I was so outraged that I picked it up and refused to give it up. I carried this dead duck with me all day, all morning in kindergarten, and my teacher couldn't get it away from me."

Her brother Danny was at the Far Hills school for one year while Christie was there, and one of Christie's favorite pastimes was tagging along with the older boys. "I can remember, I always wanted to sit with his friends because I always liked the older boys. And they would all do anything they could to get way from Danny's wretched younger sister." Occasionally, Danny and his friends would allow Christie to tag along while they were making home movies. For one movie, they dressed Christie in a red shirt and an old German helmet and turned her into a wounded soldier in a scene filmed along the Black River. At one point in the film, she was hoisted onto the shoulder of one of the boys and placed in a World War II ambulance and whisked away.

In 1952, while Christie was pestering the older boys at the Far Hills Country Day School, her parents were convincing Dwight Eisenhower to run for president. Christie's contact with national politics began that year when vice-presidential nominee Richard Nixon made a campaign stop in New Jersey. Six-year-old Christie and five-year-old Malcolm S. Forbes, Jr., together, presented Pat Nixon with two dolls for her daughters, Julie and Tricia.

However, Eisenhower's victory in 1952 meant that Christie would miss the second grade at Far Hills. Webster Todd was one of the Eastern Republican party chiefs who had helped Eisenhower win the election, and in September 1953, when Christie was seven years old, President Eisenhower appointed her father economic minister to the North Atlantic Treaty Organization (NATO).

When the Todds sailed to Paris, France, Christie's eyes filled with tears because she had to leave behind her dog, "Ike" (named after Eisenhower). To help Christie feel at home in Paris, she was allowed to pick a new dog, the first of the Scottish terriers that she would own. The impish Christie thought she had found the perfect dog because Casimir was the only puppy who got excited enough to pee on the rug at the fancy Paris home where they went to make the selection.

The Todds lived at 19 Rue du General Appert, a brownstone home where guests like Harold Stassen, the former governor of Minnesota who had vied with Eisenhower for the GOP presidential nomination the year before, would visit. They enrolled Christie in the city's American School. It seemed a perfect choice because the children spoke English and her classmates were the children of ambassadors. But Christie hated the school. She felt as if she were locked in an American cell with the excitement of Paris beyond her reach.

Bored with her classes, she decided to liven them up by telling stories that kept her classmates mesmerized during the show-and-tell period. In vivid detail, Christie described how her father would chase her mother around the dining room table with a hatchet.

Shocked at the stories, the school's headmaster called Eleanor Todd to the school for a conference. Christie recalls: "This headmaster looked at Mother and said to her, 'Well, I have to tell you, it is very disturbing to Christie when Mr. Todd chases you around the dining room table with a hatchet.' " Deciding that she didn't want her daughter educated at a school whose teachers would believe such a story, Christie's mother removed her daughter from the school.

Next, Christie was placed in a French school where nobody spoke English. "That was wonderful. I became fluent in French in no time, and I loved it."

Yet several problems soon developed. First, the school only met in the morning, an inconvenience for Eleanor Todd who had afternoon events to attend as the wife of the American economic minister. Second, while the school did supervise afternoon play at the Bois de Boulogne, a nearby Parisian park, Christie would sneak away and spend her afternoons in front of the park benches where she would watch couples necking. "I was riveted by them. I had never seen anything like it in this country."

Exasperated with the school situation, the Todds decided to send Christie to a third school, a Catholic school in Paris. But that didn't go well either. "I hated it. I finally ran away from that one."

> They used to make me eat fish eyeballs. And all the children would sit around the table and make fun of Dad's name, "Webster." And the nuns, if they didn't like you, they locked you in the dog run, and all the other kids would stand around and make fun of you. I never got locked in there, but I thought it was a horrible place.

Believing that they had exhausted all their options for schools in Paris, the Todds told Christie that she didn't have to go to school anymore. "So that was the best of all possible worlds. She [mother] would have to find somebody to take care of me, and I wouldn't have to go to school any more."

Aside from her difficulties at school, Christie loved Paris. She befriended the chauffeur to the ambassador who lived next door. "I made great friends with him. Mother was panicked one day because she lost me. She did eventually find me downstairs in the garage having a tête-à-tête with this man, which also didn't please her."

One of Christie's favorite activities was going to the race track on weekends where children were allowed to place bets. Fluent in French, she would go down to the paddock prior to the race and talk to the jockeys before placing her bet. She won every single race until her mother objected to her placing a bet on a horse that literally looked like an old bag of bones. Forced to bet on the horse her mother selected, Christie's winning streak ended: the horse she bet on came in last while the bag-of-bones won.

Still trying to figure out what to do with Christie while the family was in Paris, Eleanor Todd sent her to a resident camp in Switzerland, but with the same negative results. "I behaved miserably, but I also was miserable," says Christie with a quick hand gesture that expressed the frustration she felt at the time. "I was homesick. I was spoiled and didn't like taking orders."

The son of Buster Crabbe, the world-champion swimmer and motion picture star, was also a camper while Christie was there, and she was furious when the camp counselors (trying to protect Buster Crabbe from the prying eyes of the youngsters) locked Christie and the other campers in their cabins when the film star picked up his son. When a second camp incident angered Christie, she organized an all-out revolt.

> We had a counselor who was wonderful, but she got married, so she was no longer going to be with us. And the camp gave us this other counselor whom we all hated. So I organized a revolt and I got everybody to take their most favorite possession, a Teddy bear or whatever it was, and climb up this tree. I climbed up the bottom branch, so nobody could get down past me, but I was just high enough so no one could grab me. We staged a sit-down strike in the tree until they changed counselors, which they did. It worked.

From an early age Christie knew how to get what she wanted. "She knew what she wanted to do and when she wanted to do it," remembers her sister, Kate. "She would pursue it until it happened or didn't happen. She knew her own mind. She was pretty focused."

During their year in Paris, the Todds decided to load the Christmas gifts in trunks and travel by train to the Swiss Alps where they celebrated Christmas at a hotel in Zermatt, a village within sight of the Matterhorn.

Christie left an unusual impression on the Zermatt residents the day her father pulled her home on a sled through the village streets. She was angry because Web Todd had interrupted her sledding activities with a favorite male friend. And unbeknownst to her father, who had his back to Christie, she began making faces and sticking her tongue out at passers-by. "He noticed that everybody on the street was stopping, and they would sort of smile and shake their heads. We got half way up the hill, and he turned around to look at what I was doing. Fortunately for me, his sense of humor had reasserted itself before we got back to the hotel."

When the Todds returned to the United States, Christie went back to the Far Hills Country Day School and her old antics. One day, she convinced a baby-sitter who had spent the night that she was allowed to dress herself for school. "Unfortunately, Mother came to pick me up. I was in my khaki shorts and a baggy shirt and dirty sneakers. I was surprised they hadn't sent me home from school." (This incident later was mirrored when Christie decided to wear a royal blue Giants sweatshirt one Saturday during the 1993 race for governor. Dressed in the informal attire, she campaigned in the morning at tailgate parties in Giants Stadium and then surprised guests by wearing it to a formal brunch hosted by the New Jersey Federation of Republican Women, the organization both her mother and grandmother had chaired.)

Shortly after returning home from Paris, the Todds decided to go on a world tour, and while they were away, Christie lived with her Aunt Lib Schley, who more than forty years later at eighty-six has not forgotten the experience. "When I got home that night, Christie was crying and crying. She kept saying, 'I've got to go home.' She was paralyzed with fright."

Without success, Aunt Lib tried to explain to Christie that she had to learn how not to be selfish, that she had to allow her parents to take their vacation. Unable to get Christie to stop crying, Aunt Lib decided to entertain her by playing the card game, Old Maid, with the family dog. Soon Christie began to notice that every time the dog was dealt the Old Maid and Aunt Lib exclaimed, the dog got so excited that it farted. Once Christie started laughing at the dog's noises, she couldn't stop.

The next day, Christie brought a friend home from school. When they arrived at Aunt Lib's Island Stock Farm, Christie pulled Aunt Lib aside and explained to her that they needed to help the girl. Her friend's parents were on vacation, too, and she needed to learn how to be unselfish. "I thought, God, at that age, she is registering what an adult told her, and she is taking care of someone else," Lib Schley recalls.

Christie became active in her parents' political activities at an early age. From the age of eight, she would accompany her mother, a poll worker, to the firehouse in Oldwick where they would count paper ballots until one or two o'clock in the morning.

In 1956, at the age of nine, she attended the Republican National Convention in San Francisco, where President Eisenhower was nominated for a second term. Christie's antics drew attention from the national press corps when she attended a news conference, which had been organized by her mother and two other GOP women, wearing a Mickey Mouse hat with a novelty dagger poking out of her head. "I sat solemnly in the audience at this press conference with the hat and dagger," recalls Christie. Once the reporters saw her, they lost interest in the press conference. "All they wanted was pictures of this wretch with the Mickey Mouse hat and the dagger." One of the organizers was furious. "I mean she was livid. Here was this horrible, fat, homely child up there with this dagger through her head." Nevertheless, Eleanor Todd laughed. "I think she had given up by then. There wasn't much she could do with me."

When Eisenhower gave his acceptance speech, Christie gained more attention by standing just below the platform with a leather golf-tee holder, which she had sewn for Eisenhower, grasped in her hand. As the president came down from the dais, Christie handed the leather pouch to him. Later that day when Eisenhower was getting on a train to leave the city and reporters asked him what he was going to do next, he held up the golf-tee holder while photographers snapped his picture.

Several months after the convention, Christie, now ten years old, made her first successful attempt at political fundraising. Positioning herself six miles from Pontefract in the Hunterdon County area where an annual point-to-point steeplechase was held on the last Saturday of October, Christie and three classmates from the Far Hills Country Day School covered themselves with "Vote Eisenhower" stickers and buttons while they sold lemonade. About one thousand members of the local gentry had gathered together for the race, and at the end of the day, the proceeds of about $10 were sent to the Republican National Committee.

Even during her preteen years when she was hobnobbing with presidents, Christie still continued to test the patience of her school teachers and fellow students. In one English class, she forced the teacher to explain the proper use of the adverb "where" for an entire period. When he realized she was joking, he was furious.

Later that morning when Christie was whispering and moving around in the classroom, the angry teacher told her to put her hands on the desk and keep them there until he told her to remove them. Still furious with Christie, the teacher left the classroom without speaking to her when the bell rang for lunch. "And so I sat there through the entire lunch period because Friday lunches were gross anyway. I didn't want to eat all those fish sticks. I sat there with my hands on the desk until the headmaster came in. He was furious at me. I said I was told not to move or take my hands off the desk until the teacher told me to, and he didn't tell me to. He wasn't talking to me, so I was still there."

Christie learned to love music at an early age, but the students at the day school made it clear that she had little musical talent. "I learned in grade school that I did not have a voice that was worthy of projection. I got hissed at during one Christmas performance by the girl standing next to me, who said, 'Why don't you be quiet so you don't ruin the whole thing?' Which is devastating at age twelve. After that I never opened my mouth again."

Christie had an earlier inkling that there was a problem. "We always gave a Gilbert and Sullivan play every year. Our English teacher gave me a solo, albeit brief, one year. The best thing that Danny could think of when he came up afterward was, 'Well at least we could hear you go off key.'" (When the governor travels with the New Jersey state troopers, she tries not to sing out loud to the music played in the car, resorting to whispering under her breath.)

Even into her preteen years, Christie spent her free time outdoors at Pontefract. When she was twelve years old, she liked to go down to the Pontefract pond and use an air rifle to thin out the frog population. And one Oldwick resident told neighbors that he had difficulty voting for Christie in the fall of 1993 because as a young girl, she was always riding her horse through his property without an apology.

The farm animals remained her companions, but on one occasion a neighbor's boar gave her the most frightening experience of her early years at Pontefract.

Faith's father had a boar that we bred to our sows. Topper was huge. He was enormous: four hundred to five hundred pounds. I went into the barn one night. It was just about dusk. I opened the barn door to go in to see the horses, and there was Topper, nose-to-nose with me. He had escaped from the neighboring farm and had come over to visit our sows. I have never run so fast in my life.

But it wasn't just five-hundred-pound boars that frightened the young Christie. More than anything else, she feared her father's temper. "If you woke up and heard him whistling and the vacuum cleaner going, you knew you wanted to do downstairs the back way because that meant he was in a terrible humor," Christie said with an obvious fondness in her voice for her father. "When he was in a bad humor, he vacuumed and whistled. The house got very clean."

John, Danny, and Kate felt their father's anger far more than Christie, who, because she was so much younger than the others, had a different relationship with her father. "Dad had been very strict with the other three. Mother interceded for me. They all got whomped. He had a belt that he used with some alacrity on both my brothers." While the other children didn't want to risk testing their father, Christie was not awed by him. The two developed a more relaxed relationship, and Christie was always able to turn his anger into laughter. Yet on one occasion, Christie's father was particularly determined to spank her because she had taken her rabbit out of its cage, and when Webster Todd returned the animal to its hutch, it bit him.

> He came after me. He was going to get me. He got me up into their bedroom, and I was so paralytic with fear, I was screaming bloody murder, which I guess he finally decided was pretty funny because he locked the door. Mother was pounding on the door, saying, "Don't hit her." I was shrieking bloody murder. He had started to laugh. He said: "I'll beat the bed and you scream some more." So he beat the bed, and it didn't take anything for me to scream some more. Then he opened the door, and I went like a shot past Mother, who was sure I had been reduced to blood and pulp.

Although she escaped without the intended spanking, Christie concedes, "I didn't let the rabbit out again when he told me not to."

Ironically, Christie's mother was the only parent to ever really spank her. Christie was nine years old at the time, and the family had taken a trip out West to the A Bar A Ranch in Wyoming. "There was a rodeo, and I kept climbing in the shoot with the bucking bronco, which Mother didn't think was a great idea," explains Christie matter-of-factly. "She finally said that if I ever did it again, she would send me back to the cabin and spank me, which I did, and she did."

In the early years of her life, Christie also experienced quiet, peaceful times at the farm. She spent a great deal of time with her mother, who, in some ways, was more like a friend. In the end, it was her mother's view of the world and politics that had the most influence on Christie. The two of them would walk every day along the river while they discussed their lives, politics, and the family.

In the years to come, whether she was planning her wedding, burying her parents, or enduring the mudslinging of a gubernatorial race, Christie would return to her home base of Pontefract. "She just flourishes at Ponte-fract," says her lifelong friend Nancy Risque Rohrbach. "She gets so much strength from being home. She thrives on the earthiness of her home."

Christie had a special tree all her own at Pontefract, a sycamore whose branches stretched over the river. She would climb up in the tree and scheme, think, or write poetry. Fascinated with the Civil War, partly because her mother's family had one of the best collections of civil war memorabilia in the country, Christie wrote one particular poem about a young boy going off to the Civil War. During her final, eighth-grade year at the Far Hills Country Day School, the poem won the school's poetry prize.

But in general, Christie wasn't a good student. "The dirty secret of my life is that I never graduated from grade school because I couldn't pass Latin in the eighth grade," Christie says with a hint of personal disap-pointment. "My diploma says, over in the lower right-hand corner, if you turn it over, 'except for Latin.' I hated rote memorization, and I just would-n't do it. Poor Mother would go nuts trying to help me with things like Latin verb conjugations. I just hated it and wouldn't do it."

At the age of thirteen, just before leaving for Foxcroft, Christie became more involved in her parents' political activities. She began door-to-door canvassing with her mother, and in the summer of 1960 she attended the Republican National Convention in Chicago which nominated Richard Nixon as its standard bearer. Through her position on the platform com-mittee, Eleanor Todd arranged a convention job for Christie that made her the envy of every teenager at the event. She was the page for Efrem Zim-balist, Jr., star of the popular television show "77 Sunset Strip," who was a convention guest. "I was just walking around with my mouth hanging open," Christie recalls with a chuckle. "I would have laid down and died for him, I thought he was so attractive. And he was so nice to me, even though he was being followed around by this thing with her tongue hanging out."

In the fall of 1960, as she was about to turn fourteen, Christie left her family and Pontefract to attend Foxcroft School, the quasi-military boarding school her mother and sister had attended. The school was nestled in the fox-hunt country of Middleburg, Virginia, and it made sense to her parents that Christie would like it too. However, Christie tended to balk at the structure and rules set down for her life at the same time that she held firm to Pontefract, her parents, and her political heritage.

2

Lap of Politics

"I was steeped in government as a way to affect policy and make changes. If you are going to complain, you better do something about it or you lose your right to bitch. That's what my dad used to say."

Christie Whitman (October 11, 1993)
during an interview at her campaign headquarters.

Visitors to Pontefract would say, "It's too bad that Christie and her father have such a terrible relationship." What they did not realize was that the bantering between father and daughter was a demonstration of affection. And, in many cases, it was an instruction in politics.

Whether she was arguing with her father about politics at the dining-room table, counting paper ballots with her mother at the Oldwick firehouse, or listening to a speech at a Republican National Convention, Christie's early years were steeped in politics.

Her political heritage ran deep, coming not just from her father, who chaired the New Jersey Republican party in the 1960s and 1970s, but also from her mother, who was active in national politics, and her grandparents, who were leaders in their own right in state and national politics.

Christie was reared in a family of strong women who were politically active and became dominant forces within their communities as well as their families. The menfolk were wealthy, successful businessmen and lawyers from New York, who settled in the scenic fox-hunt country of northwestern New Jersey and made politics their avocation.

All four of Christie's grandparents were at a Republican event in the early 1930s when they met and decided that Webster "Web" Todd and Eleanor "Tootsie" Schley should be introduced. Eleanor Schley was the only daughter of Reeve and Kate Schley, part of the exclusive circle of landed gentry in Far Hills, New Jersey.

The Schley family originated in the Palatinate region of southwest Germany and immigrated to upstate New York in the late 1700s. Grant Schley, the founder of Far Hills, was working in the peach district of Canandaigua, New York, when he caught the eye of New York City banker George Baker, who talked him into taking a job with the First National Bank. Grant stood out among the workers because he was strong enough to load peaches on train cars by himself, when in most cases it took two men, and because he could quickly add whole columns of figures.

Grant Schley agreed to relocate to New York City, worked at the bank, and eventually married the boss's daughter, Elizabeth Baker. From his brother who was a land trader, Schley purchased 1,500 acres of land extending across the Watchung Mountains of New Jersey thirty-five miles west of New York City and built the first Schley home, "Fronheim" or "happy home," on the property in 1890. When Elizabeth Baker Schley arrived at the New Jersey site by wagon, she insisted on calling it "Far Hills."

The Schleys were one of a handful of wealthy New York families that purchased large tracts of land in the Far Hills countryside at the turn of the century, often using the land for weekend homes and fox hunts.

The Schley family (including Christie) still populates the area, residing in elegant country estates set in a backdrop of hundreds of acres of scenic fields and woodlands crossed by streams and dotted with ponds.

Members of the small, elite group of families that settled in the land straddling Somerset and Hunterdon counties at the turn of the century were the Bradys (including Nicholas Brady, secretary of the treasury for President Reagan) and the Dillons (including C. Douglas Dillon, secretary of the treasury for President Kennedy). Others residing in the area included New York publisher Malcolm S. Forbes; the Frelinghuysen family, which sent six family members to Congress; and late congresswoman Millicent Fenwick.

Christie's grandfather Reeve Schley was Grant Schley's nephew, and Grant treated Reeve like a son, eventually encouraging him to come from his home in New York to Far Hills by giving him land and making him his personal attorney. A graduate of Yale University with a law degree from Columbia University, the six-foot-four, pipe- and cigar-smoking Reeve Schley was vice president of Chase Bank in New York, where he handled the Russian government accounts. Reeve was president of the American-Russian Chamber of Commerce and during World War II, was in charge of the Soviet division of the U.S. Lend-Lease Administration.

Locally, he purchased the controlling shares and was chairman of the Somerset Trust Company, an investment that seemed small at the time but later proved lucrative for his descendants. When Grant Schley died in 1917, Reeve became the trustee of the Far Hills Land Corporation, which owned and managed Grant Schley's land.

After serving as fuel administrator for New York City during World War I, Reeve, a staunch Republican, was elected mayor of Far Hills. He served as chairman of the New Jersey Republican State Finance Committee in 1932. And ten years later he was named president of the board of the state Department of Institutions and Agencies, where he also served as acting commissioner until he suffered a stroke in 1956. Well-read with one of the finest collections of Civil War writings in the country, he served for years as a trustee of Yale University.

Reeve and Christie's grandmother Kate Schley, a petite, athletic woman, owned Ripplebrook, a 200-acre estate in Far Hills. They resided and entertained political guests in a thirty-room American country house of stone and brick with a paneled ballroom constructed of seventy-foot-long floor boards from the Samuel Shipman's Hotel in Rocky Hill, Connecticut. The home's balconies stretched along the south side of the estate, overlooking Mine Brook, a scenic pond populated with swans, and acres of manicured fields where Kate insisted on keeping a white horse simply for its scenic effect.

Kate was a spirited, upbeat woman, almost Pollyanna-like in her love for life and her support for whatever venture her grandchildren wanted to undertake. She had three children: Christie's mother, Eleanor; Reeve Schley, Jr.; and Jackie, who died in a fire at the home in 1931.

Family members describe Kate as strong-willed and determined to have her own way. Without excuse, the extended family was expected for Sunday lunch. When Kate celebrated her eightieth birthday, Christie's brother Dan wrote a poem about how she had managed to get her grandchildren into the tower of London during one of their many trips to England:

> I remember in London, we went to the tower,
> If we'd been in the line, we'd have waited an hour.
> At the entrance she paused and she cased the joint
> Then she turned to the keeper and drove home her point.
> Sixty people just gaped as we passed through the gate
> And somebody asked, "How'd you do it, Aunt Kate?"
> "Oh, it's really quite simple, she said with a grin,
> I talked and I talked until he let us in!"
> But the thing that surprised us was that no one got mad
> For Gran has that something that makes you feel glad—
> Glad to be living and filled up with pride,
> Glad to take all life's hardships, and not break your stride
> To look to tomorrow, forget yesterday
> And no matter what happens, to always seem gay.
> No mind how great her problems, she always has time
> To lay them aside and then listen to mine.

According to Schley family lore, it was very likely that Kate Schley, despite the family's German heritage, told the gatekeeper at the tower of London that she was related to Henry VIII. Christie talks about her grandmother with pride. "Granny portrayed the image to many of being a scatterbrain, but she wasn't. She did not take no for an answer. If she wanted something, at the end of the day, she would get it one way or the other." For example, after Reeve Schley had a stroke in 1956, Kate strapped him into a chair and placed him on top of a car so that he could continue to watch the fox hunts at Ripplebrook. Another favorite story is told about Kate's travels with the family in Europe. "Everybody was arguing the way families argue. They were handing sandwiches around the car, and they handed Granny the sandwich. She passed it right out the window, and there went somebody's lunch, which broke the ice for that day."

Despite having grown up in Brooklyn, New York, Kate Prentice Schley was an Annie Oakley-style markswoman who could shoot a hare or a grouse on the Moors in Scotland as easily as any man. An athlete, she rode well and, with Reeve, she captured numerous country club tennis championships at the turn of the century. She was willing to try anything, including trout fishing in Alaska.

Kate literally stumbled into national politics, according to her daughter-in-law, Lib Schley. When prohibition ended in 1933, Kate was appointed to lead the Republican discussion on liquor control in New Jersey. She did such a poor job at delivering a speech on the issue to a group of New Jersey Republicans that she drew a sympathy vote and was elected national committeewoman. In the position until 1952, Kate, accompanied by Reeve Schley, attended a number of Republican National Conventions. Wearing a dark dress accented by two strands of pearls and long white gloves, gray-haired Kate was a member of the escort committee for former President Herbert Hoover when he stepped to the convention rostrum in 1952.

Well-known for her political parties and women's political gatherings at Ripplebrook, Kate served as chairwoman of the Women's State Republican Club of New Jersey, now known as the New Jersey Federation of Republican Women. "I can remember those parties at Ripplebrook during Governor [Alfred] Driscoll's campaign [in the 1940s]," says Dan Todd. "The Republican women were . . . all colors and shapes and sizes and very traditional in their approach to life. I recall them as rather stout and giving their orations in stentorian tones. Nonetheless, they were enthusiastic supporters and workers." Christie recounts one particular story: "Mother always loved to describe the time one of the rather heavy women from the women's federation was walking along the balcony and fell through. But it was only one leg. As least she didn't fall all the way down, or it would have been serious."

Kate also instilled a love for Peter Pan in both Eleanor and Christie. A Peter Pan garden was built at Ripplebrook, and when there was a full moon, the children would find a fairy ring in the yard composed of little presents and flowers. (Whitman still collects books by *Peter Pan*'s author, Sir James M. Barrie, and whenever she visits England, she stops at the Peter Pan statue in Kensington.)

A religious woman, Kate traveled several times a week to St. John's on the Mountain, the Episcopalian chapel in Bernardsville, where she would take communion. However, as a child, Christie was troubled by her grandmother's failure to recover from the death of her son, Jackie, in 1931 and the death of her husband, Reeve, in 1960. "In a funny way, when my grandfather died, I remember thinking she was a bit of a hypocrite, which was a harsh thing to say, but she was so upset," Christie recalls with some discomfort. "If you believe in God that much, you've got to get over it because you believe they are going on to a better life."

Although Jackie died in a house fire at Ripplebrook fifteen years before Christie was born, she could see the effect it had on her mother, who was forced to leave college in 1931 to care for Kate. "Mother always had a little bit of a sense that Granny would have been happier if she had been the one who had died." Christie says with a touch of sadness in her voice for both women. "I mean, that's not true, and it's unfair, but obviously it's an emotion that she carried with her. That took a real toll on Mother, for which I, being a devout loyalist to my mother, always held a little bit against my grandmother."

Christie's paternal ancestors, the Todds, were Scottish Presbyterian ministers and missionaries who migrated to America from Pontefract, England, located in North Yorkshire, a county in northern England near the border of Scotland, Christie recounts. (Todd means "fox" in Scottish.) "The story is that the patriarch of the family, the sheriff, was found with the mayor's wife in a condition that was not conducive to longevity in the town, and the sons were so mortified by their father's behavior that they all came across the Atlantic. They all emigrated. . . . He was the sheriff, and he was caught in bed with the mayor's wife, and that didn't go down too well with either of the spouses. So the sons were the ones who left town."

The Todds settled in the colony at New Haven, Connecticut, and then moved westward. Christie's great-grandfather was a minister, following his calling in Wisconsin, Minnesota, and then Kansas. According to family lore, as part of his ministerial duties in the western territory, he organized two posses to try to capture outlaw Jesse James, who committed his crimes along the Kansas-Missouri border.

Christie's grandfather, John R. Todd, came to New Jersey from Kansas in 1884 by hitchhiking with his brother, William, to attend Princeton University. "They were good Presbyterians,* and that's all you needed to go to Princeton at that time," Christie's brother Dan Todd contends.

---

*The College of New Jersey, which later became Princeton University, was founded by Presbyterian churchmen in 1746.

After graduating from Princeton in 1889, John R. Todd was a teacher at the Protestant College in Beirut, Lebanon, for two years. It was there that he met Alice Bray, a schoolteacher from Wisconsin who had come to visit her sister, the wife of one of the instructors. The romance began when they left Beirut for New York on the same ship in 1891, and they were married in July 1895.

Returning to New York City, John R. formed the law firm of Irons & Todd with an old Princeton classmate, Henry Clay Irons. They intended to practice law, but when the fledgling firm acquired a half-finished apartment from one of its clients, they ended up in the construction business. Starting with apartment houses on New York's West Side, John R. eventually constructed much of New York's skyline, becoming one of the nation's most successful general contractors.

Founding the firm of Todd, Robertson, and Todd, John R. built many of New York's famous structures, including the Postum Building, the Barclay Hotel, the Ritz Towers, the Cunard Building, and the Graybar Building. During his stay in New York, John R. formed a professional relationship and personal friendship with John D. Rockefeller, and as a result, the firm of Todd & Brown (the construction company belonging to his son, Web Todd) was hired in 1928 to reconstruct colonial Williamsburg. That same year, John R. and Web Todd began a four-year association as general contractors for the construction of New York City's Rockefeller Center, at that time the largest privately owned business and entertainment center in the world.

In 1901, John R. and Alice Todd moved from New York City to Summit, New Jersey, where he served as finance chairman for the New Jersey GOP and was an active leader in the state and national party. His power and influence in the party grew for the better part of the next three decades. In 1928, according to his autobiography, *Living a Life,* published by Alice in 1947, John R. raised a record $734,000 as chairman of the Republican State Finance Committee.

Although he was a teetotaler himself, John R., of imposing, sometimes stern appearance with gray eyes that could pin an opponent to the wall, worked at the national level to convince Republicans to change their unpopular prohibition plank. He also advised national GOP leaders to broaden the party's base to attract new members. (Ironically, it was the same strategy his granddaughter would recommend forty years later during her early years with the Republican National Committee.) "The only way out, as he [John R.] saw it, was for the Republicans to broaden their political base; to create, if necessary, a new party to bring in those people in the South who for traditional reasons could not bring themselves to vote the Republican ticket," wrote William P. Vogel, Jr., in the introduction to *Living a Life.*

John R. died in 1945, a year before Christie was born. The older grandchildren remember him as a "difficult man." Nevertheless, two generations later in statements about the importance of family life, Christie would echo these sentiments John R. expressed in his autobiography: "Looking at my own life and thinking of the lives of others, I realize the serious danger that faces us all of becoming so involved in earning a living that we forget the living of our lives."

The grandchildren describe the straitlaced Alice Todd, who died in 1956, as "not a whole lot of fun" and "rigid in her ways." The Todds had a summer home on Long Island which the grandchildren would visit. They recall how "Ga Ga," who had a prominent nose and square jaw, would tap her cane loudly at 9:30 P.M. to tell Christie's sister, Kate, that it was time to send her suitor home. When playing games with "Ga Ga," the children either played by the rules or took their turn over again.

The union of Web Todd and Eleanor Schley was orchestrated by John R. and Alice Todd and Kate and Reeve Schley, who thought the two should meet. Eleanor, who was thirteen years younger than Web, had dark hair, gray-blue eyes, and a figure like a flapper. At his parents' prompting, Web asked Eleanor out for dinner, and she agreed to meet him at his New York apartment.

Web graduated from Princeton University in 1922, studied law for one year at Cambridge University, and then attended Fordham University Law School, where he graduated in 1927. After his law practice blossomed into the firm of Todd & Brown, construction engineers, he began his ten-year project to restore colonial Williamsburg.

Eleanor Schley told Christie that she was in love with Web Todd before she ever saw him. "She always described how she heard his whistle before she ever saw him and fell in love with his whistle. Then she saw him come down the stairs, and he was the most devastatingly attractive man she had ever seen in her life, and that was that." The five-foot-eleven Web had dark hair and gray eyes that twinkled when he joked and turned to steel when he was angry. He had inherited the Todds' prominent nose. Web Todd proposed to Eleanor in a horse-drawn carriage in Central Park. When she hesitated, in his backhanded way of joking, he told her, "You had better take the cookies while they are being passed."

A thirty-three-year-old man-about-town, Web went to the Chase Manhattan Bank to ask Reeve Schley for Eleanor's hand in marriage. "My grandfather kept him sitting in the outer lobby for forty-five minutes," Christie recounts. "Dad, a successful businessman, did not appreciate this. And then my grandfather brought him in and asked him the typical question, 'Can you keep her in the style to which she has grown accustomed?' He [Web] never quite got over that. I think he felt Ma was getting a pretty good deal at that point."

When Web and Eleanor married in 1933, her parents gave them their residence at Pontefract as a wedding present. (The land was not part of the original tract of land owned by Grant Schley but had been purchased by Reeve after he moved to Far Hills.) A German farmer had resided at the farm, keeping some of the animals in the old farmhouse, and the Todds, through Web's construction contacts, had the home refurbished.

The Todds had their first three children, Kate, Dan, and John, before World War II. During those early years, Eleanor, who had graduated from Foxcroft School and attended Barnard and Sarah Lawrence colleges without receiving a degree, was active in founding the Far Hills Country Day School, a large white home where about fifty students were educated from kindergarten through the eighth grade.

Before war broke out, Web managed the theater at Rockefeller Center's Radio City Music Hall. He was assigned the difficult task of turning the music-hall concept into a money-maker. During the war, he was director of the Kingsbury Ordnance Plant in LaPorte, Indiana, and Eleanor was in charge of the New Jersey Red Cross Canteen.

After the war, Web Todd became a partner in J. H. Whitney and Company and served as director of the Equity Corporation, the Cunard Steamship Company, the Bank of Commerce of New York, and Metropolitan Life Insurance Company. The Equity Corporation, which Todd owned with a handful of partners, purchased troubled companies, made them profitable, and resold them in what was an early buy-out operation.

Web Todd became interested in politics in the mid-1940s, about the same time his fourth child, Christie, was born. He was part of the liberal, eastern "establishment Republicans"—wealthy lawyers, financiers, and businessmen who dominated the Republican party from 1940 to 1964. He was a fiscal conservative, both personally and politically; he never took out a loan in his life, and he wanted government to operate the same way. Socially, he was more conservative than Eleanor, who, along with her children, was enamored with Nelson Rockefeller. Web Todd was of the mind that Rockefeller spent too much of the government's money. As governor of New York, Rockefeller became known as a liberal Republican who raised taxes and increased state services. "He [Web Todd] was not inclined to support out-and-out handouts," Dan Todd says. "He used to quote the old saying, 'Teach a man to fish and he will live forever. Give a man a fish and he will live for a day.'" Web Todd believed that people—churches and social agencies—should take care of those in need, not government.

In 1944, Web Todd served as Wendell Wilkie's New Jersey campaign manager during the presidential campaign. In 1948, he was a close friend and supporter of New York Gov. Thomas Dewey, who defeated conservative Sen. Robert Taft for the GOP nomination. And in 1952, he was one of the eastern establishment leaders who tapped Dwight Eisenhower, commander of the North Atlantic Treaty Organization (NATO) forces, for the GOP nomination over Taft.

In 1952, when the party was bitterly divided between Eisenhower and Taft, Web Todd took on the task of New Jersey primary campaign manager for Eisenhower. "He was very close to Eisenhower," says Dan Todd. "I used to fly Dad over to the Gettysburg farm where he would disappear into the study so they could 'shoot the shit.' "

Ironically, Web Todd was a high school and Princeton University classmate and lifelong friend of Adlai Stevenson, the Democrat who ran against Eisenhower in 1952. Web and Stevenson corresponded and joked to one another about the race. At one point Stevenson said he did not want to be nominated for the presidency. "I must be nuts—which will be no surprise to you!" he wrote to Web Todd in July 1952, just before the Democratic convention.

When Eisenhower won the presidency, Web Todd was appointed director of the Office of Economic Affairs for the United States mission to

NATO and was sent to Paris from 1953 to 1954. His main responsibility was to watch gold reserves and each country's balance of payments to assure that member nations remained stable.

From 1960 to 1978, Todd was active in national politics and was a delegate to all but one GOP national convention. However, during Richard Nixon's years in the White House, he became persona non grata because he had refused to endorse Nixon prior to the 1968 convention. Todd was chairman of a group of northeastern Republican state chairmen who issued a statement saying that the more moderate New York governor, Nelson Rockefeller, son of Todd's longtime business associate, would be a better candidate. In addition, Eleanor Todd was chairwoman of the Citizens for Rockefeller in New Jersey.

Web Todd's failure to support Nixon early in 1968 is believed to have cost him the only thing he ever wanted for himself during nearly forty years in politics, namely, the ambassadorship to Australia. Even though Todd supported Nixon after the convention, he wasn't forgiven by those surrounding Nixon for being a Johnny-come lately. Instead of the Australian post, Todd was appointed to the Panama Canal Company, the firm responsible for managing the canal and the canal zone's civil government. Despite his disappointment, Todd was an active member of the canal board from 1969 to 1977. "It was another one of those lessons," Christie says with obvious pride in her voice. "You didn't take something on lightly. You did it with everything that you had, and you did the best job you could."

On the state level, Web Todd chaired the Republican State Committee for two separate terms totaling eleven years and was a longtime member and chairman of the party's finance committee. He served as state chairman from 1961 to 1969 and from 1974 to 1977, years when the party was out of power or in trouble. "He served during the days when the state committee met in an elevator shaft in a building in Trenton," says Dan Todd.

The year Web Todd took over as chairman, Democrat Richard Hughes was elected governor in an upset victory. Four years later, Hughes was reelected and the GOP lost control of both houses of the state legislature in a backlash against Republican presidential candidate Barry Goldwater. Todd was credited with saving the party from a damaging primary fight that year by telling both candidates for the GOP nomination—Goldwater and Rockefeller—"to stay the hell out of the state." After serving as party chief for eight difficult years, Web Todd was replaced the year his party recaptured the governor's seat. When Republican Bill Cahill, who would become governor later that year, installed a new chairman in 1969, Cahill said of Todd, "He has a quality that I call 'class.' "

Five years later, when the New Jersey Republicans were reeling from the Watergate scandal and had lost the governor's seat, a combination of moderate, liberal, and conservative Republicans placed Todd once again at the helm of the troubled state party. Cahill had lost his bid for reelection in a primary race with Charles Sandman, who was roundly defeated by Democrat Brendan Byrne in the gubernatorial race. Sandman, who some say engineered Todd's return to the chairmanship, had a campaign debt of $300,000 that needed to be paid.

During his years as chairman of the Republican State Committee, Todd spent most of his time using his own personal money to shore up its finances and working to keep its splintered factions together. He was considered a class act, a chairman who was respected by GOP leaders throughout the state. The *Evening Times* of Trenton wrote of Todd's first stint as party chief:

> Todd has an easy-going, almost gentle personality. He dislikes confrontations, and he will go to almost any length to reconcile intra-party disputes through negotiation. There is nothing lacking in Todd's sense of partisanship, but he always seemed uncomfortable and a little out of character saying nasty things about Democrats, as Republican chairmen are compelled to do from time to time.

Dan Todd remembers his father preaching, "This isn't a game for enemies. You fight like hell over policy issues, but don't bring personal animosity to the table." Todd was casual about his wealth and political connections. He teased and joked with everyone who came through Pontefract's doors, and he cursed like a sailor. His Scottish background had taught him not to show his emotions, so he showed his fondness for people with friendly banter. "Dad had a wonderful sense of humor," recalls Christie. "It is one of the ways he showed emotion. People would misunderstand and say, 'It's too bad Christie and her father have such a terrible relationship' because we just constantly bantered, and bantering was our way of dealing with one another."

Web enjoyed working around the farm, often strapping a tank of insecticide on his back to kill bugs in the yard. He lifted weights and was an avid golfer, winning the Somerset Hills Country Club championship even when he was sixty years old.

Web appeared the comfortable country gentleman in tweed jackets and corduroy slacks. Eleanor wore serviceable shoes, shirts, and sweaters. When it rained, they walked in their rubber galoshes. They loved listening to show-tunes and dancing, especially to the tune "Cheek to Cheek." In fact, Web taught Christie how to two-step at an early age. He was a teetotaler until, at age seventy-four, he had a heart attack and his doctor recommended one gin and tonic a day. From that time forward, he became adamant about having his Beefeaters gin.

When Web Todd died at the age of eighty-nine, it was his integrity that people cited. "Webster Todd always stood for what is right and proper in public life and conduct," Gov. Tom Kean told the *Hills-Bedminster Press*.

State Sen. Wesley Lance described Todd to the *Hunterdon County Democrat*: "During fifty years in politics, I have never met a greater gentleman in public life in either party than Webster Todd. He was a modest man. Every Republican president in modern times knew him personally, but you would never learn this from him."

Because of the way her parents had reared her, Christie admits with a hint of regret in her voice that the lowest point in her difficult campaign for governor was having to reveal that she had hired two illegal aliens to care for her children. "I had done something that I shouldn't have done. I was brought up by a father who did not even deduct the farm equipment [from his taxes] because he felt that was somehow cheating the government. He was so dead honest that I just felt I had let him down and brought it on myself. If Cary Edwards [her primary opponent] hadn't had the same problem, I don't know if we would be sitting here in the statehouse today."

When it came to political philosophy, Christie adopted her father's fiscal conservatism and her mother's more moderate stance on social issues. Her political persona is a combination of the political personalities of each of her parents. While Web Todd was helping to select presidents and bailing out the state GOP, Eleanor Todd was hard at work leading Republican women in the state, working for state and local candidates, and helping to organize the GOP's national conventions. Web Todd explained the difference in their styles to the *Evening Times*: "I talk. She works."

Eleanor Todd was a large, dynamic woman, who some called shy and others described as reserved, or even gruff. She was a no-nonsense, get-to-the-point type, not as friendly as Web, according to those who worked with her on political events. She was a better public speaker than her husband, who refused to run for public office, but he was more personable one-on-one. In the 1950s, when the *Newark News* ran a list of women who would be considered as gubernatorial candidates if the state were ready to elect a woman governor, Eleanor Todd was among them. Eleanor became a Republican national committeewoman in 1952 when Kate Schley, her mother, stepped down. Four years later, in 1956, she was elected vice chairman of the Republican National Committee. She held the post of committeewoman until 1961 when she resigned after her husband was elected Republican state chairman. From 1946 to 1952, Eleanor also served as president of the Women's State Republican Club.

Eleanor attended every Republican national convention from 1940 to 1976 serving either as a delegate, an alternate delegate, or as convention committee chairman. She chaired the committee on decorations and music at the 1956 convention in San Francisco and was program chairwoman for the 1960 convention in Chicago.

During the Chicago convention, Eleanor was shown on television presenting the historic convention gavel, which had originally been handed to Abe Lincoln. Newspaper accounts said Eleanor was in charge of everything, including sending cars for entertainers, corralling speakers, proofreading speeches, and buying gifts for the daughters of nominee Richard Nixon.

When Eleanor came home from Chicago, she recounted to a local newspaper a story Nixon had told at a convention breakfast for the Republican women: "He said that a barber came in to cut his hair and told him, 'Mr. Nixon, as long as I've lived in Chicago, no Republican has ever come to my door.' Nixon then asked him if the Democrats had come, and he said, 'many times.' " According to Eleanor Todd, this was a clear indication that Republicans throughout the nation had been lazy. And being "lazy" was something Eleanor Todd, dubbed "the Hurricane" by her children, could never tolerate. Always busy with politics, she also was an avid golfer, tennis player, and rider. However, she still found time to write children's stories and poetry and to attend classes at Columbia University.

Remaining active in politics into the 1980s, the Todds hosted a fund-raiser for George Bush at Pontefract, and Eleanor was the state finance chairwoman for his 1980 presidential bid. In 1983, Gov. Tom Kean appointed Eleanor to the New Jersey Board of Higher Education, where she served until 1988. When first appointed to the position, Eleanor, who had attended private schools all her life, told reporters that her "only direct contact with public schools has been as a substitute teacher in Bedminster." (Eleanor's comment was a forerunner of some of the comments Christie would make during the 1993 race for governor, which her opponents used to portray her as out-of-touch with the average New Jersey resident.) Nevertheless, newspaper accounts indicated that while a member of the board of higher education, Eleanor promoted the interests of public colleges in New Jersey.

While Christie's family is listed among the exclusive families in the Social Register, the Todds did not restrict their politics to champagne brunches. For more than forty years they attended every GOP dinner, barbecue, and reception in the area. Eleanor was active in local get-out-the-vote efforts, making some of the telephone calls herself and counting the ballots on election night.

Christie's parents included her in many of their political activities. She watched her parents give speeches at Todd family gatherings; she participated in political games at parties with the family of Nicholas Brady and other members of the social clique in Far Hills; and she was a part of the political discussions around the dinner table. However, Pontefract has been inaccurately portrayed by the press as the meeting place for state and national political leaders. "For some reason, everybody likes that image of [people of political importance] hanging around the old Todd farm," says Christie in exasperation. "Nobody really came to dinner on a regular basis. It [politics] was the topic of conversation a lot, but there were not a lot of heavy-duty political dinners. Dinner time tended to be family time. It would be Mother and Dad and me, or Kate, John, or Dan, if they were home."

Yet every year the Todds would invite the statehouse press corps to Pontefract for a picnic of farm food, swimming, and music, including a Dixieland band, which Web Todd, on occasion, joined with his trombone. At family parties, the Todds were known for their speech-making. When the Schleys and Bradys socialized, they would sometimes play political games. One time, at Aunt Lib Schley's Island Stock Farm, family members each dressed like a different president, gave speeches, and then voted on a winner. In a long-standing dispute over the winner, Lib Schley maintains that if the Bradys had not stuffed the ballot for Woodrow Wilson, Abe Lincoln would have won.

George Melick, whose family came to the Oldwick/Far Hills area in 1735 and stayed for eight generations, describes the Todds as an integral part of the community. "They had a real sense of responsibility of what it took to be a citizen. They wanted to do their part. They were the type of people, if you had a problem in the community, they would help you." Web Todd was as comfortable washing dishes after a firemen's supper at the Oldwick firehouse as he was hobnobbing with presidents. "With a twinkle in his eyes and a cigar in his hand, he enjoyed talking with them," Melick says. "Eleanor Todd could present a gavel at the national Republican Convention, but if it was the handyman's day off, she could milk a cow."

In the 1940s, when one of the Todds' barns burned down and the firefighters were kept at the scene into the evening, Eleanor went back to Pontefract and prepared food for the men. "Who else, but Eleanor, at 10 P.M., would get coffee and sandwiches for the men?" Melick asks. And during World War II, Eleanor was one of the women who drove the Red Cross wagons in the hills near Pontefract. "The military did some training up in the hills behind Oldwick, so they needed the Red Cross to deliver coffee and donuts to the troops as they were on maneuvers," says Christie. "She would drive up over the mountain in the dead of winter in the ice and snow." Melick recalls another time when, as a Hunterdon County freeholder, he questioned a county prosecutor's expense account, received no answers, and went to Eleanor Todd for help. "She penned a letter to the state attorney general, and the guy [the prosecutor] got his ears pinned back."

Through the way they lived their lives, the Todds instilled in their daughter a sense of responsibility to the community. They didn't preach. It was an automatic attitude of returning the favor for the good fortunes they enjoyed. "It was a strong family tradition," Christie says. "I had everything I wanted. All those things gave me a responsibility, but it was not a responsibility to be undertaken grudgingly."

Neither her grandparents nor her parents lived to see Christie become governor. Web Todd died in February 1989 with a gin and tonic in his hand,

and Eleanor died two years later in January 1991. Some family members say that had Kate Schley and Eleanor Todd been alive in 1993, their strong personalities might have preempted Christie's own pursuit of a political career. Others say it was from her strong matriarchal heritage that Christie drew the fortitude she needed to accomplish something no other woman had yet achieved.

"[Eleanor] was someone whose message was very clear—that women were every bit as good as men," says Christie. "Dad was very supportive of that, as well. He was supportive of her, constantly pushing her to the fore as far as politics was concerned. So it was a good lesson in team work. They were very much a team. They complemented one another very well."

In October 1993, during one of the darkest days of the race for governor, Christie sat at a conference table in her campaign office and talked about the political heritage she had embraced at an early age. "I was steeped in government as a way to affect policy and make changes," she said, letting down for a moment from the intensity of the campaign. "If you are going to complain, you better do something about it or you lose your right to bitch. That is what my dad used to say."

3

Young Republican

"When I was about thirteen, I thought, I have to decide if I'm a Republican because my parents are or because I believe in it."

Christie Whitman (February 27, 1995)
during a statehouse interview.

Christie was never shy about what she wanted for herself or the Republican party. The first time she met her husband-to-be, John Whitman, she stole his pants when she needed something more comfortable to wear after her high school graduation party. The first time she worked for the Republican party, she told the conservative GOP that it needed to open its ranks to minorities, senior citizens, and protesting college students.

Christie developed her own brand of Republican politics around the time she turned fourteen years old and was entering the Foxcroft School in Middleburg, Virginia. Following family tradition, the Todds sent Christie to the exclusive girls' school hidden away in the rolling Virginia hills in the fall of 1960. Her mother and sister had attended the school and loved it. Mrs. Todd sat on the school's board of trustees, so Christie was given no alternative other than Foxcroft when she finished eighth grade at the Far Hills Country Day School.

45

Balking, as she often did, at the game plan her parents had for her life, there was little doubt about the way Christie felt toward the school during her brief stay. "I hated it. It was quasi-military. They made us march around in uniforms and carry wooden guns which they called 'pieces.' "

The school went so far as to bring a Marine down from Quantico to drill the freshmen. While Christie could perform the skills outlined in the manual of arms better than anybody in a Reserve Officers' Training Corps, she disliked sleeping on unheated porches in sleeping bags with nothing but rough, terrycloth sheets to wrap around her. Three girls shared a room where they changed and kept their belongings in a military style that included folding their underwear and enduring white-glove inspections each month. "I remember getting demerits once for a dusty bathtub," Christie recalls. "They gave you [cleanser] to clean the bath, and it leaves a residue."

Other than holidays and the summer break, students were only allowed to go home for one weekend during their entire four-year stay. Christie was homesick from the start. She missed her parents and Pontefract. To her, Middleburg was in the middle of nowhere, and her life was devoid of the political activities she had become so accustomed to attending with her parents. Before leaving for Foxcroft, Christie had attended the GOP convention in Chicago where Richard Nixon was nominated, and she had grown used to the excitement. The young girls at the school didn't share or understand her interest in politics. "I was basically very homesick. It was 1960, a presidential election year. I was interested in it, and nobody there cared. It is not what most fourteen- and fifteen-year-old children are interested in, so I was out of sync."

About the time that she arrived at Foxcroft, Christie made a conscious decision that would dramatically mold the remainder of her life. She decided, for her own personal reasons, to become a Republican. "When I was about thirteen, I thought, I have to decide if I'm a Republican because my parents are or because I believe in it." Most of her friends were not embracing the Republican party, even though their parents were. "It was a good time to rebel and revolt. Their parents may have been Republicans, but they were all saying they weren't. It wasn't a cool thing to be. I took a step back and said: Why was I Republican? Was it just because of my parents, or because I believed in something?"

As a young teenager, Christie embraced the party's view that problem solving was more effective at a local level, that people can do things better than big government, and that more government was not the answer to everything. At thirteen years of age, she was already a fiscal conservative who supported the gold standard and opposed deficit spending.

Discontented with the austere life at Foxcroft, Christie lost thirty pounds. "I didn't go on a hunger strike. I just worried it all off. I was so miserable. I was homesick. None of it was Foxcroft's fault. It was mine."

Christie's godmother, Barbara Lawrence, says Christie was unhappy at Foxcroft because her parents had spoiled her. "Christie was not ready to accept rules. She was allowed to do whatever she wanted to do, and all of a sudden she had all these rules."

In 1961, when Christie was nearly fifteen, she convinced her mother to remove her from Foxcroft with the understanding that she would return in a year. She was then enrolled in the tenth grade at the prestigious Chapin School, located near Gracie Mansion, the mayor's residence along the East River in Manhattan. There were no dormitories, so the school arranged for Christie to live with a nearby family whose daughter also attended the school. She stayed at school during the week and then returned home on weekends. Her friends remember how on Monday morning, she would start counting the minutes before she could go home on Friday night.

Her mother, who was working toward her bachelor's degree at Barnard College by taking classes at Columbia University, would drive Christie to school on Monday morning, and Christie would take the train home on Friday afternoons. Having married Web Todd before finishing college, Eleanor was determined to get her degree before Christie graduated from high school. She accomplished her goal with a few days to spare.

When the time came for Christie to keep her agreement with her mother and return to Foxcroft, she confided in her aunt Lib Schley about how miserable she had been at the Virginia school. She didn't want to return, yet she knew how much it meant to her mother for her to continue the family tradition. Christie had a close relationship with her mother and did not want to hurt her feelings. "I don't want to go, but Mother wants me to go so badly," Aunt Lib recalls Christie saying. "And Kate [Christie's sister] tells me I'm a coward."

Lib advised Christie to stand up to her mother and to tell her how she felt. "Have the courage to say no," Lib told her niece. "Sometimes you have to say no to be brave."

In what some family members consider a turning point in her life, Christie went to her mother and told her that she did not want to ever return to Foxcroft. This was far different from her little-girl antics at the schools in Paris, or at the Far Hills school. Eleanor Todd was devastated but listened to Christie and decided to allow her to stay at Chapin. "By not going back to Foxcroft, she stood up to her mother and became more independent," says Lib Schley. "Her mother said, 'I want her to be happy.' "

By being located far closer to home and coming home on the weekends, Christie was able to continue to attend political events with her parents; her focus during her school days and summer vacations also was on politics. While most of the girls were interested in parties and clothes, Christie took her love for politics to the Chapin School where she organized the Current Events Club and convinced her mother to take a half dozen club members to Washington, D.C., where they toured the White House and breakfasted with House Speaker Gerald Ford.

Although she firmly embraced the Republican party during her teenage years, Christie became argumentative and unwilling to espouse the same brand of more conservative Republican politics her father favored.

> When I was in high school, I used to argue about everything. Dad maintained that if he were to say the sky was blue, I would argue it was black. He got somewhat fed up with the arguments at the dinner table. Mostly, it was political. He was more conservative than I was. Some of the arguments were over Nelson Rockefeller, whom I felt was terrific, and he was never a big supporter of. He felt Rockefeller spent too much money on social programs. Dad felt people ought to be made to work.

Christie's mother was a strong supporter of Rockefeller, and because Eleanor spent far more time with Christie than her father, Eleanor had the most influence on Christie's views, including her politics. But that did not mean they always agreed. "I spent lots of time with her. We were very close, good friends, although I argued with her often. I can remember my dad getting furious at me one night at the dinner table, saying I would argue about anything, and that I should stop arguing with my mother."

Eleanor was notorious for excusing Christie from Chapin for outings.

She took her to a tickertape parade honoring astronaut John Glenn after he made the first American orbit around the earth in 1962. Because the Todds were close friends with Los Angeles Dodgers' owner Walter O'Malley, Eleanor also took her daughter out of school when the Dodgers returned to New York to face the Yankees in the 1963 World Series. While Christie loved the outings, the headmistress did not like her absences. After one such trip, Christie had to stand in the back of the room at an assembly because she was not in uniform. She listened to a lecture, obviously intended for her, on student responsibility.

In the spring of 1964, in anticipation of the upcoming presidential election, the headmistress did grant Christie one school period to run a mock Republican Convention. Those in attendance say that while a conservative Barry Goldwater would eventually capture the real GOP nomination, at Chapin's mock convention, Nelson Rockefeller, Christie's political idol, got the party's nod. In pre-balloting, Richard Nixon didn't make the cut to be among the top contenders at the mock convention, and his elimination angered his daughters, Julie and Tricia, who had just entered Chapin School. "Julie was furious and said she wasn't going to participate in anything her father wasn't in," Christie recalls with amusement.

Even as Christie's interest in politics grew, her school work still held little interest for her. She was an average student whose grades were no more than a C to C-plus average. Keeping her love for the outdoors, she was a member of the softball and field hockey teams and played some basketball during her years at Chapin.

During the summers, Christie did volunteer work or traveled with her parents because no one in the Todd family sat idle. "In the summers, I was lucky enough to be in a position where I didn't have to work in order to get spending money, but I volunteered. There was never a summer that I didn't either volunteer to work with cerebral palsy children or was a candy striper at the Hunterdon Medical Center. You always did something. All of us always did. It varied between getting paid jobs, which we did as well, or just giving of your time."

Graduating from Chapin in 1964, Christie, wearing a long, pink dress with a stand-up ruffle at the neckline, was the guest of honor at a dinner dance at Ripplebrook Farm, her maternal grandmother's (Kate Schley's) estate in Far Hills. Swans floated in the nearby brook as family, friends, and classmates partied under a tent to the rear of her grandmother's home in celebration of Christie's graduation and her formal entrance into society.

In the first chance meeting between Christie Todd and John Whitman, John attended the party as the escort for one of the young female guests. At one point in the evening, friends recalled him bragging that he had been able to sit next to the guest-of-honor. John Whitman was considered a ladies' man at the time. "His sister was at Chapin, and John and his brother knew every girl in my class, in the class behind me, and in the class ahead of me," Christie recalls. "That's how I met him. He was the date of one of my classmates at the party at my grandmother's. Actually, he was supposed to be a date of one of my classmates and instead came with somebody else."

There was an interesting twist to Christie's first encounter with John. "I don't remember much, but I'm told I ended up wearing his green pants," Christie says with a chuckle in her voice as she recounts events after the party. "Late at night or early in the morning, we went over to a friend's house where John was staying for the night. We were in dresses and wanted to get out of them, and he had extra clothes. So I think we went up to his bedroom and took his extra clothes. That's why John keeps saying that our paths kept crossing. We kept meeting at odd places like that. It was pure happenstance."

In the summer of 1964, Christie and her brother Dan worked for Gov. Nelson Rockefeller's campaign for president at a time when the Republican party was rallying around the conservative Sen. Barry Goldwater's candidacy. While Rockefeller was never a successful presidential candidate, his ability to attract the public's attention impressed the young Christie. "I supported his social programs of inclusiveness. What I admired about the man, what impressed me, was the ability he had to relate to people. It was just incredible. I can remember doing a cavalcade through Newark and Elizabeth in 1964, in the summer, before the convention, and men would come out of the barber shop half shaved and women would come out of the beauty parlors with their hair in curlers just to see him, just to say hello. He had an incredible way about him that made people want to see him. He was very much in touch with the people."

Despite his wealth, Rockefeller, with a flash of a smile, was able to communicate with truck drivers and high-ranking officials alike. He genuinely liked people, and those who met him knew it. Christie never forgot his magnetic personality. Nearly thirty years later during her campaign for governor, she would, in some ways, emulate his man-on-the-street style.

In the fall of 1964, Christie entered Wheaton College, a private women's college in Norton, Massachusetts, where she would major in government. "I took all international government courses. It was teenage snobbery. I figured I knew about as much about domestic politics as anyone who was going to teach me. What I really didn't have was international experience." Christie finally had found something she thoroughly enjoyed studying, and she did well enough at Wheaton to graduate with honors. "It was the first time I really enjoyed learning and studying."

She was, however, a typical college student. Thinking that she would get a better grade on her thesis by selecting a topic that no one at the college knew much about, Christie decided to write her thesis on Nigerian democracy because Wheaton had no courses in African studies. Much to her surprise, when she returned after a summer break to begin her senior year, the school had hired a Nigerian expert.

A natural leader, well-liked by the other students, Christie was elected president of the Young Republicans Club and vice president of her class during her senior year at college. "Everyone knew her," says her roommate Meg Moulton. "I'm not aware of anyone who didn't like her." An attractive young woman, Christie was stylish, but not trendy. Her blue eyes, dark eyebrows, and large smile were her assets. She wore her thick, shoulder-length hair pulled back from her face and earrings frequently dangled from her ears.

During class discussions on politics, it was clear which side Christie was arguing for. "It came out in classes, in activities and discussion," Wheaton classmate Susan Swift, whose father was assistant press secretary to Eisenhower and a friend of Web Todd, told the *Trentonian*. "She was very clearly Republican."

Everyone knew, even in those early years, that Christie had a definite opinion on issues and wasn't afraid to speak her mind. Attending college during the Vietnam War, Christie argued in favor of the war during the college's formal debate on the issue. "I think I would question more the whole premise that got us into the war in the first place. But once we were there, I certainly thought we should fight a war."

The only student demonstration she participated in during her college years was one for reproductive rights. When women's rights activist Bill Baird was arrested for showing a birth control pill to students at nearby Wellesley College, Christie went to Boston with a group of Wheaton students to protest at his arraignment. "I thought it was so outrageous that someone should be arrested because he was disseminating information. I believed in reproductive freedom, and this was a tool in that arsenal. I certainly felt strongly that people should not be arrested for just talking about it and showing it."

Because Wheaton was an all-girls school, Christie and her friends had to travel thirty minutes to Brown University in Providence or forty-five minutes to Cambridge and Harvard University to find boys. "We did a fair amount of partying, but I was never a social animal. We had a group of friends, and we would go skiing on the weekends. Every spring, I brought them down to the farm for what we called 'Spring Fling weekend.'"

Christie tried computer dating the first year it was available to students, but when she ended up with a date whose head was shaped like a wedge of a pie, she went back to the traditional way of finding dates. During the winter of her sophomore year, she again crossed paths with John Whitman, who was at Yale University. They dated for a semester after meeting in Stratton, Vermont, where Christie had transported a number of Wheaton students for a skiing trip. Her car, she explains, was a key factor in the brief romance. "Apparently, he had a hot and heavy girlfriend, who I didn't know about. Her car had broken down, but I had a car that worked."

The Todd-Whitman romance lasted only until that summer when John graduated from Yale. "I think his girlfriend's car got fixed," an amused Christie says of the breakup.

The incident Christie recalls most vividly from her college years was the suicide of her favorite government professor, Daniel Lewin. When Christie heard he was missing from campus, she drove around the area with a friend, and the two just happened to drive by as the professor's body was being pulled out of a nearby river. Christie was shocked to learn from the professor's wife that he never realized how much the students, including Christie, cared for him and for his ability to teach. "It drove home a very important message about letting people know how you feel about them and not presuming that they understand things like that."

Daniel Lewin had helped Christie refine the way she thought about politics. When he died, her classmates, who knew Christie to be cheerful, even in the early morning, saw her shaken for the first time. "She lost her stiff upper lip," Meg Moulton reflected. "It was the only time I was aware of her openly expressing any emotion except cheerfulness and self-containment. She felt saddened that someone who meant so much to her didn't know it."

During her years at Wheaton, and the years that would follow before her marriage to John Whitman, Christie formed some of her strongest, life-long friendships with people from a cross-section of social and economic backgrounds. "She is just very careful about friendship," said Nancy Risque Rohrbach, who met Christie in 1968 and twenty-five years later traveled with her during the final, difficult days of the 1993 gubernatorial campaign. "She calls just to say hello. She makes an effort to be there. She makes time for her friends and family, and she depends on them."

During her college years, Christie's passions were ice cream and dancer and screen star Fred Astaire. She loved to sing and dance. Her college classmates say she knew the words to every old World War II song as well as the musical productions of Fred Astaire and Ginger Rogers. She proved it while she drove to ski outings or weekends at Pontefract. "She appreciated the simple pleasures," Meg Moulton recalls. "She had the ability to jump in a hayloft, but also to have wine and cheese in lofty places. She enjoyed the moment, regardless of the situation."

While at Wheaton, Christie arranged her college schedule so she could be at home for long weekends. After she balked at being sent to Foxcroft, it was apparent that Christie had a special attachment to both her family and Pontefract. "It was friends and family that she called upon as the rock upon which she rested," says Meg Moulton.

During her college years, Christie advanced to competitive, point-to-point horse racing, and she also came home to ride. Her cousin, Reeve Schley III, who rode with her in one race, remembers her as a "wild woman" who displayed a fearless steel and verve during the competition where they rode through country fields and woodlands.

On one occasion in the late 1960s, Christie returned home to fox hunt in northern New Jersey and had an amusing encounter with Jackie Onassis. When the participants mounted their horses and went into the area where they would be checked before the Essex County hunt, Mrs. Onassis, dressed in white breeches, was positioned next to Christie, who was riding Air Travel, a horse known for its lively disposition and playful antics. "He did all sorts of strange and wonderful things, this horse. He also tended to slobber. He got all frothy at the mouth when he got excited about fox hunting."

On this particular occasion, Air Travel had grabbed some grass and had green slime dripping from his mouth. "He whipped around and put his head in her [Jackie's] lap and got her with green slime from her hip to her knee." Mortified with embarrassment, Christie apologized profusely: "Mrs. Onassis, I'm sorry, I'm so sorry." But that wasn't the end of Air Travel's antics. "[Jackie] turned her horse around, and he did it to her other leg before I could catch him," Christie remembers.

During the summer before her senior year, Christie lived in Washington, D.C., with her cousin Georgie Schley and two other women. Working as an intern in the office of U.S. Sen. Clifford Case, she was given clerical duties. But on one occasion, Sen. Case asked her to write a speech in which he blasted a New York congressman for sending a letter, on his congressional letterhead, to federal employees in an effort to solicit campaign contributions. "Case kept sending the speech back and saying it wasn't tough enough. We finally got to the point where we called it blackmail and extortion. I was leery of going that far, but that's what he wanted, and eventually, that's what he got out of it."

Georgie Schley remembers how the four Washington roommates carefully divided expenses down to the penny, and how at one point, there was a dispute over whether Georgie had wasted their food money by allowing some meat to spoil. Christie ended the bickering by arriving home from work with a bottle of sherry for the roommates to share.

Graduating from Wheaton in 1968 with a bachelor of arts degree in government, Christie spent the following summer in New York working at Rockefeller's campaign headquarters. The politician she admired was making his second unsuccessful attempt at securing the GOP presidential nomination, and Christie worked for the cause for $100 a week. After GOP nominee Richard Nixon was elected president in the fall of 1968, Christie went to Washington and worked as a special assistant to Donald Rumsfeld during a time when he was making the transition from Congress to the directorship of the U.S. Office of Economic Opportunity (OEO).

At the time, the agency was dominated by men. Christie recalls being the lone woman in a room full of men at an OEO meeting when one man began to curse and another warned that a lady was in the room. Rumsfeld quickly stopped the squabbling by telling the group: "Don't worry about her. She's just one of the guys." "That's when I figured I had made it," Christie declares.

While at the OEO, Christie had her first encounter with Bill Bradley, whom she later would challenge for New Jersey's U.S. Senate seat. Bradley, who had just started his professional basketball career with the New York Knickerbockers and was interested in politics, had come to the OEO during the off-season to work as an intern. One day, the young, six-foot-five Bradley came into the office and made the mistake of asking Whitman to fetch him a cup of coffee. "He dropped his change on my desk as he went by and told me how he liked his coffee." During the 1990 Senate race between Whitman and Bradley, newspaper accounts of the incident indicated that Christie's reply was "unprintable." However, Christie says she can't recall exactly what she said. "I don't think I said anything unprintable. I just gave him his money back. I was assistant to the director, and he was summer help, as far as I was concerned, and it did not go down well." Bradley, during the 1990 senate race, said he could not recall the incident.

In 1969, Christie left the OEO and went to work for the Republican National Committee. With Nixon in the White House and the Republicans weakening their ties to the black community, Christie convinced the GOP that it needed to reach out to senior citizens, minorities, and college students to find out why those groups weren't attracted to the Republican party. "Dad was in D.C. for a state chairmen's meeting, and I went to the luncheon with him. Rogers Morton was there as the new national chairman. I pitched the idea to him, and he said, 'Go with it.' "

Touring the country during a year-long Listening Post project, Christie, at twenty-three years of age, was given the freedom to travel around the country to colleges and universities, to ghettos, and to senior citizens' projects, to find out what it would take for the Republican party to attract the people who lived there into its fold. Traveling alone most of the time, she met in each city with a Republican party contact who arranged for her to meet and interview seniors, minorities, and students. "Her demeanor is very quiet in many ways, and that belies the assertiveness of her nature," says Nancy Risque Rohrbach, who was with Christie at the NRC and observed her Listening Post year.

On several occasions during the tour, Christie encountered dangerous situations. At one point, she was traveling across Florida with two men, one seventy-eight years old and the other eighty-seven years old, who were amusing themselves by racing through yellow traffic lights as they turned to red. They had refused to allow Christie behind the wheel, until they reached Miami. "One man was going down a one-way street the wrong way. I said: 'That's it. Get out. I'm driving.' "

On another occasion, in Galveston, Texas, Christie was forced to cancel a meeting with a group of black people because of the community's reaction. "I was as close as you can come to feeling discrimination if you are not one who's usually a target."

Christie had driven from Houston to Galveston with contact Loveland Johnson to meet with members of the black community. Arriving early, the two decided to take the sightseeing ferry that tours the bay. "I felt the white males on that ferry were going to kill him and keelhaul me. It was not pleasant. They did not like the idea of a white female with a black male, and they were not subtle in the way they looked at us and the way they acted. It got to be fairly scary." Because members of the white community threatened to disrupt her meeting with the black community, it was canceled. "The problem was not so much for me, but for those local African Americans who were planning to meet with me. They were really afraid for their jobs and concerned for what would happen to them. It was an eye-opening experience. It brought it all home."

Christie's travels also took her to New York's Harlem and to the East Ward of Chicago where she met one winter night with a street gang named the Black Disciples. Despite her privileged upbringing, Christie says she wasn't intimidated or frightened during the Listening Post project. "I went into these places and just never thought twice. I went into Harlem, and it never occurred to me that anything was going to happen. There were others who were more scared. But I had contacts in all these places, and I just went in and talked with people."

The Black Disciples had agreed to meet with Christie only if they could set the time and place. "The only time they could meet with us was after ten o'clock at night. It was January or February. It was subzero weather. And it was dark. We were in this small, narrow room. We were at one end, and the door was at the other. These kids were pretty tough when they first came in. They wore leather jackets and carried chains. We all sat at one table."

As the meeting got under way, the contact person, who had arranged the session, suddenly turned against Christie and the other GOP worker with her, setting the stage for an unexpected confrontation.

> The kids started swearing and using all the words that they knew. But I had two older brothers, and I had grown up on a farm, so that wasn't getting very far. Once they knew they weren't going to shock me, and I wasn't going to burst into tears or anything, they settled down and it was a very interesting time.
>
> It became very clear that the reason a lot of them joined the gangs was a lack of structure anywhere else. At that point in time, you didn't hear about the dysfunctional family, yet it was very clear from these kids that they were missing something in their lives, that the family wasn't there for them.

According to Nancy Risque Rohrbach, "She was determined to listen to everybody. Christie received good dialogue from people who were having their own revolutions." Christie drafted memos to the Republican party with advice on how to attract the varied groups she had visited. Her final report, containing quotes from people around the country, had no immediate impact on the Republican National Committee, although it may have influenced the development of programs for the elderly poor. Nevertheless, for Christie, it was preparation for the future. "It gave me some valuable training in listening and hearing what people have to say and in learning that we have more in common than what divides us. I made a strong appeal to the party to understand this and to be willing to reach out."

Visiting college campuses where students were protesting the Vietnam War, Christie learned another lesson that would serve her well in later years. "The knee-jerk reaction, the Beltway view, was that these students were wide-eyed liberals, that they were radicals, smart-ass kids who didn't know what they wanted and were just against everything."

But that was not what Christie heard on the campuses. "When you listened to them, it wasn't that they hated the country. They were really saying that the Vietnam War had the United States in a position of being less than what it should be, of not living up to its ideals, of repressing people. These were not young kids who hated government. These were not young kids who hated the United States. These were people who felt this country was letting itself down." The contrast between the prevailing viewpoint in Washington and the reality on the streets taught Christie to be cautious about how she gathered information. "I certainly got from that experience how important it is not to just take what you hear from the pundits or what you read in the papers, but try to get behind it a little bit and to really listen to what people are saying."

During the summer of 1970 when Christie was back in Washington but still working for the RNC, she and the other young workers at the Republican National Committee became active in the War on Rats being waged in the poorer sections of the city. "We were twenty-two years old going on forty," says Nancy Risque Rohrbach. "We had nothing to do but make the world a better place. Our lives centered around our work, but we also played well, partied and traveled together."

Wearing blue jeans and gloves, the RNC staffers, whose average age was twenty-four, would shovel out debris from ghetto neighborhoods to clear the way for the city to go in with rat poison. Preparations started Friday night when bulletins were sent throughout Capitol Hill to solicit help. Later the RNC staffers gathered to make hundreds of baloney sandwiches for the workers and people in the neighborhoods. After spending the day cleaning the neighborhoods, the staffers would open the valves on fire hydrants so that the children could cool off, and then people from the neighborhoods would gather together for a picnic. "What people needed was a little help," Whitman said. "They were so busy trying to survive they didn't have time to keep the neighborhood clean."

Most of the RNC staffers had not come from Christie's privileged background, but they had a common purpose. The Listening-Post program, combined with projects like the War on Rats, broadened Christie's outlook beyond Pontefract and New Jersey. "All of it made an impression. It reminded me of how good we had it, and how lucky we were."

During her years at the RNC, staffers recalled that Christie had the courage to disagree with her superiors and to stand up for what she believed in. When Nixon nominated G. Harrold Carswell to the U.S. Supreme Court in 1970 and the RNC staffers were asked to make calls to encourage people to support him, Christie told the RNC leadership that it was not something that she could do, because of his background. In 1948, during his campaign for the Georgia legislature, Carswell had said that he would always be governed by the principles of white supremacy. Even though Carswell disavowed the statements in 1970, the Senate rejected his nomination.

In 1970, Christie returned to work at the Office of Economic Opportunity but decided that she hated being a part of the federal bureaucracy. When the elections got under way that fall, she convinced the Republican National Committee to send her to Colorado to work on a congressional race. Returning to Washington after the elections, Christie spent 1971 working as the deputy director of New York State's Washington, D.C., office at a time when Nelson Rockefeller was still governor of the state.

In 1972, she went to work for her brother Dan at the Committee for the Reelection of the President, the Nixon campaign committee whose illegal activities eventually led to the Watergate scandal and Nixon's resignation.

Appointed national director of older Americans for the campaign committee, Dan Todd hired his sister as the eastern regional coordinator. From Maine to Florida and as far west as Ohio and Michigan, Christie organized senior citizens in support of Nixon's reelection. "We had the interesting experience of being accepted into some states where regular committee-for-the-reelection people had been chucked out because they had been a little arrogant in their treatment of the local Republicans. Since both of us had a state chairman for a father, we knew how to be deferential and work with the party officials, so we had a pretty good relationship."

Christie was working at the Committee for the Reelection of the President when the Watergate break-in occurred in June 1972, but she said she was unaware of the committee's illegal activities. However, she did recall the committee's concern for security. "You weren't allowed to leave anything on your desk that had any writing on it. I got a note saying that I had been bad because I had thrown out a typed list of the state coordinators. I thought, hey, if you are a state coordinator, people are supposed to know who you are. But I was supposed to have shredded it."

After the break-in made national news, Christie recalls how her brother tried to find some humor in the situation. While an office manager in the state in which they were working was away from his post, Dan issued a memo, under the office manager's letterhead, saying that all members of the president's reelection committee should only identify themselves on the street by a secret handshake and that they should report to the manager's office for their cotton gloves. When three people, who didn't get the joke, called for their cotton gloves, the manager learned of the stunt and was furious.

After Nixon was reelected, the White House found jobs inside a variety of federal agencies for those who had served on the reelection committee, and Christie requested a stint at the Peace Corps. Discovering that the agency was unhappy about being forced to hire her, Christie left the office under an arrangement that allowed her to design a personnel appraisal system for the agency as an outside consultant.

In 1973, Christie moved from Washington to Manhattan where she became a freelance consultant for the national Association of the Junior Leagues of America. Hired to organize a five-day training institute on criminal justice in Houston, she made her first contact with the National Council on Crime and Delinquency. (Florio tried to use Christie's association with the council against her during the 1993 race for governor.)

While glad for the work, Christie was embarrassed about her association with the Junior League because of its sorority-like reputation, which she said was inaccurate, but nevertheless worried her. "I couldn't stand it. The job was good, but the thought of being affiliated with the Junior League killed me. . . . I was worried that it would stay with me for life."

By the time Christie moved to New York, John Whitman had reappeared in her life. This time, it was serious. They already had started to talk about her future as a wife, a mother, and a politician.

4

Wife and Mother

"There is nothing more important than the family. This all will pass. I am not going to be governor forever. I will be a mother for all of my life, if nothing happens to the kids. And that's more important than anything else."
Christie Whitman (March 28, 1995)
during a statehouse interview.

On April 20, 1974, at the Presbyterian Church in Lamington, less than a mile from Pontefract, Christine Temple Todd married John Russell Whitman. It was a perfect political match. The bride was the daughter of an East Coast Republican party chieftain. The groom was the son of a New York City judge and the grandson of a former New York governor. But this was no arranged marriage. The head-strong Christie had selected her own mate, and they were a perfect match for more than political reasons. They both were keenly ambitious and competitive; they loved sports, the outdoors, dancing—and each other.

John, a financial consultant and banker, resurfaced in Christie's life in 1972. After graduating from Yale University in 1966, he had volunteered for the army, serving a tour of duty in Vietnam and returning home with two bronze stars. He relocated to Washington, D.C., on a Harvard University fellowship, and not long thereafter he encountered Christie. They started

61

playing tennis, but that was as far as it went. "We kept meeting in different places," John says about the years between 1964 and 1972. "Sometimes we got along, and sometimes we didn't. There were times when we distinctly didn't like each other. These were different events and different times, and we had different reactions to each other. But, basically, nobody else in my life kept coming around again just sort of by happenstance over a ten-year period. We literally kept running into each other in places."

When Christie needed a date for Richard Nixon's second inaugural ball in January 1973, she asked John because she knew he loved to dance. That's when the relationship sparked. The two began dating, and by the time Christie had moved to New York City later that year, the relationship had become serious.

On New Year's Eve 1973, John proposed. Nancy Risque Rohrbach was at the New Year's Eve party in a New York apartment with Christie and John when he pulled Christie into a side room to propose. When they emerged from the room, they shared the news with all their friends.

They were deeply in love, "goo-goo eyes" over each other, according to Rohrbach. Christie had found her perfect mate. John was gregarious and fun-loving, yet competitive. He could surprise her by doing things like offering her a glass of champagne with a pair of magnificent earrings in the bottom of the glass. But when they were on the tennis court, he was out to win—and vice versa.

Some family members say that John and Christie discussed the possibility of her running for governor even before their marriage, and that they planned exactly how they would do it. John was supposed to earn the money in the early years of their marriage, and then Christie would have the foundation she needed to make the run.

However, the Whitmans maintain that they talked in a more general sense about her future in politics. When they were married, Christie made it clear to John that she wanted to be a wife and mother, but she also wanted a political career. "Our marriage vows should have said in sickness and health and in politics," John quips.

Published reports have hinted that the Todds selected John for Christie because they considered him the last single man on the East Coast acceptable for their youngest daughter. But family members laugh out loud at the notion that anybody other than Christie could decide anything for her life.

But there was little doubt that John Whitman came with the proper credentials. A New York financial consultant, he was the son of a New York City municipal judge and the grandson of former New York Gov. Charles Whitman, Sr. His grandfather, who was fictionalized in E. L. Doctorow's novel *Ragtime,* was a New York City district attorney who convicted a corrupt police official of murder. As a result, he was catapulted to the governorship in 1914. "He has alternately been called a great lawyer and a gin-soaked social climber," John Whitman says of his grandfather, who died when John was four.

John's father, Charles Whitman, Jr., also a lawyer, worked in the general counsel's office for New York Gov. Thomas Dewey and then helped with the Dewey presidential campaign in 1948. Charles Whitman, Jr., was the only Republican judge elected in New York City in 1955, and he sat on the bench for more than thirty years representing the silk-stocking district on the upper East Side where some of the most prestigious addresses in the world are located.

John Whitman graduated from St. Paul's School, Yale University (where he played rugby and ice hockey), and Harvard University's School of Business. A decorated war hero, he was awarded the bronze star for valor after he helped drain a burning diesel fuel tank during a nighttime rocket attack at an army base along the Mekong Delta, thereby preventing a petroleum tank farm from exploding.

After agreeing to marry John, Christie returned home to Pontefract to tell her parents, and within twenty-four hours, Eleanor Todd had organized an engagement dinner. Between January and April 1974, Christie and Nancy Risque Rohrbach traveled to Pontefract on weekends to plan the wedding.

Six hundred people attended the large, formal ceremony that in some ways was bittersweet for Christie because Web Todd was hospitalized with his first heart attack and could not attend the ceremony. Christie, at twenty-seven years of age, was given away by her uncle Reeve Schley, Jr., after her father insisted that the ceremony not be postponed.

A poised and pretty bride, the five-foot-eight Christie wore a white, high-necked, short-sleeved dress with lace at the neckline and covering the scalloped skirt. A floor-length veil, trimmed with satin, was attached to her hair, which was worn up and away from her face. Her sister, Kate, was the matron of honor; her best friend, Nancy Risque (Rohrbach), was the maid of honor.

Dressed in an ascot, tails, and a top hat, John, who is five-foot-eleven, was sporting sideburns on his wedding day. Otherwise, with short brown hair and glasses, he fit the role of a banker. During the ceremony, John, who had insisted on memorizing his vows rather than repeating them after the minister, surprised everyone by becoming so nervous that he forgot his own name. When he was supposed to say, "I, John, take thee, Christie," he got as far as the "I," and could go no further. Christie started to prompt him, then decided that wasn't a good way to start her marriage, and allowed the minister to take over the task. "He literally could not remember his name," Christie recalls. "And it wasn't one of those things where you could just prompt him once and he would take off. We have a great picture where you can see all the bridesmaids and ushers in hysterics at the alter." John took a considerable amount of harassment for the slip-up. Later, in the receiving line, he joked with Christie, saying he was prepared to deck the next person who said, "She's one up on you now."

When the ceremony was over, the newlyweds opened a bottle of champagne and rode in an open carriage to Pontefract. The carriage was pulled by Christie's hunter Vagabond and driven by Meryl Stiles, the Pontefract farmer who was dressed in a tuxedo and top hat. Christie and John danced wildly at the reception, hosted by Eleanor and Web Todd under a huge, white tent in the back yard.

For their honeymoon, the Whitmans were supposed to spend a week at Virgin Gorda in the British Virgin Islands, but ended up coming home early. "We got bored on our honeymoon," says Christie, tipping her head to acknowledge that most people would be surprised by the statement. "I think everyone thought we were destined for divorce."

A friend of the family had invited the Whitmans to use his mountain home on the island. "It was all by itself, way on top of a mountain, which might have been terribly romantic, but we were paralytic most nights because we could hear these noises all night long. There was no club or anything down there, so there was nothing to do. There is only so much snorkeling and swimming you can do. We like to be active, so we came back early."

John returned to his job as a financial consultant and officer of The

First National City Bank in New York, and Christie returned to her consulting work for the Junior League. On Wednesday evenings they taught English as a second language in Harlem.

Shortly after their marriage, the Whitmans began building a home called Twenty Springs on fifty-four forested acres in Far Hills, a portion of the Ripplebrook farm estate where Christie's grandparents had lived. From Twenty Springs, located on a hill overlooking the south side of Ripplebrook, Christie could see the home where Reeve and Kate Schley had lived. The ownership of the land had been passed from Kate, to Eleanor, to Christie. "We did a lot of that construction ourselves. We laid the hardwood floors, tongue in groove. I got very good at that. We could paint. We could put in a window. The only thing that we just absolutely couldn't do together was wallpaper. All we had to do was just mention wallpaper, and we would start to fight. Hanging it was impossible."

The house, designed with cathedral ceilings in every room, was finished in September 1975. But before they ever lived in it, Citicorp assigned John Whitman to establish the Citicorp International Bank Ltd., a corporate-financing branch in London, and the Whitmans moved to England for two and a half years. They lived in Chelsea, one of the inner boroughs of London along the north bank of the Thames River. Traditionally the city's artistic and literary quarter, Chelsea became fashionable after World War II. "During the two and a half years we were there, we went from the smallest house on Godfrey Street to the second largest house on Godfrey Street. It was wonderful. At the end of Godfrey Street was something called Chelsea Green. There was an iron monger, a grocery store, and a butcher. It was your own little community."

Without her green card, Christie was unable to work, and she found that to be a difficult adjustment. "For the first six or seven weeks, I was not all that pleasant to live with," Whitman admits with a smile. "I started doing things like baking. The first loaf of bread I baked over there, I had an American recipe, and I didn't realize that English measures were different. I turned out something that the Irish Republican Army would have been proud of. You could have used it as a lethal weapon with no problem at all."

Christie gradually began to enjoy the slower pace of her life. She and John left the city on weekends, staying in a borrowed home in Surrey, a popular woodland resort just south of London. She began taking courses in criminology at the London School of Economics because she was contemplating getting a degree in the field. She also attended several courses, sponsored by the London City Council, on London and silver. Unable to keep her hands out of politics, Christie became active with the United States Republicans abroad and eventually chaired the Republicans for the United Kingdom. In 1976, she returned to the United States long enough to watch the Republicans select Gerald Ford as the nominee at the Republican National Convention.

While Christie and John were living in England, their first child, Kate, was born on April 18, 1977. "We were married two years, and we thought we would have a child. It wasn't all bad being that far away from the in-laws on both sides. It gave us a little breathing space."

Christie, however, did not always get along with the British doctors who provided the family's medical care. When a very proper British doctor discovered that the unborn baby was in the breech position, he told Christie that because she was an "elderly primipara" the baby would have to be delivered by Caesarean section. The doctor was explaining that because Christie was thirty years old and having her first child, a Caesarean was necessary. But that's not the way she took it. "I kept thinking they called me an elderly primate, which insulted me to no end. I came back to John seething. I didn't think I was an elderly anything."

Kate had some health problems during her first year. Both of her hips were displaced at birth and required special care. And when she was six months old, there was an epidemic of whooping cough in the city, and Kate contracted the disease. The national health care service had stopped vaccinating children, and by the time Whitman convinced the British doctors to give Kate her first vaccination, it was too late.

But in 1978, when John and Christie returned to Far Hills, they brought with them a healthy Kate, a Bentley automobile, and some cheap champagne. John remained with Citicorp through the early 1980s at a time when the bank was handling a number of leveraged buyouts. He was involved in the high-profile Penn Central Railroad Company bankruptcy and reorganization case and later joined Citicorp Venture Capital, the leveraged-buyout division of the bank. Meanwhile, Christie was a full-time wife and mother. Her only government involvement was as a member of the board of directors of the Somerset County Community College.

In January 1979, shortly after the Whitmans returned home from England, their son, Taylor, was born. From the beginning, both Whitman children had an independent nature. "I don't remember when they first said, 'Ma' or 'Pa,' or whatever their first words were, but I do remember their first phrases," Christie states proudly. "Kate said 'by self.' Taylor said, 'All by self.' " Kate, who had been a kicker in utero, had the more aggressive nature. Taylor, who liked to swing punches before his birth, failed to sleep soundly for more than two years after he was born. "He would wake up three or four times a night." Christie quips, "If he hadn't been so cute every time we got to the crib, he would have been dead."

John and Christie, who had kept her long hair and youthful figure, made a point of spending time outdoors with the children, doing many of the activities that Christie had enjoyed when she was growing up at Pontefract. "We were lucky. At Twenty Springs, we had a lot of paths in the woods, and we spent a lot of time hiking along the streams and hunting for salamanders and things like that."

Bedtime was a special time at the Whitman home. "She spent a lot of time with the children," recalls Nancy Risque Rohrbach. "She and John, these are people who put their children to bed, sang songs to them at bedtime, led them through their prayers." Christie read the children entire books, like *Indian in the Cupboard, The Tale of Two Cities, Tom Sawyer, Uncle Tom's Cabin,* and *Treasure Island.*

When Christie was growing up at Pontefract, she went to church with her parents nearly every Sunday, and she continued the tradition, taking her children each week to the Lamington Presbyterian Church. "It is an important, but quiet, part of our lives," reflects Christie. "I am always aware that there is something a lot bigger than us or me in anything that we do or try to do. It is just an integral part of who I am."

When she returned to politics, Christie adjusted her work schedule to meet the children's needs. "She would be here when we got home from school and would cook for us," Kate explains.

Taylor and Kate inherited their parents' love for sports, and from an early age, Christie and John hauled them to athletic events, ice hockey, football, lacrosse, and stayed to watch—or participate.

Each summer, the Whitmans put aside a week for a family trip. "We would rent a van and go out West to the Bad Lands and to the national parks," says Christie. "We did some camping and a lot of hiking and things like that with them. We always tried to get away as a family in a situation where we experienced things together for the first time."

As the children grew older, the family started mountain biking out West. Taylor jokes about his mother's demeanor on the trail: "When she is not swearing at herself for going on the trip, she is having a good time."

During the 1993 race for governor, Christie sent a clear message to New Jersey voters about the importance of her family. At a time in late July when her campaign was experiencing serious difficulties, she decided to accompany her family on a week-long, trail-bike trip to Idaho. When reporters, critical of the trip, gathered at Newark International Airport for the family's return home and began firing questions at her mother, Kate cried.

Kate and Taylor were students at Deerfield Academy in Deerfield, Massachusetts, and the airport incident was one of the few times the campaign directly touched their lives. "We had just come from being very close and very private—from being a family—and all of the sudden you walk off the plane and there is the campaign," Christie recalls with a look of concern in her eyes.

Christie, who describes the incident as one of the low points in her campaign for governor, never backed away from her decision to take the trip. "There is nothing more important than the family. This all will pass. I am not going to be governor forever. I will be a mother for all of my life, if nothing happens to the kids. And that's more important than anything else."

As the children were growing up, Christie had a close relationship with both of them, but there was a period when she did not get along with Kate. Kate has inherited her mother's ability to make her feelings known when things do not suit her or if she thinks something is a waste of time. At the age of seven, Kate made a quick switch from figure skating to ice hockey. "We were at Lake Placid and they dressed me in this blue Smurf costume with a white hat, and that was it," says Kate.

"It's a family that has a lot of respect for each other, that listens to each other," recounts Nancy Risque Rohrbach. "But like all families, they have their moments." Christie describes her relationship with her daughter with frank amusement: "Kate was very strong-willed, and she and I fought like tigers until she was about thirteen. From the time she was ten until she was thirteen, John used to come home and laugh because he said I was behaving just like Kate. The two of us would be just bellowing at each other."

John admits enjoying the situation. "I would come home from the office and the two of them would be sitting there sort of spitting at each other. The question I had was, 'Who was the more mature one of the two of them?' They both would be fighting about nothing. It was really very funny, and I would just sit there and laugh at both of them, and they would get redder and redder in the face." The situation reversed itself when Kate turned thirteen. "At a time when everyone starts to have bad times with their children as teenagers, it [her relationship with Kate] was wonderful." says Christie.

Taylor, on the other hand, was an easy-going child. "He didn't have the high spikes, the emotional roller coasters that Kate subjected us to. He was much easier from that perspective."

Kate, who inherited her mother's blue eyes and thick, straight hair, was more like Christie had been during her younger years at Pontefract. "Taylor is too nice," Christie says bluntly. "He always conned every teacher he had. They were always in love with him. He was always able to slide through things when he shouldn't have, when they should have been making him stay after or do more homework. But he had them all wrapped around his little finger. He would just smile and be nice, and they would fall for it. Kate would always argue with everybody, so she didn't get the same breaks from the teachers as Taylor."

Along with her mother's ability to argue, Kate inherited Christie's love for horses. When the Whitmans were on a trip to Santa Fe, Kate fell in love with an Arabian horse named Cozmo.

"I asked the lady how much, and she said probably around twelve," Christie recalls.

> I looked at Kate and said, "We are not paying any $12,000 for a four-year-old that we have to truck home. You can forget that."
>
> Well, she [Kate] was just in love with this horse at that point. We went out to dinner, and when we came back, Kate said, guess what, Mom, it's not $12,000, its $1,200 and here is the name of the person who can ship it and here's the name of a vet. She had done everything. She had gone back and checked this out. So we got Cozmo for her, and she had a ball with him. He was a four-year-old that had never done anything but

trail riding. She turned him into a fox hunter and had many happy years on him.

As they were growing up, Kate and Taylor told their mother things that they would share with no one else. "We used to have this joke," says Kate. "She would come into my room, and in this deep, joking voice say, 'Tell me your deepest, darkest secrets.' I could really tell her anything. I could tell her about problems with friends and at school."

When Taylor was about ten years old, Nancy Risque Rohrbach, his godmother, invited him to Washington, D.C., to view the filming of an NBC Christmas special. After the event, Taylor had the opportunity to meet film star Arnold Schwarzenegger, so he headed in the actor's direction to secure an autograph. When he returned without the autograph, no one could ascertain why—except Christie. For weeks after his return to Far Hills, he talked to his mother about how he was dumbstruck by the beautiful Maria Shriver, Schwarzenegger's wife, and had been unable to ask for the actor's autograph. "We can talk to each other," Taylor says. "All of us."

Christie handles family problems head-on with frank, open discussion. When there was a crisis, like the time Taylor had an appendectomy, she reacted with a calmness and sureness about what needed to be done. "Christie is very matter-of-fact about life and that sometimes can be read as not having an emotional attachment, but she is quite romantic with deep feelings," says Rohrbach.

Taylor (who plays football and ice hockey at Deerfield and is six feet tall, having grown half a foot since his mother was elected governor) recalls his mother's reaction to the inconvenient timing of the operation. "We were just about to go on a family vacation out West. They canceled the trip, and she stayed with me night and day, reading and watching TV."

In the early years, when there was a problem with the children—for example, when Taylor refused to pick up his room—the situation was handled with a "kitchen meeting." As a result of some of those more serious family discussions, punishment was doled out. "They have their rules, and we follow them," Kate says. "I don't want to disappoint them."

(In the mid-1980s, the Whitmans' lifestyle took an upward turn. In 1987, John left Citicorp to run the leverage-buyout division of Prudential-Bache Securities. In 1990 he opened his own financial consulting firm,

Broken Bridge Incorporated, which encouraged United States investment in countries previously behind the iron curtain. In 1995, he formed his own leveraged-buyout corporation, City Growth Funds.)

In a decision that would return to haunt Christie's political career (in the way similar disclosures damaged some of President Clinton's cabinet nominees), in 1986 the Whitmans hired two illegal aliens, a Portuguese couple, to care for the children and Pontefract. And according to family members, Christie and John were no longer drinking the cheap brand of champagne that they had brought from London, but were toasting with a more expensive brand.

Even as she began to gain a toehold in politics, Christie's extended family was the main focus of her life. She devoted herself, not just to her husband and children, but to her aging parents. It was a matter of family tradition. She had been reared in a family of strong, influential matriarchs in a social setting where the entire family—from the newest baby to the great-grandmother—gathered for holiday celebrations and parties.

In 1986 when Eleanor Todd suffered a stroke, underwent brain surgery, and lapsed into a coma, Christie visited her every day in the hospital, shuffling back and forth between the hospital and ice hockey games for Kate and Taylor. In an incident that fused three generations of women, Eleanor awoke from the coma and spoke for the first time in three weeks when she overheard Christie bragging to the nurses about Kate's skating competition.

Kate is the most recent recipient of the matriarchal heritage passed from Kate Schley to Eleanor Schley Todd, to Christie Todd Whitman, and now to Kate Whitman. The young Kate compares herself to her mother: "She is strong-willed and opinionated. She has opinions and ideas, and she stands by them—so do I." Declining to follow her mother's footsteps to Wheaton College or the Todd family's path to Princeton, in 1995 Kate enrolled at Wesleyan University in Middletown, Connecticut.

Christie's family has always been the rock upon which she relied. First it was Eleanor and Webster Todd, and then John Whitman. "He is clearly my best friend," Christie Whitman said, as she sat forward in her seat. "We were friends before we started serious dating, as it were. That formed a very good basis for a relationship. We just had a lot in common."

While breaking the glass ceiling for women in a number of areas, Whitman has never downplayed the importance of her family and her husband.

Friends and family say John Whitman assumed the role of "Mr. Mom" as Christie became more active in politics. John also plays a role in picking Christie's clothes, and according to those close to the Whitman family, he is an active participant in the choices made about house decorations and food preparation. I sat across a desk from Christie Whitman seventeen months after she had been elected New Jersey's first woman governor and heard her credit John for her success. "I obviously couldn't have done what I am doing if it weren't for his support and understanding, because he has had to step in on more than one occasion with the kids when I haven't been able to do things. And just his overall support has made it all possible."

John loves to surprise Christie, and his biggest surprise was delivered in 1989 when she was president of the state Board of Public Utilities.

> For our fifteenth wedding anniversary, I said, "The only thing that you have to do is you have to be the hostess at a dinner party Friday night." I organized all of our ushers and bridesmaids to meet us in Paris. I hadn't bothered to tell her where the dinner party was, just that there was a dinner party and that she was the hostess.
>
> I had spent the week or ten days before this with Christie's secretary at the Board of Public Utilities. She [Christie] would make an appointment, and we would cancel it, but leave it in the book. She had a whole calendar of things that she had to do, at least she thought she did. Every one of which had been canceled.
>
> I have always spent a lot of time picking her clothes. I like doing that. I had to pack for her. The dinner was at a very chichi restaurant, so I decided what she was going to wear that night and put it all together. I rented a car for the evening to take us around.

However, there was a glitch in the plans. On April 19, the day before their wedding anniversary, the State Commission of Investigation issued a report focusing, in part, on the BPU's inability to adequately set trash hauling rates in New Jersey. "I nearly got away with it entirely . . . but there was some crisis at the Board of Public Utilities the afternoon of the party. I couldn't just spirit her away. I had to tell her just before we were going to go. I asked if she thought we should stay because of this crisis. Since we were going to Paris, she didn't think we had to stay."

Like Christie's parents, the Whitmans never just sit around doing nothing. John and Christie spend their free time together, playing tennis and golf, fishing, and biking. "He doesn't go off with the boys for nights, nor do I go off with the girls for nights or weekends or vacations or anything like that. We always do them together."

Between husband and wife the competition can be keen, Christie explains. "I'm much better as his partner for tennis. It's bad when I'm on the other side of the net. Most husbands and wives say they can't play together because they get so mad at one another if one makes a mistake. That doesn't happen with us. We are much better playing together than we are on opposite sides. I hate losing a point to him."

Similar to the relationship Christie had with her father, she constantly banters with John and the children. "Every person in the family is strong-willed, strong-minded, and determined," says Nancy Risque Rohrbach. "According to Christie and Mr. Todd, you had better be able to stand the heat to be a person of character." Christie likes to tease John about his propensity for accidents. "She teases him, and he takes it," Georgie Schley says.

The challenges go in all directions in the Whitman family. "She basically challenges everybody to try and keep up with her," says John. "It is kind of a friendly challenge . . . part of the structure of the family, this competitive spirit of challenging everybody all the time: . . . 'Are you good enough to do this, or even more so, do you have enough energy to do this and keep up?' And that's fun."

At times, Christie is on the receiving end of the banter. According to John, "Everybody's ego suffers. I think it's frustrating to her when she either isn't as good at something as somebody else or she plays badly at something. And you can get her goat about that all the time. And you have to. Whenever you get a chance, you've got to take advantage of her because she is going to [take advantage of you]."

While there is a lively give-and-take going on inside the family, it's not visible to the public. The Whitmans work hard to protect the family's privacy, as John, Kate, and Taylor maintain a low profile. This was especially true during Christie's ascent to the governorship.

At a statehouse news conference the day after Christie Whitman was elected governor, John, who loves to talk, was asked for a comment on his wife's victory. Wearing a dark business suit and glasses, he pushed his way through the crowd to the rostrum where she was standing, and kissed her.

That was it. A simple, quiet show of support. "John has his own strong personality," said Malcolm S. Forbes, Jr., Christie's friend since kindergarten. "There is no feeling of weakness or jealously. He has a strong ego. And he is proud of what she is doing." At times, during the heat of the campaign when New Jersey newspapers were filled with articles critical of her campaign operation, John was openly upset over what he considered unfair media coverage. "Some days, we have to peel him off the ceiling," Christie declared during the campaign.

Christie Whitman was questioned throughout her campaign for governor and during her first years in the office about the amount of influence John Whitman has over the political and governmental decisions she makes. As an expert in banking and finances, John Whitman played a key role in Christie's decision to peg her campaign for governor on a 30 percent income tax cut. "He just offers his opinion, and that's that. He doesn't push. He knows perfectly well that at the end of the day, I'm going to make the decision."

John responds: "I have a point of view, and I am not shy about telling my wife about what my point of view is. But she is not shy about not taking it either. She has much better political judgment than anybody. Every time we have made a mistake in things like the campaign, it has been by doing things that she didn't want to do but that she got talked into doing. The major part of my job is to be a cheerleader, to convince her to do what she thinks she should do and not what other people think she should do."

As a mother, Christie Whitman has the ability to leave her all-consuming job at the statehouse. "She doesn't bring it home with her, but she is more than willing to talk to us about it, if we are interested," Taylor says. In a May 1995 commencement address at Wheaton College, she told the graduates that they needed to consider the importance of their families, as well as their careers, when they planned their lives. It was the same point her paternal grandfather, John R. Todd, had made in his autobiography. "I don't mind saying I have the most important and fulfilling job in the world. It demands responsibility, knowledge of finance, being on-call twenty-four hours a day, combining firm leadership with careful negotiation, and keeping one's promises. That job is being a parent."

In the final days of the race against Gov. Jim Florio, when the Whitman campaign for governor was in serious trouble, Kate made a radio ad for her mother. "We were looking at the polls, and I was not doing well among women," Christie explains. "It was clear that I needed to do more about being a wife and mother and understanding those things."

Christie's Washington-based ad man made the suggestion that Kate record a radio ad, and she instantly agreed. The media firm sent someone to Deerfield with a copy of the ad. "She rewrote it a bit to make it more like her own words," her proud mother recalls. "It was a really good ad, and it really had an impact on people."

Kate's ad countered the image Gov. Florio had painted of Christie Whitman as a soft-on-crime candidate who favored drunken drivers, assault weapons, and carjackers. Kate said to radio listeners:

> I want to tell you about a wonderful woman I know. She's been my role model for sixteen years. She's taught me about honesty and integrity, and about the challenges facing working mothers. She's also taught me that no matter what your fight, stand up for what you believe, whether it's equal rights or equal pay.
>
> Her name is Christie Whitman, and she's running for governor. Jim Florio has said a lot of nasty things about her. He says she doesn't care about people, but I know that's not true. Christie Whitman wants to bring jobs back to New Jersey, so that moms and dads can go back to work.
>
> And as the mother of two children, Christie Whitman wants schools that give kids a great education and she wants the streets safe from assault weapons and drunk drivers. So when Jim Florio tells you Christie doesn't care, don't believe him.
>
> I know Christie Whitman cares. She's not running for governor because she wants to be a politician. She wants to see New Jersey working again. I know, because Christie Whitman is my mom. I'm Kate Whitman, and I hope you'll vote for Christie Whitman for governor.

Christie Whitman had adjusted her life and her political goals for Kate by staying home with her for the first five years of her life to nurture her and to help her grow. Kate, in her own way, was continuing the family heritage, and returning the favor.

5

Political Seeds

"I categorically deny that there was anything wrong with what happened. It was all done in the full light of day."

Christie Whitman (October 6, 1993)
on being asked about the votes she cast as a Somerset County
freeholder to deposit millions of dollars into the Somerset Trust Co.,
a bank in which she and her family had substantial financial interests.

"My intention was that the land be preserved forever as open space."

Christie Whitman (May 29, 1993)
on a maneuver during her final hours at the New Jersey Board
of Public Utilities to sell 287 acres of protected watershed land.

When the Somerset County Republican party asked Christie Whitman if she would run for a freeholder position in 1982, she jumped at the chance. In New Jersey, freeholders are the part-time officials, elsewhere known as commissioners, who direct county government. Whitman, thirty-six, had been out of politics for nearly a decade, since 1973 when she left Washington, D.C., moved to New York, and married John Whitman. With Taylor now three years old and Kate five, Whitman was ready for the challenge.

Her only public service had been membership on the Somerset County Community College board of trustees and participation in the Upper Raritan Watershed Association. Now, she would help run one of the wealthiest counties in New Jersey during an economic boom when residents were moving into the suburbs and demanding more services.

In 1982, because of her family's name recognition and involvement in politics and business in Somerset County, Whitman won a three-year term on the board of freeholders even though she challenged a formidable incumbent Democrat for the position. When she was successfully reelected three years later, she was the top vote-getter on the Somerset County Republican ticket.

During her five-year tenure as a Somerset County freeholder, Whitman, who served as both deputy director and director of the board, was praised by her colleagues for her hard work and honesty. Workers were surprised at the way they were treated by the wealthy newcomer who rose to the status of freeholder director. "She would come out of her office and say, 'I'm going down for tea. Does anybody want something or would you like to go along?' " recalls Barbara Lucas, clerk of the board. "She would go to the coffee shop so people could talk to her. She always had an ear for everybody." If a mistake was made, instead of spending time searching for the culprit, Whitman would focus on solving the problem.

Whitman was serious about her work, turning the elected position into a full-time job, but at times she also could be silly. Her hair cut to chin length, Whitman often wore tailored dresses and blouses with notched collars to work. However, on her fortieth birthday in 1986, she wore a T-shirt with a picture of a diamond and the words "Forty and Flawless" across the front and enjoyed being the brunt of jokes about the milestone.

She always put the children first, dropping them off at school in the morning and then picking them up in the afternoon. If they were sick, she stayed home. If need be, she brought them to work, giving Taylor paper clips to make chain links and allowing Kate to write stories about her horse on the computer.

Her performance as a freeholder was given high marks by editorial writers and surprised some professionals who dealt with the county. The *Home News* of East Brunswick, New Jersey, praised her service on the board:

Since her election, Whitman has been the most visible, the most active, the most engaged member of Somerset's all-Republican board. Issues that Somerset's freeholders had ignored or dithered about for years . . . she pushed to resolution.

When Whitman was placed in charge of the construction of a new courthouse, the construction contractors and workers considered it a joke for a woman to have been appointed to the position. But the laughter stopped when Whitman, whose father and grandfather had constructed Rockefeller Center and restored colonial Williamsburg, showed up in her hard hat to inspect the construction site. And she went toe-to-toe with the contractors in boardroom sessions to complete the construction at $2 million below cost estimates. In another move that surprised county workers, when the county initiated a recycling program, Whitman jumped aboard a truck and traveled one of the pickup routes to make certain the system was working properly.

Yet in many cases, Whitman's decisions as a freeholder came back to haunt her during the 1993 race for governor. When her freeholder record resurfaced during the campaign, more often than not, it hamstrung her efforts to win.

While she was on the gubernatorial campaign trail promising to lower taxes and cut government spending at the state level, Whitman had to answer to her Democratic and Republican opponents for a county record that showed budgets that literally soared.

From 1985 to 1987, Whitman's final three years as a freeholder, the Somerset County budgets increased by more than 44 percent. Whitman and the other freeholders, like the state's leaders in the mid-1980s when the economy was booming and tax revenues were flowing into the public coffers, spent the public's money at a fast pace. While she was on the board, the freeholders authorized the construction of the new county courthouse, a new two-hundred-inmate jail, a renovated and expanded county administration building, a seven-hundred-car parking deck for county employees, and a county library. During her tenure, the county also opened its first homeless shelter and a halfway house for alcoholic male teenagers.

As an example of the speed in which Somerset County money was spent, the $12.7 million bond ordinance to fund the jail was introduced the same night in May 1987 that the freeholders authorized the final payment on the $15.5 million courthouse. Meanwhile, renovations to the administration building had already begun and its $4 million addition was planned for later that year.

During Whitman's tenure as freeholder, the Somerset County property tax rate fell almost 3 percent, but the value of the real estate to which the tax was applied increased 75 percent (because of the construction of new buildings and higher assessments on old buildings), bringing an additional $64 million into the county coffers. To her credit, during the boom years, Whitman insisted on planning for the future, and by 1987, the county had a surplus totaling 14 percent of its budget. "She did not believe in major swings in the tax rate, where you drop it ten points when times were good and then raise it back up," Republican freeholder John Kitchen told the Associated Press during Whitman's 1993 campaign for governor. "We knew the boom would not last forever."

Somerset County budgets reveal the details of the spending frenzy during Whitman's tenure as freeholder. In 1985, the county budget increased 17 percent to $59 million. It funded a 6.5 percent pay raise for the freeholders, twenty-four new county jobs, a 15 percent increase in county debt, a 32 percent increase in road and bridge work, and a 9.4 percent salary increase for county workers. The county ended the year with an $8 million surplus, saving $3 million and transferring $5 million into the 1986 budget.

The 1986 budget increased spending by another 17 percent to $69 million. It funded thirty new county workers, 4 percent to 6 percent raises for county employees, and a 4 percent raise for freeholders. A separate capital improvement budget of $36 million, including the jail, land for a five-mile-long park, and improvements to roads and bridges, was funded mostly through borrowing.

The 1987 budget increased spending by yet another 10 percent to $76.5 million. The county debt service alone increased by $2.6 million because of the large number of building projects undertaken by the county in the 1980s; the number of workers on the county payroll grew by forty-seven; and the Board of Social Services received a $1 million increase, including $460,000 for a homeless shelter.

For the fourth year in a row, the freeholders gave themselves a raise, the same 6 percent they gave to other county employees. Freeholders' salaries increased from $15,335 to $16,255, and Whitman's salary, as free-holder director, rose from $16,335 to $17,255. Freeholders justified the increases by saying that their salaries were still less than those paid to free-holders in the two neighboring counties of Union and Middlesex.

When the 1987 budget was passed, Somerset County Democratic party chief Norman Weinstein blasted the freeholders for excessive spending. The freeholders, in turn, defended the budget by saying the increase was needed for the county to keep pace with its growing population.

During her campaign for governor, Whitman's Democratic and Republican opponents were quick to point out the increased spending and salaries during her years as freeholder. "I laugh when she talks about controlling costs," Weinstein told the *Press* of Atlantic City. "If you look back at those budgets, they had some of the fastest rates of increases the county has ever seen." While Whitman served on the freeholder board, the county devoted some of the money flowing into its coffers to preserving open space. By matching $2.5 million in county money with state funding to purchase the development rights to area farms, the county preserved them forever as farmland. Participating farmers were paid the difference between the value of their land as farmland and what it would bring if sold for development. In return, the farmers signed agreements never to develop their land.

During her tenure as freeholder, Whitman had the courage to grapple with the county's politically sensitive trash crisis. The county had been ignoring the state's instructions to take care of its own waste and was continuing to dump its trash in nearby Middlesex County. Attacking the problem head-on, Whitman defended controversial plans to build both a landfill and an incinerator inside county lines.

"I think there's no question that wherever the landfill is located, people who it will have an impact on will protest," Whitman told the *Courier-News* in June 1987. "Our responsibility is to find a suitable site for a landfill . . . and understand we're not going to make everyone happy."

After the board came under fire for going behind closed doors to select a landfill site, Whitman scheduled a public hearing on the plan and allowed the meeting to continue until 1 A.M. Five charter buses brought in protesters, and as public outrage over the landfill erupted, the freeholders, including Whitman, were called potential killers and were described as immoral, dispassionate, and asinine. When the freeholders tried to build an incinerator in another part of the county, angry residents, carrying signs painted with skulls and crossbones, charged that the freeholders were endangering their homes and health. In the face of the public outcry, the freeholders signed a contract to transport Somerset County's trash to Pennsylvania. However, they did move forward with long-range plans to build the landfill. When the freeholders finally approved the site in December 1987, just before Whitman resigned from the board, she told the *Courier-News* that the vote was "one of the toughest and most far-reaching decisions the board has made in recent history." (The county, which still takes its trash to Pennsylvania, never followed through on plans to construct a landfill within its own borders.)

During Whitman's tenure on the board of freeholders, it was criticized on several occasions for its closed-door policies. In October 1983, the board was successfully sued under the state's Right to Know laws for withholding information and excluding the public from a decision on the site of the county's new landfill. Ruling in favor of two newspapers, a Superior Court judge said the freeholders had to reveal the location of proposed landfill sites, which had been withheld from the public.

Again in March 1986, the *Courier-News* reported that Whitman had presided over a closed-door meeting, in violation of the New Jersey Sunshine Law, during which freeholders voted on the site for the county jail. The next day, Whitman said she misspoke when she said an actual vote had been taken. "We did not vote. We came to an agreement."

The *Courier-News,* in its endorsement of a Democratic candidate for freeholder in 1987, wrote:

> The all-Republican freeholder board in this very Republican county is clubby and sometimes displays an assurance of power that borders on arrogance. An example is when they decided the final siting of the new jail behind closed doors.

The most serious issue to arise from Whitman's tenure on the freeholder board did not become an issue until the fall of 1993 while she was running for governor.

As Whitman's campaign for governor stumbled through Labor Day and into October, Republican party leaders in New Jersey grew increasingly anxious over Whitman's failure to openly attack Gov. Florio on the scandals of his own administration. Florio's chief of staff, Joe Salema, had been forced to resign in the wake of a federal investigation into bond deals in New Jersey, and a Camden County lawmaker, and Florio crony, was accused of ethics violations after the *Trentonian* reported that he had been handed a $2.8 million sweetheart office lease by the Florio administration. Yet Whitman had failed to use the scandals as ammunition against Florio.

Her ability to do so was damaged when on October 6, 1993, the *Courier-News* published a story on Whitman's own bank dealings. During her tenure as a Somerset County freeholder, Whitman had watched her own stock portfolio, as well as her family's, grow, as she voted to deposit millions of county dollars into a bank where her family held substantial financial interests. During a press conference in Trenton, Whitman confirmed that the *Courier-News* story was accurate, but she maintained that there was nothing wrong with her casting the votes to deposit money in the Somerset Trust Company because everyone in Somerset County knew of her family's ties to the bank. "I categorically deny that there was anything wrong with what happened," Whitman told reporters. "It was all done in the full light of day."

The votes were taken in meetings open to the public, and no one had challenged them at the time, Whitman said. Besides, the Somerset Trust Company had been used for county deposits for ten years before she was elected as freeholder, and Whitman maintained that she had never cast the deciding vote in favor of the bank. "There was no visible change in the relationship [with the bank] from before Christie got there and when she left," Carl Golden, Whitman's campaign spokesman, stated. "The [county's] relationship with the bank was the same in 1974, as it was in 1985, as it is today."

Margaret Maccini, longtime clerk to the Somerset County freeholders, told reporter Pat Politano of the *Courier-News*: "It was known not only to the freeholders, but to the whole town [that] her family was involved. I don't remember ever discussing her association with the bank. What would there be to discuss?"

Whitman's maternal grandfather, Reeve Schley, and two other investors had purchased the controlling shares of the bank in the 1930s, thereby saving it from going out of business during the depression. The old investment, which appeared unimportant to Reeve Schley at the time, proved to be a lucrative investment for the Schley family, including Christie Whitman.

The Democrats charged in 1993 that Whitman had violated conflict-of-interest rules when she cast the old freeholder votes, and an aide to the Whitman campaign conceded privately that she should have abstained on the votes. Whitman argued that her votes on matters related to the Somerset Trust Company were approved by the freeholders' attorney, William Ozzard. However, Ozzard later resigned as board attorney in 1991. Conflict-of-interest questions were raised regarding his law firm representing both the county and a waste-hauling company in a garbage dispute.

County records show that Whitman, at times, abstained on votes designating Somerset Trust Company as a depository for county funds, but in other instances, she chose to vote. Golden said she had abstained on votes that specifically related to Somerset Trust Company, but chose to vote on board motions that listed the trust company together with other banks selected for county deposits. Yet in one instance, 1983 county records show that Whitman personally introduced a resolution specifically designating Somerset Trust Company as the depository for the county sheriff's account.

During the five-year period that Whitman served as a freeholder, the county deposited $74 million into eleven bank accounts at the Somerset Trust Company where Whitman and other family members held millions of dollars in stock, the *Courier-News* reported. During Whitman's tenure on the board, the county's yearly bank deposits into the Somerset Trust Company ranged from $5.1 million to as much as $35.6 million. The *Courier-News* story stated that over that same period, the value of the bank stock owned by Whitman family members, including Whitman herself, grew from $2 million in 1983 to $6.5 million in 1988, as the value of a share of stock in the bank jumped from $17 to $34. Whitman, herself, owned 1,000 shares of stock in Somerset County Trust Company, and while sitting on the freeholder board, she watched the value of those shares grow from $17,000 to $34,000. However, Whitman's shares were minuscule when compared with investments in the Somerset Trust Company owned by other family members during her tenure as freeholder. Whitman's mother, Eleanor Schley Todd, and her uncle, Reeve Schley, Jr., were among the bank's top three investors, with her mother owning 5.5 percent of the trust company and her uncle's share fluctuating between 10 percent and 13 percent.

In addition, many of the bank's investors and board members, including those from the Whitman family, were prominent Somerset County Republicans. During Whitman's tenure as freeholder, her brother John R. Todd II and her cousin Reeve Schley III, served on the bank's board of directors and owned stock in the institution. After leaving the freeholder board, Whitman joined its board of directors and expanded her financial interests at the institution through gifts of stock from her mother. By 1990, when Whitman filed the financial disclosure form required for her entry into the 1990 U.S. Senate race against Sen. Bill Bradley, the Somerset Trust Company stock held by herself, John, Kate, and Taylor was worth between $151,000 and $355,000.

While the controversy surrounding the bank votes failed to have a long-lasting, negative impact on the Whitman campaign, behind the scenes, the damage was more significant. The bank vote, combined with a controversial vote Whitman cast as president of the New Jersey State Board of Public Utilities (BPU) to sell protected watershed land, made the campaign staff cautious in its attacks on Gov. Florio's ethics. Whitman's tenure as a freeholder and her stint on the BPU were the only government experiences she had prior to running for governor. And in a larger sense, when opponents referred to the Somerset Trust Company issue or the controversial land sale at the BPU, Whitman was quick to point out that the two incidents were the best examples that anyone could find to criticize her past performance.

In early 1988, Whitman left the freeholder board two-thirds of the way through her second three-year term to accept an appointment by Republican Gov. Tom Kean to the state Board of Public Utilities. The New Jersey BPU, a three-member panel, sets state policy and consumer rates for electric, gas, telephone, and water utilities, as well as the cable television and garbage disposal industries. Whitman was appointed to the board amid charges that she wasn't qualified for the position and in the face of evidence that sitting members of the board had been guilty of ethical misconduct.

While there were no specific qualifications for the $90,000-a-year post, questions were raised about whether Whitman was qualified because she totally lacked expertise in the field of public utilities. Ed Lloyd, general counsel to the New Jersey Public Interest Research Group, called the practice of appointing inexperienced people to the board "a very serious problem." Gov. Kean defended Whitman's nomination by saying that the most important qualifications for the post were common sense and the ability to weigh issues fairly. "I didn't want a technocrat," he told the Gannett News Service.

BPU board members are appointed by the governor with confirmation required by the state Senate. During her January 21, 1988, confirmation hearing before the Senate Judiciary Committee, Whitman faced some tough questioning from Sen. John Lynch of Middlesex County, where Somerset County had hauled its garbage during the debate for the construction of a landfill within Somerset's own borders. When Lynch tried to saddle Whitman with the responsibility for planning delays on the landfill, she turned the question to her advantage by citing one of her accomplishments as freeholder. "Who had vision down the road in Somerset County in the early 1970s when they first got reports from their consultants saying they needed some landfills?" Lynch asked Whitman. "Not being on the board at that time, Senator, I wouldn't try to answer that," Whitman reported.

"But you're privy to that. You know that that was recommended back in those days," Lynch countered. "I know they've been looking," Whitman answered. "It's a little bit like the courthouse, Senator. That had been something that had been seen as a need for fifteen years before I went on the board, and it's now open. That was my responsibility."

Somerset County's *Courier-News* defended Whitman's appointment against attacks by Democratic state Sen. Daniel Dalton.

> Whitman has shown that she is bright, level-headed, committed to public service and able to move projects along while carefully balancing competing interests. Moreover, it's hard to imagine her taking freebies from utilities or otherwise compromising her credibility—as a number of current and former utility commissioners have done. Christie Whitman's appointment was a political one, but she is not, as Dalton suggests, a political hack. She's a public servant who deserves a promotion.

Kate, ten, and Taylor, eight, held the Bible while Whitman, wearing a long-sleeved paisley dress, was sworn in as BPU president in a ceremony presided over by Gov. Kean. Pictures of the event show Kate with the same serious, almost bored expression that early pictures of her mother had captured during political events in the 1950s.

Whitman had some problems waiting for her when she arrived on the job. The year before she was appointed to the BPU, the state's Executive Commission on Ethical Standards found that the BPU had lapsed into a period of "unprecedented, widespread ethical insensitivity and backsliding" by accepting social favors from utilities. Not only did the ethics commission find that board commissioners and staff were using utility companies' boxes at the Meadowlands Sports Complex, but one commissioner had been honored with a $64,000 banquet paid for by the utility companies while another had accepted an invitation to the dinner, worth $300.

In addition, the board had been criticized for its controversial decision to reject recommendations from some of its top staffers and allow the Public Service Electric and Gas Company to bill its customers for the $4 billion cost of the company's Hope Creek nuclear power plant, a project plagued by cost overruns. Whitman had just been appointed to the BPU board when she attended her first New Jersey Legislative Correspondents' dinner, the annual dinner hosted by the statehouse press corps, and she was greeted by reporters carrying banners that read, "BPU Ethics—P.U."

When Whitman arrived at the BPU's headquarters in Newark for her first day on the job, she also discovered that her landlord was the American Telephone and Telegraph Company, one of the utilities the agency regulated. "I couldn't believe it when I walked in," Whitman told the Gannett News Service. "If the state does any construction of government buildings, we'll move." (In 1995, AT&T was still the BPU's landlord.) Whitman's first task at the BPU was to address the ethics problems. During her term on the board, she implemented an ethics code aimed at halting the acceptance of favors from utility companies. "If there is ever a hint of someone not obeying it, I'm going to come down very, very hard. And they know it."

On the fiscal side, the BPU's budget, derived from fees paid by the utility companies, grew 13 percent, from $12.9 million to $14.6 million, while Whitman was on the board. Gov. Tom Kean had rejected Whitman's request to have it grow even more. During Whitman's tenure at the BPU, published reports indicated that electric rates statewide dipped in 1988 and increased in 1989. Customers at seventy-seven water and sewer systems and three gas companies saw their rates increase, yet New Jersey Bell kept its rates the same.

In a controversy over privacy rights, Whitman voted against allowing New Jersey Bell to offer its customers Caller ID, a system that allows customers to view the telephone number of a caller before answering the telephone. Whitman sided with the state's Public Advocate, who opposed the service on privacy grounds. The other two BPU commissioners voted in favor of the service. Whitman said Caller ID service threatened the privacy of battered women and people contemplating suicide who call police or counseling services for help. "I have a real fear that people will not avail themselves of these services when they most desperately need them."

On another issue, Whitman voted in favor of the customers in 1988 when the BPU board ordered Public Service Electric and Gas Company and Atlantic Electric Company to pay more than $35 million in refunds for the poor performance at the Peach Bottom nuclear power plant in Pennsylvania.

By the end of her first year on the BPU board, Whitman, was receiving high marks from her critics. "I think she has learned a lot in one year, and she has brought a certain air of dignity to the board," Raymond Makul told Gannett News Service. Makul was the lawyer for the state's Public Advocate, the state agency that frequently challenged BPU rulings. (Ironically, one of the first things Whitman did when she was elected governor was abolish the Public Advocate.)

Sen. Dalton, Whitman's early critic, said he was surprisingly pleased with Whitman's performance. "The Board of Public Utilities is as powerful an entity as we have in this state, and yet no one knows much about it. In the past, the only time you heard from them was in a reactive manner, either defending the decision they made or defending the status quo. I'm seeing Whitman being more aggressive."

The workers at the BPU were so fond of Whitman that when she ran for governor in 1993, many of the clerical workers who had been Democrats all their lives crossed party lines to vote for her. They said she had been fair. And when she could, Whitman opted for training those who were already at the BPU, allowing them to move into higher-level positions rather than bringing others in from the outside.

Whitman had been appointed in February 1988 to serve the final two years of an unexpired term on the BPU board. In February 1989, Gov. Kean nominated her to a full six-year term on the board, beginning in January 1990. During her confirmation hearing for the full term, the BPU was again rocked by charges of ethics abuses. It was revealed that the State Executive Commission on Ethical Standards had launched a new investigation into misconduct at the BPU. The investigation centered on charges that board member George Barbour and a top staffer at the agency had dined privately with a consultant for a county utility authority a week before the board granted a rate increase for the utility.

The incident had occurred in 1987, before Whitman was appointed to the board. Nevertheless, the senators' questions at the confirmation hearing left Whitman defending statements that one of her top priorities had been to clean up the board's ethics. Whitman said that she was the one who had initiated the ethics probe by turning the information on Barbour over to the ethics commission several days after learning about the incident. "I can only say that I don't think I'm the most popular person at the Board of Public Utilities because I have enforced the code of ethics."

In October 1989, the ethics commission filed three complaints against Barbour for violating conflict-of-interest laws. The commission learned that the consultant who dined with Barbour billed the utility $350 for the dinner and justified it by saying that he had talked to utility board officials about the rate request. Barbour, who reached an agreement with the ethics panel and paid an $855 civil penalty to settle the issue in January 1990, remained on the board until Gov. Florio replaced him in June 1991.

However, Whitman continued to maintain that she had cleaned up the agency's ethical problems. She told the *Courier-News*: "What the public should be assured of is this agency's commitment to the highest standard of ethical conduct from the top down." Despite her assurances to the lawmakers, another incident in 1989 raised questions about the agency's ethics. Three attorneys employed as BPU regulatory officers were found to be conducting private legal business during agency hours. When the attorneys were confronted with violations of the new ethics code, they challenged it in court and won when a Superior Court judge ruled that the code had been adopted improperly. Stating that the BPU would appeal, Whitman maintained that the code was valid and had been properly adopted.

During her second year at the BPU, Whitman joined other board members in the unpopular decision to allow Jersey Central Power & Light Company to force its customers to pay for the $189 million cost of the accident which had occurred a decade earlier at the Three Mile Island nuclear power plant in Pennsylvania. Whitman also came under fire from the state's investigatory agency during her tenure at the BPU for the utility board's handling of trash-hauling rates. New Jersey, like many of its neighboring states, was facing a waste-handling crisis. With landfill space shrinking and plans under way for expensive and controversial waste-burning incinerators—and residents wanting neither in their back yards—the cost of waste hauling had more than doubled in some New Jersey counties.

In April 1989, a scathing report by the State Commission of Investigation (SCI) stated that the BPU lacked both the money and the staff to properly regulate trash-hauling rates or to deal with the influence of organized crime in the trash-hauling industry. The commission described the BPU's regulation of trash-hauling rates as "conspicuously ineffective." (In another interesting move, after becoming governor, Whitman balked at giving the SCI the permanent status it was seeking as a state agency. Instead, she gave it an eighteen-month lease on life and appointed a commission to study whether it was needed at all. When the SCI was created, the state required that its right to exist be periodically voted on by the state legislature.)

The SCI charged that the BPU was so slow in setting rates that many trash haulers ignored its directives and charged customers whatever they wanted. The report indicated that the problems had begun several years before Whitman was named BPU president and continued during her tenure. After the report was issued, Whitman moved to correct the problems by transferring staff from other divisions to address the backlog of rate-setting cases and by approving a uniform pricing system for garbage haulers. However, she maintained that the SCI's proposed reforms—which where never adopted—would have been just as slow at setting rates.

Raymond Makul said that waste haulers were permitted to charge high rates on a temporary basis with the expectation that the rates would be lowered when they were made permanent, but the lawyers for the haulers were able to continually delay the permanent rates by bouncing minor issues back and forth between the BPU and the state's courts. In a statement to the *Record* of Hackensack, Makul claimed that Whitman could have stopped the delay with stronger leadership. "At no point did I see anybody calling these people in a room and reading them the riot act. My impression was that she [Whitman] relied pretty heavily on staff. . . . She was definitely a layman in the utilities field. She wasn't there long enough to acquire the technical skills to make independent judgments." Yet Makul told the *Atlantic City Press*: "I would never accuse her of not having her heart in the right place."

Several incidents from Whitman's years at the BPU surfaced during the campaign for governor. In one case, Whitman's Republican and Democratic opponents accused her of using BPU workers to conduct a survey for the installation of a satellite dish at Pontefract. While her GOP opponents were able to produce evidence that the BPU wrote Whitman a lengthy memo on the subject and proved that staffers did accompany a cable company during the survey, there was no evidence that Whitman had requested the personalized service. Murray Bevin, Whitman's chief of staff at the BPU, labeled the BPU work done on Whitman's behalf merely employees too eager to please their boss.

A far more serious issue, a maneuver by Whitman during her eleventh-hour at the Board of Public Utilities to sell protected land, haunted her campaign for governor. Whitman had orchestrated two controversial votes in which state and BPU rules were skirted in order to sell watershed property that was protected from development. In a statement to the *Record*, state Assemblyman John Rooney, a member of Whitman's own party, termed her final days at the BPU "an example of a BPU commissioner doing a favor for a rich and powerful utility company."

When the controversial votes were taken in January 1990, Whitman knew that her days were numbered as president of the Board of Public Utilities. Democratic Gov. Jim Florio was about to take office, and it was certain that he would replace Whitman with his own appointee.

Awaiting approval at the BPU was a special request by the Hackensack Water Company to sell 287 acres of protected watershed land to its unregulated sister company, Rivervale Realty. The state had imposed a moratorium on the sale of watershed lands, and any such transaction would need to be approved as a special exception to the state-imposed restriction on watershed sales. Hackensack Water Company, as a regulated utility, could neither sell nor develop the environmentally sensitive land surrounding the Oradell Reservoir in northeastern New Jersey without BPU approval, but Rivervale Realty was not subject to BPU jurisdiction.

The land in question, which was being leased by three golf courses, was some of the last undeveloped land in northern New Jersey, and environmentalists and New Jersey residents were arguing that it should be kept that way in order to control runoff and flooding and as protection for the drinking water supply of nearly one million people. On the other side of the issue, the Hackensack Water Company had powerful political connections to the outgoing Kean administration, as Gov. Kean's brother Robert sat on the board of directors of United Water Resources Incorporated, the parent company for both Hackensack Water Company and Rivervale Realty.

Whitman, appointed to her $90,000-a-year position at the BPU by Gov. Kean, accomplished the approval for the land sale in a half hour. Between 2 P.M. and 2:30 P.M. on January 12, 1990, Whitman presided over the two meetings required for the approval of the controversial sale. At 2 P.M., Whitman convened a meeting of a special Watershed Property Review Board, a three-member board including Whitman, which had the authority to grant the exception to the moratorium on watershed sales. The vote was two to one approving the sale. Helen Fenske, acting commissioner of the Department of Environmental Protection, joined Whitman in voting in favor of the sale. Anthony Villane, commissioner of the Department of Community Affairs, voted against it.

At the property review board session, Whitman said that despite the vote, the land would remain undeveloped. "I would like to emphasize that these deed restrictions will continue to keep these lands open."

Yet a second approval was needed, and at 2:30 P.M. Whitman convened a meeting of the three-member BPU board of commissioners. Via a conference telephone call made by Whitman from the public meeting room at the BPU's Newark office, she and George Barbour, who was on the other end of the telephone line, ignored the BPU's standard competitive bidding process for land sales and voted two-to-zero to allow the sale of the 287 acres.

Giving the New Jersey residents who opposed the plan little time to object, the vote allowed Rivervale Realty to purchase the 287 acres of watershed land at what newspaper reports claimed was a below-market price of $16.5 million. Whitman justified the vote by saying that the board wanted to complete a difficult case, initiated on its watch, before the Democratic administration took control.

At the BPU meeting, Whitman said, "I have reviewed the entire record in this proceeding, including a form of revised deed restrictions which BPU staff and the Attorney General's Office have found offers full and sufficient assurances that the property to be transferred will be permanently dedicated to golf course and country club uses."

Despite her assurances, it was discovered that the agreement of sale included a "poison pill" provision linking protection of the 287 acres to the unhindered development of 700 acres transferred from the Hackensack Water Company to Rivervale Realty six years earlier. The sale document for the 287 acres said that if any governmental body blocked development on any part of the 700 acres sold in 1984, then the owner of the 287 acres was allowed to develop an equivalent amount of that property.

In statements to reporters, Carolyn Hague, the Republican mayor of Oradell, was blunt in her criticism of Whitman's maneuver to allow the land sale. "This is a snow job if I ever heard one. Government's in the pocket of the water company. . . . I had thought a lot of her [Whitman] because she was a very intelligent lady. I really admired her because she was so ladylike, but I really put two and two together in the end because she was so close to Kean. She was a real smart politician."

When the hurried votes were cast, Whitman was well aware of the public's opposition to the plan. Hackensack Water Company's request to sell the 287 acres had been awaiting BPU approval for two years. Opponents of the sale had packed a hearing room on the issue in June 1988. Just twenty-nine days before Whitman organized the approval of the sale, the BPU's Watershed Property Review Board had formally rejected the proposal, and Whitman had voted against selling the land because she said it made the land too easy to develop.

Documents obtained by the *Record* of Hackensack revealed that the sale had been hammered out in private meetings between regulators and water company attorneys prior to the January 12 vote. Just one week before the sale was approved, the Hackensack Water Company indicated, in writing, that an agreement had been reached between the water company and the BPU on a modified plan for the sale. Four months after the controversial vote, the Environmental Defense Fund filed suit against the BPU's decision to allow the sale of the 287 acres, which the environmental group said was needed for open space and to protect the county's drinking water. When the case came to court, the Appellate Division of the New Jersey Superior

Court ruled that the BPU's actions were illegal. Striking down statements by Whitman and others at the BPU who said they were confident the agreement protected the sensitive watershed area from development, the court overturned the land sale. "The BPU board stated that the restrictive covenants* contained in the modified proposal were unqualified, permanent and indefeasible," the court stated. "Clearly, they are none of these."

The court also said that the Watershed Review Board had violated the state's Watershed Protection Law by granting the exception to the moratorium and that the BPU had no basis on which to waive the normal bidding procedures for the land sale. In addition, the court found that both boards had known, in advance, what the decision on the land sale would be before holding their meetings on January 12, 1990, and had failed to allow adequate time for public comment. There were clear indications that the decision had been made in advance, the court stated, noting that "comprehensive, carefully written decisions and orders of both agencies, which required some time to prepare, are dated January 12, 1990," the day the meetings were held.

During the 1993 gubernatorial primary, Whitman blamed the controversial vote on bad advice from her BPU staff. She denied ever discussing the land sale with Gov. Kean. However, in an interview with the *Record* of Hackensack, she admitted that she knew there was a possibility, although she believed it was remote, that the land could be developed. It was later revealed that Whitman did offer to delay the decision on the watershed land if the Florio administration wanted to handle the matter, but incoming BPU commissioner Scott Weiner apparently declined the offer.

Trying to put the issue to rest in May 1993, Whitman sent opinion letters to the state's major newspapers. "My intention was that the land be preserved forever as open space. The appellate court found that the language in the restrictions did not guarantee that the land would remain green forever. That ruling said the language was not as tight as I thought it was and the language should be tightened, as was my intent all along."

During the 1993 campaign for governor, environmentalists termed Whitman's statement a whitewash. "She squelched public comment and

---

*The restrictive covenants, which could be reversed by the "poison pill" provision, restricted the land to golf course and country club use and limited construction to 15 percent of the property.

disregarded the call for protection of environmentally sensitive watershed lands," Jeff Scott, chairman of the Vote Environment Committee of the New Jersey Environmental Federation, said in a press release. "Since this is the only real environmental decision in Whitman's record, her conduct in this matter shows how she might manage and lead in the future." Whitman said that the watershed issue had undergone a number of public hearings prior to the vote, but Oradell mayor Carolyn Hague said in a statement to the *Record* that the public never had a fair chance to speak at the hearings. "The public had to speak through the Public Advocate . . . but the water company attorneys were allowed to have full rein. . . . We felt the public was shut out."

Fortunately for Whitman, the watershed vote had no immediate impact on her political career. Six months after Whitman left the BPU in 1990 to run for the United States Senate, the public's attention had turned away from the environment to another pressing issue. When Whitman emerged as the Republican challenger to the popular United States Sen. Bill Bradley, only one issue was on the minds of New Jersey voters: Gov. Jim Florio's taxes.

6

David and Goliath

"The more people tell me I can't do something, the more I want to try."
Christie Whitman (March 14, 1990)
upon announcing her Senate campaign against Bill Bradley.

As the 1990 U.S. Senate race approached, New Jersey Gov. Tom Kean and the Trenton press corps liked to joke about whether the Republicans would be able to find anyone foolish enough to run against Sen. Bill Bradley, the state's most popular politician with one of the largest war chests in the U.S. Senate.

When Christie Whitman entered the Senate race in the spring of 1990, no one, including the GOP, thought she had a chance. She was considered a sacrificial lamb, the only Republican willing to take on the formidable task of challenging the revered two-term senator and former basketball great. The Princeton All-American, Rhodes Scholar, and star forward of the New York Knickerbockers was considered unbeatable.

Jim Florio's landslide win over Jim Courter in the 1989 gubernatorial race had devastated the Republican party, as Florio's coattails cost the GOP control of the state assembly that same year. A year earlier, Democratic Sen. Frank Lautenberg had defeated Republican Pete Dawkins in an unusually nasty campaign, and more of the same was expected for anyone brave enough to challenge Dollar Bill, the nickname given to Bradley because of his lucrative basketball contracts, but which also applied to his ability to raise campaign funds.

In 1984, Bradley had crushed his opponent, former Montclair mayor Mary Mochary, winning 64 percent of the vote to her 36 percent, even as Republican Ronald Reagan swept the nation at the presidential level with a landslide victory over Democrat Walter Mondale. Mochary, who had spent $956,000 to Bradley's $4.6 million on a campaign that no one was interested in, told Whitman not to challenge the powerful senator. "Christine Todd Whitman has taken on one of the most unpromising political tasks in the country," an editorial in the *Home News* of East Brunswick, New Jersey, declared.

From the beginning, there was speculation that Whitman was laying the groundwork for a race for the governorship. While no one wanted to take on Bradley, it was understood that any candidate willing to run on the GOP ticket would be making an investment for a future campaign. Whitman believed she had no chance of winning. When her children, Kate, thirteen, and Taylor, eleven, expressed concern about having to leave their friends and move to Washington, Whitman told them that they had nothing to worry about. However, Whitman realized that the Senate race would allow her to get her foot in the door of state politics and perhaps someday the governorship. "When I ran for the U.S. Senate, I certainly had thought about running for governor too. It was always there as something that clearly you are interested in."

Because Congressman Jim Courter had decided not to seek reelection in the district in which she lived, Whitman could have made the far easier leap to the U.S. House of Representatives. When she opted instead for the Senate race, some people within her own party saw the decision as political arrogance, as an unwillingness on Whitman's part to pay her political dues. She says, "I decided if I was going to do it, I might as well go for the Senate and get the statewide exposure." Those close to Whitman contend that New Jersey's Republican leaders saw the Bradley race as a way to push Whitman aside permanently with no risk to other gubernatorial aspirants. While Whitman came from a prominent Republican family, she was little known outside of her home base of northwestern New Jersey, and other potential candidates for governor saw the 1990 campaign as a way to end her hopes of statewide popularity. "The irony is that it was a throw away," says Nancy Risque Rohrbach. "The boys thought they would get rid of her."

As Whitman announced her challenge to the seemingly invincible Bradley on the steps of the Somerset County Courthouse on March 14, 1990, she told the crowd of supporters that she was entering the race to protect the party's future:

> If we Republicans simply choose to retreat from a statewide race and lick our wounds from our losses in 1989, it will be years before we recover. Of course, taking up this challenge means taking on a two-term United States senator who has lots of staff and lots of money. However, if on the heels of 1989, we Republicans just roll over and play dead, the voters of New Jersey will count us out.

Tom Kean, one of the most popular governors in the state's history, had already eyed Bradley's seat and decided the popular senator was unbeatable. State Sen. William Gormley of Atlantic County had turned down a request by party leaders to run against Bradley. He told the *Courier-News* of Bridgewater: "I know enough about politics to not take on an American hero." And Lawrence Bathgate III, the Republican National Committee's finance chairman, was estimating that the GOP would be lucky to get 35 percent of the vote in a race against Bradley. When reporters asked Whitman why she was taking on the impossible task, she said: "The more people tell me I can't do something, the more I want to try." Then she added, "Mike Tyson didn't expect to lose either."

However, there was something afoot the importance of which no one knew at the time. On the day that Whitman made her formal announcement entering the Senate race, an event that would prove to be the single most important factor in her political future occurred: Gov. Jim Florio unveiled his record $2.8 billion tax increase, a maneuver that would so enrage voters that it would dramatically affect every New Jersey election for the next four years. Surrounded by arrogant advisers and believing he had a mandate from his overwhelming defeat of Republican Jim Courter, Florio decided to ram most of his policies through the Democrat-controlled state legislature during his first six months in office. He was convinced that by the end of his first term, voters would forget about the tax increase.

While Republican leaders in Washington were hoping that Whitman could tarnish Bradley enough to hurt his chance to run for president, Whitman made it clear that she did not intend to sling mud, even if ordered to do so by GOP leaders in Washington or in Trenton. Whitman promised an issue-oriented campaign with criticism focusing on the Democratic Congress rather than directly at the popular senator. Running on a fiscally conservative, socially moderate platform, Christie Whitman favored a line-item veto for the president, a constitutional amendment to require a balanced federal budget, the deficit-cutting Graham-Rudman Bill, a woman's right to choose an abortion, the death penalty for cop killers, and President Bush's "commitment to world peace through a continued military presence."

Whitman acknowledged that she would have little money for expensive media buys and would run an old-fashioned, people-oriented campaign using party organizations and word-of-mouth to reach the voters. She planned to rely on cable television ads, rather than those aired on the major New York and Philadelphia networks, an unusual strategy for someone running for office in the Garden State. Because New Jersey is located in the heavily populated area between Philadelphia and New York with no major television networks of its own, statewide candidates are traditionally forced to buy air time in New York, the most expensive media market in the nation, or Philadelphia, the fourth most expensive. In what appeared to be a ludicrous strategy, within a month, Whitman met with the Atlantic County Republican Committee to ask each of its members to send postcards to ten people in an effort to spread the word about her candidacy. Later, she would produce audio tapes for commuters to pop into their cassette decks while they were stuck in New Jersey traffic.

When Whitman stepped down as president of the state Board of Public Utilities to run against Bradley, she entered the race knowing that the senator was likely to have a campaign war chest ten times larger than hers. Before taking on Bradley, Whitman sought assurances from the Republican party that she would have at least $1.5 million to spend, one third or $600,000 of it from the National Republican Senatorial Committee in Washington. By February 1990, before either Bradley or Whitman had formally entered the race, Bradley, who would be challenged in the primary by a little-known Democrat, had already raised $4.1 million in campaign contributions. Despite speculation that he was saving some of his money for a possible presidential bid, Bradley's Senate campaign chairman announced that whatever he raised would be spent on the Senate race.

Whitman quickly used the disparity in the amount of money the candidates would have to spend to her advantage by questioning Bradley's need for such a huge war chest. She gained the support of several newspapers that wrote editorials questioning why Bradley intended to spend so much campaign money against a weak challenger. "Political analysts agree that Bradley could probably win reelection in November if he just put his name on the ballot and then went fishing," the *Courier-News* said.

Even before Bradley formally entered the race, Whitman announced that she was seeking an agreement whereby each candidate would cap campaign spending at $3 million, even though Bradley already had far more. Taking aim at the large amount of money Bradley had raised from out-of-state contributors, Whitman also proposed to limit contributions from special-interest Political Action Committees to 10 percent of a candidate's campaign fund and to limit contributions from out-of-state sources to 10 to 12 percent.

Election records showed that since his last Senate race in 1984, Bradley had raised about $9 million in campaign funds. He had spent nearly $5 million on staff, national-issue polling, computers ($500,000 to keep track of his contributions), and fundraising, leaving his campaign fund with $4.1 million at the start of the 1990 race. In ratings by the citizens' watchdog group Common Cause, Bradley ranked number two in the Senate with a war chest second only to that of Sen. Phil Gramm of Texas. Newspapers reported that during the last six months of 1989, 10 percent of Bradley's contributions were from special interest PACs and 80 percent were from contributors who lived outside of New Jersey. He had held more than a dozen fundraisers around the country, accumulating more than $800,000 from two California outings alone.

Whitman suggested that Bradley donate $1 million of his campaign funds to charity, leaving him with the $3 million she proposed that each candidate spend. Bradley immediately turned down the suggestion, labeling it a "political tactic" from a candidate who knew she would be raising far less money than the candidate she was challenging. Bradley justified the large war chest as protection against the negative campaign tactics that had characterized recent New Jersey political races. "I like to be prepared. In the age of slimeball politics, you have to be ready for anything."

Bradley termed his campaign a "conversation with voters" that would need funds to pay for television advertising and explained that he had raised much of his money outside the state to keep his fundraising from interfering with the fundraising efforts of Jim Florio and Frank Lautenberg. While the Whitman campaign was able to score some points on the issue of campaign finance reform, the *Philadelphia Inquirer* reported that neither Whitman nor Common Cause could produce any evidence that Bradley, who had accepted hundreds of thousands of dollars from Wall Street firms while sitting on the Senate Finance Committee, had allowed those special-interest contributions to influence his votes.

The day before Bradley officially announced his entry into the race, a *Star-Ledger*/Eagleton Poll showed what an uphill battle Whitman faced. Sixty-seven percent of those polled said Bradley was doing a good to excellent job as a U.S. senator; 18 percent rated him as "fair;" only 3 percent said he was doing a "poor" job. On April 2, Bradley announced his reelection bid at Montclair State College where his wife, Ernestine, was a professor of German and Comparative Literature.

Born in Crystal City, Missouri, Bradley came to New Jersey in 1961 to attend Princeton University. Majoring in politics and economics, he was an All-American basketball player and captain of the 1964 Olympic basketball team that brought home the gold medal for the United States. He was a Rhodes Scholar at Oxford University in England before joining the New York Knicks in 1967. As a result of his ten-year stint with the Knicks, during which the team won championships in 1970 and 1973, Bradley was elected to the basketball Hall of Fame.

At the time of the 1990 Senate race, Bradley was best known in the U.S. Senate for his work as the primary architect of the 1986 tax reform law (a tax simplification plan), for his knowledge of Third World debt, and for his expertise on U.S.-Soviet relations. When announcing his candidacy, Bradley mentioned his tax-reform accomplishments, but said his 1990 campaign would focus on the issues of children and the environment. Whitman had already questioned his commitment to the voters and issues of New Jersey by claiming that he really had his eye on the presidency, and he wanted his efforts on behalf of the state known. Cynical GOP consultants speculated that Bradley believed he had captured the male vote with his status as a former basketball star and was now appealing to female voters with his emphasis on children. Ever since his embarrassingly poor delivery in a 1988 speech to the Democratic National Convention, Bradley had been battling his image as a methodical speaker with a dull personality. In his 1990 campaign announcement, he had some unusually harsh words for people who endanger New Jersey's children: "For corrupt government officials who take money meant for housing or child nutrition and put it in their pocket, I say throw them in jail. For drug kingpins who murder to make their millions off the destruction of a generation, I say give them the death penalty."

While Bradley tried to focus on the environment and children, reporters covering the campaign wanted to know two things: Did Bradley intend to run for president in 1992, and was he prepared to defend his huge war chest? Trying to deflect Whitman's criticism, Bradley formally announced his support for federal campaign finance reform, including public financing of campaigns, spending caps, and limits to PAC contributions. But the senator said he would continue to follow the current rules until those reforms became law.

Bradley's statement left the door open for Whitman to suggest a plan to reform federal campaign finance rules for U.S. Senate races. On April 4, she proposed increasing the amount individuals could contribute and suggested cutting in half—from $50,000 to $25,000—the amount of money PACs could contribute to a candidate. She continued to call for overall spending limits and restrictions on the total amount that out-of-state donors could contribute. "The status quo of excess spending, nonstop fundraising, and PAC-influenced voting has turned off even the most idealistic citizen. The influence of PACs must be curtailed at the same time we should be encouraging citizen support. That's why I propose allowing individuals to give more than PACs." Whitman charged that Bradley was trying to have it both ways by favoring reforms, but not practicing them until they become law. "Everyone is for improving the present system. The real issue is whether or not one's campaign activities reflect a commitment to positive reform."

The following day, on April 5, feeling the sting of Whitman's barbs, Bradley blinked. Criticizing the current campaign-financing system, Bradley announced that he was cosponsoring a bill to extend public financing to congressional races. Attending a press conference in Washington with Massachusetts Sen. John Kerry and Delaware Sen. Joseph Biden, Bradley was hounded by reporters asking whether his support for the reforms, which were unlikely to pass through Congress that year, was a politically motivated response to Whitman's recent charges. "This is an attempt to get public financing," was all that Bradley would say before abruptly leaving the news conference. When reporters followed him down the Senate corridors, he repeated his intention to continue to conduct business as usual until the reforms were enacted. "We will play by the existing rules. This is not hypocrisy."

Whitman took credit for Bradley's cosponsorship of the reform legislation: "After we raised the issue, I am thrilled that my opponent has responded by taking a responsible position on campaign finance reform." She pointed out that under the bill Bradley had introduced, he already would have exceeded the spending cap on the Senate race by $4.6 million. "Supporting [the bill] and keeping his $9 million war chest is a little bit like eating a donut during Lent after having given up sweets," Whitman charged.

The Whitman campaign's opening shot in the Senate race generated a considerable amount of publicity for her. She had obviously found one of Bradley's weak spots. Her statements generated additional newspaper editorials supporting her position—quite an amazing accomplishment since, in the past, Bradley had been so popular that no one dared challenge him. Taking the typical challenger's stance, Whitman began to pressure the Bradley camp for a commitment to at least six debates, a number so high that it was obvious Bradley would never agree to all of them. "There are at least that many issues of importance to New Jersey," Whitman stated, as she continued to keep the pressure on.

Throughout the campaign, the fundraising and spending contrast between the two candidates remained laughable. By April 16, Bradley had raised $9.5 million, compared with Whitman's $70,000. By August 8, Bradley had acquired a fifty-to-one lead in campaign funds, raising $11.5 million to Whitman's $227,765. Whitman was paying two staffers and had collected no money from special-interests. In contrast, Bradley paid sixty-three staffers and had received $1.1 million from Political Action Committees.

Whitman visited Washington in late March where she met with U.S. Sen. Bob Dole and tried to drum up financial support for her candidacy. Meanwhile, Bradley was preparing for a large $1,000-a-plate fundraiser at the New York Grand Hyatt. The event took in $650,000. Newspaper accounts described the sports, film, and music celebrities—Bill Cosby, Whitney Houston, Paul Simon, Dustin Hoffman, Ron Silver, and Bradley's former New York Knickerbocker teammates—who were among the special invited guests. According to published reports, in California, Bradley's friend Michael Eisner, chairman and chief executive officer of Walt Disney Productions, had helped tap Hollywood coffers. Bradley told the *Los Angeles Times,* "I come from a quasi–show business background." (Some observers would speculate later that Bradley believed his status as a former basketball great would shield him from the anger over taxes.)

On April 16, Whitman criticized members of the U.S. Senate, including Bradley, for wasting taxpayers' money on overstaffing and constituent mailings. She charged that Bradley had spent $750,000 in 1989 on mail to his constituents. "You don't need sixty aides or millions of dollars for constituent mailings to be an effective senator. What is required is leadership and a willingness to challenge past practices," Whitman said. "As New Jersey's next senator, I will significantly reduce the amount of staff and office expenses allotted to me. I won't just talk about fiscal responsibility, I'll set an example." Whitman proposed a "Ten Commandments" of ethics that she said she would follow, if elected. The commandments included restricting constituent mailings, declining to serve more than two terms, declining money for speaking engagements, and limiting overseas travel. Bradley spokesman Bob McHugh responded by saying that the money Bradley spent on mailings wasn't "inappropriate." Whitman also criticized Bradley for a September 7, 1989, vote in the Senate on constituent mailings. When California Republican Sen. Pete Wilson proposed abolishing costly unsolicited mass mailings to constituents, Bradley was among only eight senators who disagreed and eventually convinced the others to drop the issue.

By the middle of April, it was clear that Whitman was denting Bradley's armor. For example, an editorial in the *Record* stated, "Wretched excess is the best way to describe Sen. Bill Bradley's fundraising." And *Courier-News* columnist Tom Perry wrote of Whitman's campaign, "Never did she expect to nick Goliath in a month's time." Whitman contended that she had burst the protective bubble surrounding the popular senator. "Nobody's seen that happen before. I think that showed you can ask some questions about him and the world won't come to an end." Whitman told the

New York Times: "I don't think he is as good as the aura that has built up around him."

On April 30, Whitman, who had not yet seized on the tax issue that would propel her to political stardom, refused to take a pledge not to raise taxes. She told the *Record*: "In honesty, I can't look people in the eye and say, 'No, never ever.' We have some serious problems. There may well be a need for some revenue increases."

Yet only two days later, on May 2, Whitman made a statement to a South Jersey audience that gave the first hint of the issue that would crack the campaign for the U.S. Senate wide open. While Florio was busy in Trenton trying to strongarm his tax increases through the recalcitrant Democratically controlled legislature, Whitman criticized the tax proposal and predicted: "As long as we keep Jim Florio in Trenton, we'll elect a lot of Republicans next fall."

Meanwhile, Whitman, who was unopposed on the GOP ticket, spent her time attending every Republican event she could find. Despite the rigorous schedule, she kept her sense of humor. On May 12, after nine hours on the campaign trail, she took a ride in a hot-air balloon tethered at the end of a Far Hills playground where she had been shaking hands. "It's one way to get taller than Bill Bradley," Whitman quipped to reporters as she ascended into the evening air. Later in the month, Whitman told a crowd of sixty senior citizens in Manitou Park, "A lot of people think I'm nuts."

Whitman's wealth was not an issue in the race against Bradley because of his own wealth. Whitman went further than Bradley in terms of financial disclosure by releasing her income tax form for 1989 while Bradley would only release the financial disclosure form required by the Senate. Financial reports filed by Whitman showed that she and John Whitman were worth at least $2.4 million that year. In 1989, Whitman's state salary as the head of the Board of Public Utilities was $95,093. She was a limited partner in Whitman Associates, a family partnership including members of her husband's family, and she was a director of the Somerset Trust Company, for which she earned $4,800 in director's fees. She filed an individual income tax return showing earnings of $62,371 in dividends and $65,287 in capital gains, mostly from the sale of stock.

Whitman reported holding stock in railroads, banks, automotive companies, defense contractors, chemical and pharmaceutical companies, com-

munications and bottling companies, and in utilities. The holdings in utilities and oil companies, which she inherited from her father, were placed
in a blind trust in 1988 when she joined the BPU. (The trust would later become an issue in the 1993 campaign for governor when it was reported that
the trust was held by Somerset Trust Company while Whitman was on its
board of directors.) Whitman's stocks were worth more than $309,000,
with her largest holdings being in General Electric. She also owned stock
in American Brands, Summit Bancorp, General Motors, Ford, First Fidelity
Bank, Monsanto, Eastman Kodak, DuPont, and Upjohn. John Whitman,
who at the time was chairman and chief executive officer of Prudential-
Bache Interfunding Incorporated, a New York City–based leveraged buy-
out firm and subsidiary of Prudential-Bache Securities Incorporated, had
his largest holdings in Prudential-Bache Capital Partners' accounts.

In 1990, Bradley and his wife had a net worth of at least $915,000, ac-
cording to his financial disclosure forms. His largest holdings were treasury
notes and a pension plan from the National Basketball Association. He reported owning part of a ninety-five-acre farm in Crystal City, Missouri,
eighty acres of unimproved land in Missouri, eighty acres in Nova Scotia,
and sixty acres and three vacation houses in Greece.

As the primary race came to an end in June 1990 and the general election campaign started, political pundits believed the Senate race had turned
into two separate races, one for the governorship and the other for the presidency. However, Whitman told the *Courier-Post* that she wanted to be in
the U.S. Senate, not the statehouse. And Bradley, who said he would serve
a full six-year term in the Senate if elected, contended that he was not running for president, nor would he accept the vice-presidential nomination in
1992.

By primary election day the tenor of the Senate race was already set.
The *New York Times* indicated that for a two-term senator and one of the
most popular politicians in the nation, Bradley was showing an unusual
caution. Asked if he supported a federal tax increase, Bradley refused to answer. "I'll save my advice for the president." At the same time, Republican State Assemblyman Walter Kavanaugh, longtime friend of Whitman,
predicted something no one else would believe. He told the *Courier-News*:
"She's a talented, talented woman who has the ability to do anything she
sets her mind to. I hate to use clichés, but she's a thoroughbred. She's had

the training and she's ready to go to the derby. When the stretch run comes, she's going to be very close and be able to win."

Bradley coasted into the June 5 primary election, making only a few campaign appearances and defeating challenger Daniel Seyler by capturing more than 90 percent of the votes. Whitman, unopposed on the Republican ballot, selected primary election day to seize on the issue that would nearly oust the popular senator. Going against the advice of her own political consultants, Whitman decided that she wanted to try to tap into the voter anger over Gov. Florio's record $2.8 billion tax increase by tying Bradley to Florio. Becoming the standard bearer for the antitax movement, Whitman pressed Bradley for his opinion on Gov. Florio's record tax increase. When Bradley refused to comment on the taxes that were infuriating New Jersey voters, Whitman's campaign began to gain some steam.

The Whitman campaign rhetoric began in early June and continued until election day. "If this is what Florio is doing to New Jersey, imagine what Bill Bradley would do to the country," Whitman adviser Bill Palatucci told the *Record*. "There's a lot of dynamite in this [state] budget. The Democratic party is going to have to stand up and be counted, Bill Bradley included." Bradley's spokesman, Bob McHugh, downplayed the impact of the taxes on the Senate race: "They're going to try to paint Bill Bradley with the same brush? Good Luck. That's grasping at straws." Bradley had no immediate plans to take a stand on the state budget, or the taxes, McHugh said in a statement to the *Record*.

More than the taxes themselves, Bradley's refusal to give his opinion became the issue. As the antitax sentiment mushroomed in New Jersey, Whitman continued to ask Bradley what he thought of Florio's tax increase. And Bradley kept giving the same answer: Florio's taxes were a state issue, and this was a U.S. Senate race. Voters, furious over the tax issue, saw Bradley's failure to respond on the Florio tax increases as arrogant and as an indication that he was out of touch with the problems at home.

On June 20, the New Jersey Legislature gave its final approval to Florio's tax package. One week later, Florio put his signature on a budget that would increase taxes on nearly everything that touched the lives of New Jersey residents, including the sale of beer, toilet paper, telephone services, gasoline, and trucks. By the end of June, the tax issue in New Jersey had reached a fever pitch as angry taxpayers, organized by the grass-roots antitax group Hands Across New Jersey, prepared to march on Trenton. Whitman took full advantage of the situation, attending a rally at the statehouse where more than eight thousand angry taxpayers, hurling rolls of toilet paper at the gold dome and waving anti-Florio signs, gathered to protest the record tax increase.

Whitman urged Bradley to "break his silence and take a stand" on whether the tax package was good for New Jersey. Bob McHugh told the *Asbury Park Press* that Bradley would not comment: "We're not going to have any response to that." Whitman continued to hammer on the issue. Six days later, she told the *Home News*: "The way this [tax and budget] bill was rammed through was partisanship at its worst. It allowed no debate on the issues. As a leader of the Democrats, Mr. Bradley should be embarrassed by this excuse for lawmaking." McHugh again said it was not Bradley's role to discuss state policy: "He's taking the position that he's going to speak out where he can make a difference—at the federal level."

Every time Whitman mentioned the tax issue, her support soared, as members of Hands Across New Jersey supported her campaign. Also working to elect Whitman were members of the Coalition of New Jersey Sportsmen, led by activist Richard Miller, who literally worked night and day, from the time Florio enacted a ban on semiautomatic guns in 1990 until the governor's defeat in November 1993, to unseat the Democratic governor. In his book *Senator,* an insider's look at Bill Bradley's Senate career published in 1992, William Jaspersohn said that Bradley had either to dump on his old friend Jim Florio, or announce that he favored the tax increase, and Bradley was not willing to choose either option. Unwilling to comment on state or federal taxes, Bradley gave the appearance of a candidate who was unwilling to take a stand on another issue in June 1990. When Congress took up the issue of flag burning, Bradley hemmed and hawed over which side he would be on. Saying flag burning was an affront to an important American symbol, Whitman supported a constitutional amendment banning the act. "This is not a test of free speech or an undermining of the Constitution. This would not limit the right of someone to say they hate the flag, only burning it." Bradley remained uncommitted on the question, and then finally issued a long, rambling statement opposing a constitutional amendment. While he used the term "ungrateful lowlife" to describe someone who would burn an American flag, Bradley said tampering with the Constitution to deter such activity would set a dangerous precedent.

On June 26, Whitman's campaign got another boost when the *Washingtonian,* a magazine with a wide circulation in the metropolitan Washington area, assessed Bradley as the most "overrated" Senator on Capitol Hill. He was one of five Washington personalities shown on the cover of the magazine's annual edition featuring its "Best & Worst" awards. The ratings are based on ballots sent to congressional offices. A Bradley spokesperson said the rating resulted from disappointment on Capitol Hill about Bradley's reluctance to run for president. When Gannett News Service asked to speak to the senator about the rating, his spokesman, Michael Jones, replied, "You can not!"

While Whitman continued to focus on the tax issue, Bradley tried to change the subject with what the Associated Press on July 10 termed "an innovative new campaign commercial." The thirty-second ad made no mention of Bradley's reelection campaign, but urged viewers to use a toll-free telephone number to tell the senator how they felt about his bill to eliminate lead from gasoline. Some political consultants said the ad could help Bradley expand his extensive list of campaign contributors. However, Whitman termed the ad a self-promotional gimmick and suggested that it was paid for by "the same people who are a part of the problem," the oil and chemical companies that contributed to Bradley's campaign.

In August the candidates harped at one another over campaign advertising gimmicks. Whitman criticized Bradley for failing to label a lead poison brochure as funded by the campaign. Whitman called it a "slick attempt to camouflage the real source of funding." That same month, Bradley's campaign fired back, criticizing the Whitman campaign for the use of unauthorized campaign literature. In the midst of the antitax rage that continued to grow throughout the state, Whitman campaign manager Kayla Bergeron ordered and distributed two thousand bumper stickers saying, "Get Florio. Dump Bradley." When the bumper stickers began appearing all over the state, the Bradley campaign complained, accusing the Whitman people of "sleazy" tactics.

The Whitman campaign described the incident as an unauthorized purchase. Bergeron had used her own money to purchase four hundred dollars worth of the bumper stickers from the Coalition of New Jersey Sportsmen, which produced numerous anti-Florio bumper stickers between 1990 and 1993. In an interview five years later, Bergeron said the only mistake she made was not ordering thousands more.

Christie Whitman opened the official Labor Day campaign season with a radio ad that did not even mention her opponent, but, instead, attacked Florio's tax increase. The ad asked: "Are you angry about the Florio tax plan? How mad are you at Jim Florio and business-as-usual in Trenton and Washington?" The sixty-second commercial said a vote for Whitman would "send a message" to Florio and Washington politicians that "higher taxes are just not acceptable." The Bradley campaign refused to comment on what it described as "Mrs. Whitman's ad for governor." At the same time, the Whitman campaign was accusing Bradley, who was spending time in Iowa and Illinois campaigning for Democratic candidates, of running for president. While Bradley was stumping out of state, the Whitman campaign faxed the lyrics of "Won't You Come Home Bill Bradley?" to reporters covering the race.

From Labor Day to election day, Whitman set a grueling schedule for herself, as she logged in more than thirty thousand campaign miles crisscrossing New Jersey. Aware that her candidacy had little chance of success, she was determined to make campaigning fun for herself and her staff. Eating one of her favorite sandwiches, a tuna melt, wherever she campaigned, Whitman was notorious for spilling part of the sandwich on her clothing. Trying to inject some humor into the campaign and to contrast her travels to all of the state's twenty-one counties with Bradley's sparse traveling schedule, in September, the Whitman camp issued a list of New Jersey's top ten restaurants for tuna melts.

Bradley had spent the first week of September visiting schools and other children's facilities. Never mentioning Whitman, rarely referring to Florio, and ignoring the tax issue, he unveiled legislation to fund the development of a single vaccine to protect children from major diseases. While Whitman was issuing two dozen position papers on every subject from abortion to gun control, Bradley was handing out buttons to students that said "Study, Dude!" GOP consultants and editorial writers began criticizing Bradley's decision not to enter the campaign fray and debate the real issues. "Bradley ought to get off his high horse," the *Gloucester Times* editorial declared. The *Asbury Park Press* said Bradley's strategy "smacks of arrogance."

Meanwhile, Whitman continued her antics in an effort to boost the morale of her small staff. When she wasn't eating tuna melts or root beer floats on the campaign trail, she was dieting, according to Bergeron. At one point, the campaign did suffer a brief slowdown when Whitman and Bergeron were consuming a diet drink that forced them to stop at every ladies' room along the New Jersey Turnpike. To break up the monotony of the campaign trail, Whitman would sing along with a wide variety of music played in the campaign car. She would accompany Johnny Cash, Bruce Springsteen, country music star Johnny Horton, her childhood friend and opera star Frederica von Stade, as well as the show tunes and songs used by the dance team of Fred Astaire and Ginger Rogers. Bergeron warned her, however, that it would cost her votes if anyone heard her. Whitman also passed the time doing tick-tack-toe on the car's dirty windshield and, on occasion, would surprise her staff by doing bird calls out the car window. "She never took herself too seriously," Bergeron said of the wealthy candidate who was seeking one of the highest offices in the nation.

Whitman, who was living in Far Hills at the time, tried to have breakfast with her children and her husband and then would make an effort to be home in time to do some evening reading with the children. No matter what time she got home, even if they were asleep, she would kiss the children "good night." On Sunday evening, she would have dinner with her mother, who was ill. Bergeron remembers saying, "This isn't practical," when viewing Christie's family schedule. "But she had her priorities in order. Even now, her family comes first. She could walk away tomorrow and lead a happy life."

Bergeron says people misunderstand Whitman by trying to make her what they want her to be rather than seeing her the way she is. "She will cook Thanksgiving dinner for thirty people, no maid, no nothing. She can do everything on the farm. She has no air conditioning in her home. She uses a NordicTrack®, rides horses and trail bikes, plays basketball and tennis, shoots darts, and goes fishing. The thing she enjoys the most is just to walk along the property with her dogs." Whitman also enjoys a challenge, and that is why she ran against Bradley. "She likes to prove people wrong," explains Bergeron. "It only makes her more determined. The more negative it got, it just made her more determined." Bergeron says she watched Whitman grow more skilled as a politician during the months of intensive campaigning. "She polished herself. She gained a lot of confidence. She was a much better speaker." In September Bradley underestimated Whitman's ability to turn a situation to her advantage. He had been stonewalling the Whitman campaign for months, refusing to commit to a series of public debates. Frustrated by the situation and unable to come up with a solution, Whitman turned to an old family friend, Lyn Nofziger, a former adviser to Ronald Reagan. Nofziger counseled Whitman to accuse Bradley of being a sexist for refusing to debate a woman candidate. Two hours after Whitman called Bradley's attitude on the debates "cowardly and sexist," he agreed to a debate schedule. Ironically, it was also in September that abortion rights and women's groups endorsed Bradley instead of Whitman because he was likely to win. Bradley was endorsed by the National Abortion Rights Action League, the Right to Choose, Choice PAC of New Jersey, and the New Jersey Women's Caucus. The abortion-rights groups, in addition to Bradley's ability to win, cited his opposition to David Souter's nomination to the Supreme Court. Pro-choice groups were worried because they had no record of Souter's stand on abortion.

It was not until October 6 that a *Star-Ledger*/Eagleton Poll indicated that Bradley was beginning to feel the wrath of those New Jersey voters who were angry about taxes. Bradley had fallen 8 percentage points in three months, although he was still leading Whitman by thirty points—56 percent to 26 percent. The poll reflected a "knee-jerk reaction" against taxes and incumbents, according to Janice Ballou, director of the *Star-Ledger*/Eagleton Poll. Bradley had fallen the most—14 percentage points—among married couples with joint incomes above $70,000, those most affected by the Florio tax hike.

During a televised appearance by the candidates on October 7, Whitman hammered Bradley on the tax issue. Yet each time Whitman tried to get Bradley to comment on the state budget, he answered with a comment on the federal budget. After taping the television show, Bradley told reporters that he would not be giving his views on Florio's taxes at any time during the Senate campaign. He said the voters recognized the difference between his federal duties and state issues. "We have different roles, different responsibilities. My record on federal taxation is very clear. That's where I work for the people of New Jersey." Whitman charged: "Not to have an opinion is ducking the most important issue in the state."

There was a second signal in October that Bradley should have been reconsidering his silence on state taxes. Another *Star-Ledger*/Eagleton poll showed that 76 percent of the state's residents believed Bradley and Whitman should be debating the issue of state taxes. Even though the poll showed that a majority of voters believed Bradley was the better candidate, the number of people interested in the tax issue should have been a red flag for the Democratic senator. Continuing to ignore the tax issue, Bradley launched a multimillion-dollar television ad campaign during the second week of October which focused on his role as a senator and made no mention of Whitman or taxes.

Michael Kaye, Bradley's friend and media consultant whose clients include Walt Disney Pictures, produced the series of positive ads aimed at attracting New Jersey's independent voters. The first showed Bradley in a school gym with a group of students while the voiceover talked about legislation he had supported for New Jersey's youth. "Shoot! shoot! shoot!" the students shouted when the basketball was tossed to Bradley, and he fired off a perfect shot. Some ads showed him walking along the shore, greeting New Jersey residents during his annual beach walk, while others talked about his programs for the elderly. The final ad cited the difficulties of being a United States senator and ended with Bradley putting his sneaker-clad feet on his desk in Washington.

During the first official debate on October 14, Bradley went on the attack. He criticized Whitman's record as a Somerset County freeholder, pointing out that residents' tax bills grew and county spending increased during her tenure on the board. The issue, however, failed to do much damage, as Whitman countered that the tax rate was actually lowered at a time when the area was experiencing a boom. Sticking to the issue she had been harping on since June, Whitman tried to needle Bradley into commenting on Florio's taxes.

> I'm in this race because I don't think New Jersey can afford a part-time senator with one eye on the White House. I don't think we can afford a senator who lacks the political courage to take a stand on the Florio tax plan. And I know we can't afford a Congress that spends more on itself than we do on drug treatment. I want to be a leader for New Jersey, and,

strange and simple as it sounds, leadership requires taking a lead. Leadership is not [spending] five hundred thousand dollars in public opinion polls and then not having a public opinion on the Florio taxes.

Bradley would not budge on the issue. "I hear their anger, but I'm not going to exploit that anger for political purposes. Mrs. Whitman is trying to exploit that anger and mislead them into thinking a United States senator can do something about state taxes." Whitman charged that Bradley lacked the courage to take a stand. "It's outrageous to consider it political pandering to answer the people of New Jersey."

Whitman also pointed out that Bradley was supporting campaign finance reform at the same time when he was raising huge amounts of money for his own campaign. By October Bradley had raised $12 million to Whitman's $513,000, as he held his annual $500-a-plate fundraising dinner and hosted a concert at the Meadowlands with recording star Paul Simon among the headliners.

The senator likened the fundraising to a basketball player's need to practice. "I want to be the best-prepared candidate." Whitman shot back: "It's funny that the definition of being the best prepared is spending more and more money."

After the hour-long debate, Whitman stayed to answer reporters' questions, but Bradley, apparently angry about Whitman's harping on the tax issue, walked out of the Secaucus television station building without answering reporters questions and still wearing the microphone he'd worn on stage. He returned to the WWOR-TV office forty minutes later, entered the press room, sprawled on the floor with his arms and legs spread-eagled, and said, "Here I am." His explanation to the *Home News* of the unusual behavior was, "I was never a good interview after the game." Whitman's retort to Bradley in the *Philadelphia Inquirer*: "One wonders how many other times he has lain down on the job."

In one-on-one interviews and conversations with people on the streets of New Jersey, Whitman's vocabulary often belies her privileged background. Yet when challenged in public or in private, she is capable of quick, biting retorts and witty, offhanded comments.

With Bradley's ads airing on television, Whitman suffered a setback in mid-October when a poll conducted by the *Star-Ledger* and Eagleton between October 16 and 22 showed that she was once again losing ground. Bradley had pulled ahead by an additional 6 percentage points. He now enjoyed a huge, thirty-six-point margin. He was favored by 62 percent of the voters, compared with Whitman's 26 percent. Still, 12 percent of the voters remained undecided.

During the second debate on October 23, the Senate candidates sparred over international issues. To prepare for the confrontation, Whitman spent two hours with former president Richard Nixon at his home in Saddle River, New Jersey. But even with the coaching from Nixon, the *New Republic* reported that Bradley's "forceful and authoritative answers" on international affairs made Whitman appear to be a minor state official challenging a major national leader. "Nobody knows what's going to happen in the next six years," Bradley said. "So, ultimately this is a race about whose judgment the people trust and who they want making what could be life-and-death decisions about their future."

Dressed in a collarless white blouse, pearls, and a dark suit with padded shoulders, her hair full and formally sculptured, Whitman appeared less than comfortable at times—a symptom of her meteoric rise on the political scene. At one point in the evening, Whitman stretched a point to turn a question about the Berlin Wall into a question about congressional term limits. "We see the Berlin Wall coming down, but we still have a wall around Congress." Whether Whitman appeared less of an expert than Bradley on foreign affairs mattered little because toward the end of the debate, she was able to turn the focus of the evening back to the issue New Jersey residents cared about the most: taxes. Whitman stumbled a bit over the words of the prepared question, but made her point. Do you think, Whitman asked Bradley, that the United States would be competitive in world markets if Congress enacted tax increases similar to those enacted in New Jersey by Jim Florio? "That's a creative way [to mention Florio]," quipped Bradley, who still avoided answering the state tax question.

The stunt drew applause from the audience, many of them members of the New Jersey Chamber of Commerce, the traditionally pro-business, pro-Republican organization sponsoring the debate. Whitman obviously had violated the ground rules, but Bradley said, "I've taken enough elbows to the jaw to know there are rules, and there are rules." Whitman also drew applause when she tapped into the anti-incumbent sentiment growing among New Jersey voters. "My opponent is one of the best examples of how twelve years in Washington can change well-intentioned people into status quo politicians. As much as we have witnessed a revolution of freedom across this world, we need a revolution in Congress."

Record columnist James Ahearn described the patrician image Whitman projected to the New Jersey voters: "Blond, curly hair, carefully coiffed. Collarless, brightly colored suits. Tailored blouses. Aquiline nose. Sometimes a double strand of Barbara Bush-style pearls." He also accurately assessed what she had accomplished with her feisty debate performances: "Whitman can stand toe-to-toe with Bradley and slug away. She held her own against him."

In the end, Whitman raised $1 million for her campaign, compared with Bradley's $12 million. In the final days of the race, the Republican National Senatorial Committee gave Whitman only $420,000, $180,000 less than the amount it had promised. Bergeron said the decision was made to send the money to Massachusetts where GOP leaders believed Republican Jim Rappaport (who lost to Democratic Sen. John Kerry) had a better chance of winning. The state GOP donated a mere $5,000 for Whitman. In the final days, Whitman loaned the campaign $100,000 of her personal money to finish the race. During the last week of the campaign, Whitman had just enough money ($250,000) for a week-long television ad campaign. She spent $200,000 airing the ads on New York television stations and only $50,000 in the Philadelphia television market where she did not have enough money to reach voters in the critical area of South Jersey, Bergeron recalls.

In one ad, Whitman looked directly into the camera and talked about the need for change, the need for holding the line on taxes, and the need for fiscal responsibility. Mentioning Florio's name three times in the thirty-second spot, Whitman said, "Mr. Bradley is a resident of the state of New Jersey, and supposedly a tax expert. Yet he doesn't have an opinion on the Florio tax plan."

Whitman had no money for private polling to track her progress in the race. But in the final weeks of the campaign, Whitman aides detected a sentiment on the campaign trail they believed indicated she was within striking distance of the powerful senator. According to Bergeron, Whitman appealed to the Republican National Senatorial Committee for more money, but party leaders would not listen. Whitman wanted the remaining $180,000 she had been promised for a last-minute media buy on Philadelphia television in order to reach south Jersey, and the party turned her down. "In the beginning, I just wanted to run a good race, but in September and October, I knew the atmosphere was different," Bergeron explains. "People were insulted by Bradley's reaction. He was playing basketball in the middle of a tax revolt. People felt that was arrogant. We knew we had a good shot. The response was just too positive. We were mobbed with volunteers."

Realizing he had misgauged the voter anger over Jim Florio's record tax increase, Bradley hit Whitman with two weeks of negative television ads, focusing on her tenure as a Somerset County freeholder. The ads, the first to mention Whitman's name, said Somerset County taxes went up 90 percent and spending increased 70 percent while she was a freeholder. At a televised appearance with Whitman on October 26, Bradley mocked her for failing to explain how she would cut the federal deficit and for failing to justify voting for tax increases as a Somerset County freeholder. "She's the original tax-and-spend Republican," he declared.

However, the Whitman campaign believed that the ads merely boosted Whitman's name recognition. Despite the discouraging news from the most recent *Star-Ledger*/Eagleton polling, Whitman, relaxed and smiling in a paisley dress, told Republicans at a champagne brunch at the Parsippany Hilton on October 28, "We're going to pull an upset. . . . Throughout this state, we're going to start a Republican tide that will take us to next year, when we'll win the Assembly and Senate back, and after that we're going to win the governor's chair."

On October 31, Whitman visited a south Jersey shooting range with the New Jersey Coalition of Sportsmen, the gun advocates who hated Florio. While the campaign stop was insignificant at the time, later, Florio would use newspaper photographs of Whitman shooting at the range in campaign ads that would tie Whitman to the National Rifle Association.

Whitman's family connections to the Republican party proved useless during the Bradley race. Even though Bradley was viewed as a threat to George Bush's 1992 reelection efforts, Bush declined to make an appearance or attend a fundraiser for Whitman. All that Whitman received from him was a handshake at the Newark International Airport when the president made a brief stop in New Jersey on his way to a New York fundraiser. Whitman and Eleanor Todd were in the receiving line with about a dozen

Kate and Reeve Schley, Christie's maternal grandparents, aboard the Queen Mary in 1948. The Schleys were one of a handful of wealthy New York families to settle in Far Hills, New Jersey, at the turn of the century.

Alice Bray Todd, Christie's paternal grandmother, was a schoolteacher from Wisconsin, who met John R. Todd while he was teaching at the Protestant College in Beirut, Lebanon.

John R. Todd, Christie's paternal grandfather, was a construction magnate who built Rockefeller Center and colonial Williamsburg for John D. Rockefeller.

Eight-year-old Christie is riding her Welsh pony, Stuffy, with sister Kate behind her during a Todd family picnic at Pontefract in 1954. Brother Dan is to her left and John to her right while Eleanor and Web are seated at the picnic table.

Young Christie obviously is unimpressed as her mother (*second from left*) presents a book to Mamie and Dwight D. Eisenhower in the mid-1950s.

Ten-year-old Christie shares a quiet moment with her sister Kate prior to Kate's 1956 wedding ceremony at Pontefract.

Thirteen-year-old Christie (*upper right*) attends the 1960 national convention in Chicago with her brother John, Eleanor and Web Todd (*front row*), brother Dan, and sister Kate (*back row*).

In 1968, twenty-one-year-old Christie graduates from Wheaton College in Norton, Massachusetts, where she majored in government.

Christie (*right*) and her sister Kate flank New York Governor Nelson Rockefeller at a 1968 fundraiser for the presidential hopeful. The event was hosted by Eleanor Todd at Ripplebrook, the country estate in Far Hills, New Jersey, owned by Christie's maternal grandparents.

Christie and John Whitman leave the Presbyterian Church in Lamington, New Jersey, on April 20, 1974, after their wedding ceremony.

The Todd clan gathers at the Somerset Hills Country Club in 1981 to celebrate Eleanor Todd's seventieth birthday. Christie, front center, is flanked by Kate and Taylor. Standing left to right are John Whitman, brother John Todd, and Eleanor. Standing third from the right is Web Todd. Sister Kate is kneeling beside young Kate, and brother Dan is at the window.

Kate, five, and Taylor, three, help Christie fill a family album with election results after she won a position on the Somerset County freeholder board in 1982. (*Bernardsville News*, December 30, 1982)

In February 1988, Christie was sworn in as president of the state Board of Public Utilities. Her husband, John (*second from right*), and her children, Taylor and Kate, attended the ceremony. Governor Tom Kean, who appointed Whitman to the post, is at the far left.

Christie Whitman takes her campaign on a whistle-stop tour throughout New Jersey to generate her come-from-behind victory in 1993. (Craig Orosz, *The Trentonian*)

Christie's brother, Dan Todd, lights up a cigar during a campaign interview on July 16, 1993. (Chris Edwards, *The Trentonian*)

At a September 21, 1993, press conference, Christie Whitman tries to explain her plan to cut taxes to skeptical reporters. Flanked by former Governor Tom Kean, she points to a chart depicting the jobs that were lost in New Jersey after Governor Jim Florio raised taxes. Assembly Speaker Chuck Haytaian watches from the far right. (Chris Edwards, *The Trentonian*)

Christie Whitman gives a victory wave beside a "Whitman For People" sign during the celebration at the Princeton Marriott on election night, November 2, 1993. (Chris Edwards, *The Trentonian*)

Governor-elect Christie Whitman leaves the Princeton Marriott on November 3, 1993, the morning after her defeat of Governor Jim Florio. Only a few state troopers, reporters, and photographers witnessed her early-morning exit. (Tom Kelly, *The Trentonian*)

Christie Whitman delivers her victory speech on November 2, 1993, to a jubilant crowd of Republican supporters at the Princeton Marriott after the returns showed her narrowly defeating Governor Jim Florio. At her side, *left to right*, are Assembly Speaker Chuck Haytaian, sister Kate Beach, former Governor Tom Kean, and campaign cochairperson Hazel Gluck. (Tom Kelly, *The Trentonian*)

John, Taylor, and Kate are at Christie's side on January 18, 1994, when New Jersey Chief Justice Robert Wilentz swears her in as the state's first woman governor. (Tom Kelly, *The Trentonian*)

On January 18, 1994, Christie Whitman delivers her Inaugural Address at the War Memorial in Trenton while outgoing Governor Jim Florio and his wife Lucinda watch the proceedings. Chief Justice Robert Wilentz, who swore in Whitman as the state's first woman governor, is to her left. (Chris Edwards, *The Trentonian*)

At a statehouse ceremony on March 7, 1994, Governor Whitman signs her first round of income-tax cuts into law. Flanking Whitman (*from left to right*) are Senate President Donald DiFrancesco, Assembly Speaker Chuck Haytaian, and Senate budget chief Robert Littell. (Craig Orosz, *The Trentonian*)

On December 16, 1994, Governor Whitman appears on New Jersey Network, the state-funded television station, to discuss gang violence in the United States with actor Edward James Olmos. (Craig Orosz, *The Trentonian*)

Governor Whitman watches the television broadcast of President Clinton's State of the Union Address on January 24, 1995 while she waits at the Trenton statehouse to deliver the nationally televised Republican rebuttal. Christie is the first woman and first governor selected to deliver a response to the president's annual address. (Mike Orazzi, *The Trentonian*)

On April 10, 1994, Governor Whitman officially opens trout season in New Jersey and then, unlike male governors who would wet their lines and depart, stays to fish in the Pequest River at Oxford. (Robert Brunisholz, *The Trentonian*)

people who greeted the president as he made his way from Air Force One to the helicopter that took him to Manhattan. "Give 'em hell," Bush advised Whitman. Eleanor, seventy-nine at the time of the Whitman-Bradley race, had been a fundraiser for Bush when he first ran for president in 1980 and had hosted a political party for Bush at Pontefract. Now, when Whitman needed his help, he wasn't willing to return the favor.

The only help Whitman received from Washington was an October visit by Marilyn Quayle, who delivered a brief comment at a $150-a-plate breakfast in Newark. While helping Whitman raise much-needed campaign funds, the vice president's wife delivered a backhanded blow to the Whitman campaign by appealing for support for President Bush's compromise budget, which Whitman opposed. On the federal budget issue, Whitman was once again able to capitalize on Bradley's indecisiveness. When Bush unveiled his budget compromise calling for new taxes and spending cuts, Whitman opposed it. Bradley, however, "reserved a decision" on the budget, waiting until after the compromise failed in the House of Representatives before saying he would not have voted for it.

Despite the lack of support from her own party, a *Star-Ledger*/Eagleton poll released on November 3, two days before the election, showed that Whitman had now cut Bradley's lead in half, from thirty-six points to seventeen points. Fifty percent of the voters polled said they would vote for Bradley, and 33 percent said they would cast their ballots for Whitman. Seventeen percent of the voters remained undecided.

There was, however, a piece of the polling results that was not made public until after the election. Among voters who considered themselves very interested in the senate race, Bradley was leading by only 2 percent, the *Star-Ledger*/Eagleton polling data showed. In light of the other favorable information on Bradley, the *Star-Ledger*/Eagleton pollsters had looked at the 2 percent difference among those voters describing themselves as "very interested" in the race and decided it was not significant enough to publish, the *Trentonian* reported later. Whitman told the *Courier-News* that telephone calls of support and comments from residents she met on the campaign trail indicated that the momentum was moving in her favor. "Anything can happen. That's what I've been saying all along. I'm going to make believers out of a lot of people." Dressed in a striped shirt, skirt, and cardigan sweater, Whitman emerged from the voting booth in Far Hills smiling.

Throughout October Bradley was hamstrung by Congress's inability to pass a federal budget, as he and other incumbents were kept in Washington and away from the campaign trail. Taping sponges to the dashboard of a new, smaller campaign car to cushion his knees, the former basketball star traveled to all of New Jersey's twenty-one counties after Congress adjourned from the budget debate on October 28. But what he saw and heard was not heartening. Everywhere he went, people were angry at Florio and were not interested in listening to political rhetoric, even from the popular senator. At the end, Bradley knew he was in for the political battle of his life.

On November 6, 1990, when 1.9 million New Jersey voters cast their ballots, Whitman lost the election by only a 3 percent margin, giving Bill Bradley the scare of his political career. Bradley won by 58,936 votes, capturing 50.4 percent of the ballots cast to Whitman's 47 percent. In the end, 918,874 people voted for Whitman, as she captured eight of twenty-one counties.

Whitman lost in all seven of the southern New Jersey counties that can be reached by ads on Philadelphia television. "To me, that's where we lost it," says Bergeron. "In most campaigns, you want to have three weeks of campaign advertising. We could only afford one." And the money had been spent in north Jersey.

On election night, when the returns came in, Bradley's celebration at the Meadowlands Hilton in Secaucus was more like a wake. The party atmosphere died when Whitman pulled ahead by three thousand votes with 43 percent of New Jersey's precincts reporting. By 9 P.M., Whitman and Bradley were locked in a dead heat. With 52 percent of the precincts reporting, each had 50 percent of the vote.

When Whitman pulled ahead in the ballot count, it scared both the Democrats and the Whitman family. Taylor was frantic when he brought what for most candidates would have been good news to the Whitmans, who were dining at the Birchwood Manor in Whippany. Taylor reminded his mother of her promise that the family would not be moving to Washington, D.C. "I told them not to worry about going down to Washington. We were downstairs in the restaurant having dinner with the family, and he said, 'Mom, you had better come upstairs because you are ahead.' They were getting very worried. I said, 'Don't worry, Hudson and Essex [the state's urban, traditionally Democratic counties] aren't in yet. It's OK.' " The family joked that if Whitman won, she could always demand a recount.

Whitman's election-night lead faded quickly, as the second half of the ballots were counted and Bradley pulled ahead. At 10:05 P.M., CBS declared Bradley the winner, and by 11 P.M., Whitman was ready to concede. The Bradley camp was shocked and bitter about the near loss, and according to Bergeron, when Whitman placed a telephone call to Bradley to concede, his campaign refused to accept the call. A humbled Bradley, with his wife and daughter at his side, delivered a subdued victory speech. "What can I say? It's been a few years since I was in a double overtime. This was definitely a double-overtime election. To all of those who voted for me, I want to thank you for your confidence in these difficult and uncertain times. For all of those of you who are dissatisfied with government . . . even for those who voted against me as a sign of protest, I hear your voices too."

An upbeat Whitman thanked her supporters gathered at the Birchwood Manor: "I think we made politics fun again tonight. I think we can be really proud if you think about what we did. . . . When you think we had less than $1 million, no name ID and . . . a paid staff of less than ten, it tells you what the people can do when they want to talk about issues, when they want to be heard."

As a result of the close election, Whitman instantly became the front runner in the upcoming contest for the GOP gubernatorial nomination. Media attention normally reserved for winners went to Whitman instead of Bradley. When Ted Koppel's "Nightline" did its postelection interviews, Whitman was the one called. "Clearly, losing has its benefits," she joked at a statehouse news conference the next day before an array of cameras. Asked whether she would take on Gov. Florio in 1993, she said the gubernatorial race was a long way off, but she was keeping her options open. "I just know I want to stay involved."

In statements to the *Record,* Republicans praised Whitman. Assemblyman Robert Franks, chairman of the state GOP which had given her so little support, acknowledged Whitman's rise in stature. "She'd have to be considered a leading candidate, if not the leading candidate." Senate Republican leader John Dorsey called her "courageous." Republican and former state attorney general Cary Edwards said, "The Republican National Committee is now kicking themselves around the world that they put so little money into Christie's race." In a congratulatory telephone call to State

Sen. Richard Zimmer, who was elected to Congress, President Bush said, "That darn Senate race was amazing."

Whitman, in her post-election analysis, said Bradley's mistake was refusing to address the issue people wanted to hear about, Gov. Florio's tax hike. She said Florio had ignored New Jersey voters when he pushed through the record tax increase, and voters took Bradley's silence on the taxes as another instance of political arrogance. With a little more money from the Republican party, Whitman said she might have accomplished the impossible, unseating the Democratic superstar. Republicans, editorial writers, and Democrats had a lot to say about the results. "He was a chicken," Republican State Sen. Jack Ewing told the *Asbury Park Press.* "He didn't have the guts to come out and say where he stood on taxes for New Jersey." A *Courier Post* editorial said Bradley had plummeted to the level of the mundane and evasive. "It is ironic that a patrician from Somerset County spoke more directly to the voters in this campaign than the man who has so ably represented them in the Senate for the past twelve years."

Record columnist Mike Kelly wrote that while Whitman may live amid the silk-and-sherry set in Far Hills, she talked with all the simple directness of a Hudson County ward boss. As for her advice to Bill Bradley about the race, Whitman said, "He ought to be able to figure that out. He's a Rhodes Scholar." Florio, who usually demonstrated little sense of humor, tried to make light of the situation: "It reminds me of the joke. Besides that, Mrs. Lincoln, did you enjoy the play?"

While Christie Whitman's political career was launched, Bradley's was beached by the election. By nearly losing to a political unknown, Bradley watched his chances of becoming a presidential contender in 1992 evaporate. Rider College political science professor David Rebovich said, "Bradley always said he did not plan to run for president in 1992. Well, he'll be held to that now." (Saying he was disillusioned with Congress, Bradley announced in August 1995 that he would not seek reelection in the following year.)

Bradley was not alone in feeling the sting of the New Jersey voter anger. Scores of incumbent Democrats, from Cape May County to suburban Trenton, were booted out of office in the fall of 1990 and 1991. Even on Florio's home turf of Camden County, Republicans who ran on a "Send Florio a message" slogan unseated incumbent Democratic freeholders to seize control of the county for the first time since 1971. Trenton mayor Doug Palmer, a Democrat, termed the election a "Florio backlash" and a wake-up call for the Democratic party. "The lesson learned is that you have to listen to the voters and hear what they're saying."

Voters, interviewed at the polls by the *Trentonian* explained why they voted for Whitman. "I voted straight Republican," said Democrat Leon Cohen. "I've never done that before. It's anti-Florio." Bob Fanelli, an employee at Johnson & Johnson who had supported Bradley in the past, said, "Florio influenced me to go away from Bradley. Bradley avoided discussing the tax issue."

The day after the election, Bradley said he got the "message" from those who voted for Whitman, but apparently he had not. In a post-election press conference, he was asked about Florio's tax hike, and once again, he refused to comment. The issue that had dashed Bill Bradley's chances for a presidential run now would propel Christie Whitman to the top in the race for the statehouse.

7

The Primary Run

"There is no point to giving an election year tax break when you have to come back next year, and the year after, and hit them [taxpayers] for two times the cut."

Christie Whitman (February 24, 1993)
during the primary race for governor

Christie Whitman was a Cinderella candidate for governor. Because the political air in New Jersey was filled with a passionate hate for Gov. Jim Florio, Whitman was able to capitalize on her near win against Bill Bradley and bypass the traditional route to the governorship. Instead, she went to the ball without a formal invitation.

Whitman began to build a statewide political base in New Jersey immediately after nearly ousting the popular Bill Bradley from the U.S. Senate in November 1990. On December 9, 1990, one month after the election, a small circle of GOP operatives were already urging her to run for governor. One hundred Whitman supporters paid $200 each to attend a cocktail party at a country estate in Hunterdon County in an effort to help her pay off a $100,000 debt from the campaign. Former Gov. Tom Kean joined other top Republican leaders in a toast to Whitman that, in an informal way, launched her campaign for governor.

After the Senate race, Whitman made a postelection visit to Washington. Apparently feeling guilty about its failure to help Whitman's Senate race, the Bush administration forwarded her an application for a federal post. When Whitman returned from Washington without a position on President George Bush's cabinet, she decided to concentrate on state politics. While in Washington, she had told the Bush aides, "If you're not talking about cabinet-level, I'm not interested."

Already beginning to lay the groundwork for the race against Gov. Jim Florio, even though it was three years away, Whitman immediately began to forge a relationship with the keenly independent and unpredictable New Jersey voters. Every Thursday, from noon to 2 P.M., she hosted a call-in talk show at New Jersey 101.5, the radio station that, along with the *Trentonian,* had helped spark the grass-roots revolt against Florio's record $2.8 billion tax increase in the summer of 1990. Every week, she penned a column on public affairs in Somerset County's *Courier-News.* In an effort to solidify her political base within the party in March 1991, Whitman announced the formation of a Committee for an Affordable New Jersey, a political fundraising committee to help GOP candidates with position papers, research, and dollars. Whitman warned Republicans that even though Florio had become one of the most unpopular governors in the state's history, he could not be written off.

"Nobody's a dead duck—not in this business," Whitman told cocky Republicans. She urged the GOP not to merely attack Florio, but to tell the public how the Republican party would do things differently.

While publicly praising Whitman's formation of the new committee, behind the scenes, Republican party leaders, part of the good-old-boys network in Trenton, began to fret. The Whitman committee would be competing with other GOP fundraising efforts for scarce political donations at a time when the Republicans were making a bid to capture control of the state legislature. Besides, party leaders weren't at all sure that they wanted a woman building a strong enough political base to run an effective primary in the 1993 governor's race.

For a year and a half, Whitman used the Committee for an Affordable New Jersey to build goodwill among Republicans throughout the state. In November 1992, as she announced the creation of her gubernatorial campaign committee, People for Whitman '93, she began to capitalize on that support. Whitman was in the race for the party's nomination. Edward Rollins, the influential Republican consultant who ran former President Reagan's 1984 race and later walked away from Ross Perot's campaign for president, was a family friend and had already agreed to work for the Whitman campaign. Whitman had contacted family friend Lyn Nofziger, who recommended Rollins for the position. Meanwhile, Democratic superstar consultant James Carville had been hired to polish Florio's image, and the media were already starting to bill the Whitman-Florio race as a battle between the two powerful consultants.

In 1993, New Jersey had a population of 7.5 million people, and 3.9 million of them were registered voters. Democrats made up just over one million of those voters while only 22 percent, or 857,244 voters, were Republicans. In the end, the battle for the governorship would center on the nearly two million undeclared voters who were not affiliated with either party. In the primary race, Florio had no challenger on the Democratic ticket. On the Republican side, less than 400,000 voters were expected to go to the polls to choose one of three candidates. On January 13, 1993, former state attorney general Cary Edwards was the first to declare himself a candidate in the race for the Republican nomination for governor. In 1989, Edwards had come in second in the Republican gubernatorial primary, losing only to Congressman Jim Courter. When Florio trounced Courter in November 1989, many party leaders saw Edwards as the leading candidate for the Republican nomination in 1993.

Just four days after Edwards entered the race, a *Trentonian/Asbury Park Press* poll showed that neither Whitman nor Edwards would have the easy shot at Florio that the Republicans were expecting. Florio's approval rating had crept to 34 percent, the highest point since September 1990, when his popularity had reached a near-record low of 18 percent. In a Whitman-Florio match-up, the poll showed Florio trailing Whitman by six percentage points, 36 percent to 30 percent. In a Florio-Edwards contest, Florio trailed Edwards by one point, 32 percent to 31 percent. About 30 percent of the voters were undecided.

Despite her efforts to become known around the state, Whitman was recognized by only 38 percent of those polled. Edwards, however, had a name recognition of only 28 percent. He was working at a decided disadvantage because Whitman had a two-year head start. She had lined up support from a number of Republican county leaders, the GOP conservative leadership, numerous Republican clubs, and professional organizations. In addition, she was championing the popular causes of the grass-roots antitax group Hands Across News Jersey including the right of initiative and referendum (giving New Jersey residents the right to put laws on the ballot) and term limits for lawmakers. Yet before Whitman had a chance to officially announce her candidacy, she stumbled for the first time in what would prove to be a year of missteps and misfortunes. The damaging issues that surfaced during the primary would dog Whitman into the general election and provide fuel, not only for her primary opponents, but for Florio as well.

In January, when Zoe Baird, President Clinton's nominee for United States attorney general, confessed that she had hired illegal aliens and withdrew her name from consideration, Whitman immediately knew she had a problem. Whitman had employed two illegal aliens, a Portuguese couple, to care for her two children and watch over the Oldwick estate from December 1986 to July 1990 while she was a Somerset County freeholder. While working to gain legal status for the couple, Whitman had failed to pay $23,000 in Social Security and unemployment taxes. As several newspapers began preparing stories on Whitman's hiring of the illegal couple, she came forward with an announcement. Admitting she had made a mistake, Whitman said she would pay the money owed in taxes, along with a pending $2,205 federal fine. "To pretend you don't know anything and didn't do anything wrong—that's politics as usual," Whitman said about the announcement.

After the Whitman revelation about her illegal aliens, newspaper reporters covering the race awaited a vicious attack from Edwards. But when the Edwards statement came, it was an admission that he, too, had hired an illegal alien as a housekeeper. Ironically, the information about Whitman's illegal aliens is believed to have been leaked to the newspaper by members of Cary Edwards campaign staff who had no knowledge of his own hiring of illegal aliens. The few members of his team who knew about Edwards's past hiring were crestfallen when Whitman made her admission.

The Edwards announcement removed the alien issue from the former attorney general's primary arsenal. And when newspapers reported that Gov. Florio's top aide, Brenda Bacon, also had hired an illegal alien, the issue appeared neutralized. But while the political candidates might be calling it a draw, the voters of New Jersey were fuming. According to public opinion polls, 44 percent of the New Jersey voters said they would not vote for a candidate who had violated the law and 37 percent said they considered the illegal alien issue "very serious." By early February, polls were showing that Whitman and Edwards were in much trouble with the New Jersey voters and that either one could lose to Florio. The Whitman campaign was outraged as Republican party leaders conducted their own poll and hinted that both candidates were tainted and someone new should consider jumping into the race.

In an early hint of Whitman's ability to adeptly handle a sticky political situation, she was given points by the media—and political observers—for the contrite way in which she handled the admission of the illegal hirings. Accepting blame for hiring the aliens, Whitman said, "The bottom line is we did something wrong. When you make a major screw-up like I did a while ago, it's good to get it out."

Edwards continued to say he believed he did nothing wrong and would only pay $2,820 in back Social Security and Medicare payments for the alien and a $1,102 fine to put the issue behind him.

The alien issue sullied Whitman's January 27, 1993, formal announcement of her candidacy for governor. While she tried to focus her statehouse press conference on Florio's $2.8 billion tax increase and the three hundred thousand jobs that were lost in New Jersey during his tenure, reporters hounded her with questions about the illegal aliens issue. Struggling to keep the discussion focused on taxes, Whitman pledged to "roll back every one of those [Florio] taxes. We have got to look at cutting programs so we can cut those taxes."

What the alien issue was doing, however, was bringing to the forefront the issue of Whitman's wealth. The public perception, especially among women, was that the hiring of illegal aliens for housekeeping was something the wealthy did to save money while hard-working, middle-class couples were paying top dollar for childcare services. Because all of her opponents believed it was her Achilles' heal with the public, Whitman's wealth was an issue that would first dominate the primary and then become a major issue in the general election campaign.

Edwards's campaign biography, painting him as having come from a humble background, began with this quote: "I know what it's like to struggle to make ends meet." Yet in 1993, Edwards was an attorney at the prestigious international law firm of Mudge, Rose, Guthrie, Alexander, & Ferdon, and he had become one of the state's most prominent lawyers, a key player in the good-old-boys network inside the Republican party, and a wheeler-dealer with the Democrats on financial projects. Edwards kicked off his campaign for governor in the Fair Lawn, New Jersey, neighborhood of small homes where his mother, divorced since he was eleven, struggled to own a home. "Christie Whitman never had to decide between paying the mortgage and paying for food. That is the difference in our backgrounds," Edwards declared in biting comments that launched his candidacy.

Whitman admitted that her most difficult challenge would be combating the "rich bitch" image painted by her opponents, and at times during the upcoming months, she stumbled over the issue. "I have been fortunate, privileged. I don't apologize for it."

During the primary campaign, Whitman wore her hair short with the sides trimmed to reveal about half of her ears. She wore makeup, but no nail polish. She occasionally wore a suit or blouse with a collar, not yet going to the completely collarless look she would wear for the general election campaign. When asked whether, if elected, she would live in the governor's mansion, Whitman said that she and John, a political consultant and grandson of a former New York governor, were, again, "privileged to live" at the family estate in Oldwick and would probably have no need for the the white-pillared governor's mansion in Princeton. Following the death of her mother in December 1990, the Whitmans moved to Pontefract, the Todd family estate, in 1992 while retaining ownership of the home that they had built in Far Hills.

In one of the most damaging comments of the 1993 race for governor, Whitman said she favored keeping a homestead rebate program that gave a maximum of $500 to New Jersey property owners, and then added: "As funny as it seems, $500 is a lot [of money]." No opponent failed to use the comment to paint her as rich and out of touch with the average New Jersey resident.

As the primary battle progressed, Edwards continued to try to use Whitman's background of wealth and privilege to improve his odds of winning. During the first days of February, newspaper reports surfaced about Whitman's use of a farmland tax assessment to lower the property taxes on land surrounding Pontefract and her previous residence in Far Hills. New Jersey's Farmland Assessment Amendment, passed in 1964, permits dramatically reduced tax rates on land used for farming. The law defines farmland as land that produces at least $500 an acre each year in gross agricultural sales for the first five acres and at least $5 an acre in sales on the remaining acreage. The law, similar to legislation in other nearby states, including Pennsylvania, is intended to encourage New Jersey farmers to continue to farm their land, keeping it from development.

Tax reports for 1992 showed that Whitman paid $17,189 in property taxes on her Oldwick estate (Pontefract) and four surrounding acres and $9,310 in taxes for the Far Hills home (Twenty Springs Farm) and 2.8 adjoining acres. Because of the farmland assessment, the taxes for the 228 farmland acres surrounding Pontefract were only $4,535, and taxes on the additional 50.8 acres at Twenty Springs were $47.27. Campaign spokesman David Marziale said Whitman participated in the state's farmland assessment program in the same way as other farmers throughout the state. "There's no special privilege."

Pontefract was a working farm when Whitman's parents, Web and Eleanor Todd, purchased the land in 1933. Like her parents, the Whitmans employed a farmer to manage the farm operations. Tax documents showed that the land was used to grow hay and to raise two beef cattle, four to six dairy cattle, two horses, twelve to twenty-five sheep, two to fourteen pigs, and ten to twenty-four chickens. In 1992, the Whitmans earned $12,291 from the sale of hay, hogs, sheep, and wool. At Twenty Springs Farm, the Whitmans owned three or four beef cattle and harvested four to seven cords of firewood and five thousand board feet of hardwood, including oak and walnut for furniture, according to their application for farmland assessment. After the Whitmans purchased the property in 1974, they hired a forester and developed a forest management plan to harvest the trees.

The *Star-Ledger* reported that the value of the Pontefract farm also was lowered in 1989, the year Web Todd died, when Eleanor deeded the development rights for most of the Pontefract property to the New Jersey Conservation Foundation. The permanent conservation easement reduced the value of the farm property by $5 million, according to John Whitman who estimated that its value dropped from $7.2 million to $2.2 million, as the state gained 231 acres of "green land forever." Even as Christie Whitman was hounded by charges from the Democrats that she wasn't paying her full freight in New Jersey property taxes and that she had failed to pay federal wage taxes for two illegal aliens, Hands Across New Jersey, which had protested Gov. Florio's record $2.8 billion tax hike, broke its nonpartisan pledge and endorsed Whitman. Disregarding its concern about endorsing someone from a privileged background, Hands Across New Jersey threw its support to Whitman because of her early stand on taxes, her support for the concept of initiative and referendum, and her refusal to accept campaign contributions from PACs representing special interest groups. However, the endorsement drew a caustic reaction from Democratic State Committee Chairman Raymond Lesniak: "I find it ironic that the organization founded to protest taxes endorses somebody who doesn't believe in paying her own."

After appearing to have overcome some of her bumblings, Whitman managed to shoot herself in the foot on the tax issue, losing considerable ground in the primary race, when at a February 24 press conference in the statehouse, she denounced a plan by the Republican-controlled legislature to cut taxes for the middle class. "There is no point to giving an election year tax break when you have to come back next year, and the year after, and hit them for two times the cut." Providing additional fodder for Florio's campaign ads in the upcoming general election, she added, "It insults the intelligence of New Jerseyans and shows contempt for their finances to dangle election-year handouts before the voters."

Florio, in marked contrast to Whitman, who was supposed to be carrying the banner of the tax revolt, said that he would be willing to discuss any proposal to lower taxes if the revenues were available. As if she had a death wish for her candidacy, at the same time she criticized the GOP's proposed tax cuts, Whitman backed away from the pledge she had made to roll back what remained of Florio's $2.8 billion tax increase. (After seizing control of the legislature in 1991 in the wake of the backlash against Florio, Republican lawmakers had rolled back $600 million of the tax increase by cutting the sales tax by a penny, returning the tax to its original 6 percent.)

Backtracking on statements she had made when she announced her candidacy for governor, Whitman denied that she had pledged to cut taxes. She said that from the start, it had merely been a goal she would strive for if elected. "I still believe that should be a goal. It may not be accomplished in six months. It may not happen in six years. But if you don't have that as a goal . . . you are not going to engage in the type of discipline you need to begin to see cuts."

However, Whitman did promise business-tax cuts that she said would encourage growth in the private sector. They included giving companies tax breaks for money spent on research and development, waiving first-year corporate taxes for new businesses, and exempting professional partnerships from the corporate tax. At the state level, she pledged to cut nine hundred middle-management positions from state government, to privatize the New Jersey Sports and Exposition Authority, to cut the governor's office staff by 20 percent, and to institute uniform curriculum standards for New Jersey's schools.

Cary Edwards, who supported the Republican plan to cut taxes, reacted quickly, taking full advantage of Whitman's misstep. "She is turning her back on the need to provide tax relief, create jobs, and boost the economy. Her positions are clearly those of someone who is out of touch with working people."

Several days later, on March 2, former state Sen. James Wallwork, casting himself in the role of a conservative populist businessman like Ross Perot, entered the Republican party primary in New Jersey and notched up the pressure on Whitman by promising to roll back all of the Florio tax hikes. His plan was to cut state government 4 percent a year for four years to reduce the tax burden. Despite the tax flap, Edwards, realizing that he was still clearly trailing Whitman, went on the attack in what the Whitman campaign would soon label his "scorched earth" policy.

On March 19, in statements to the newspapers covering the race, Assemblyman John Rooney, an Edwards supporter from north Jersey, charged that Whitman had abused her position when she served as Board of Public Utilities president by having BPU staffers advise her on the purchase of a satellite dish for her Oldwick estate. Edwards's strategy was to paint Whitman as a wealthy woman willing to abuse the privileges available to her. Rooney told reporters that BPU staffers, on state time, researched satellite-dish technology for Whitman and prepared a three-page report on the subject when she was considering buying one. In response, Whitman said the staffers had done nothing that they would not routinely have done for any member of the public. She said the staffers, in order to learn more about satellite technology, spent an hour observing a survey team from Northeast Satellite Systems conduct a survey, which she paid for, at her estate.

Edwards also attacked Whitman on another issue that Florio would pick up and use in the fall campaign. He used Whitman's leadership role in a San Francisco-based prison reform group, the National Council on Crime and Delinquency, to paint her as soft on crime. The organization favors prison alternatives, opposes mandatory prison sentences, and has been critical of the establishment of drug-free school zones.

By March 24, a public opinion poll revealed that Florio was benefiting from the bitter Republican primary and Whitman's inept handling of the tax issue. The poll, conducted by the *Record* of Hackensack, stunned political observers by showing that if the election were held in March 1993, Florio would have defeated both Edwards and Whitman. In a Whitman-Florio face off, Whitman would have captured 30 percent of the vote to Florio's 39 percent. Edwards would have fared worse. The poll showed he would have receive only 25 percent of the vote, compared to Florio's 40 percent.

That same month, Whitman willingly placed another bomb in the mine field she would cross to the statehouse. By announcing her support for a voucher program that would use public money to help send children in Jersey City's troubled public schools to private school, Whitman pitted herself against the most powerful lobby in the state, the New Jersey Education Association, whose members saw the plan as a threat to the state's public school system. Even though the teachers' union was still angry with Florio over his attempt to switch the financial burden of teachers' pensions from the state to local school boards, it was livid over Whitman's proposal.

By April 1, with two months remaining in the primary race, Whitman was seen as a weakened frontrunner. Running a cautious, reserved campaign, she was giving standard stump speeches and announcing "blueprints" on issues such as the economy and education. Rather than counterattacking Edwards, she had ordered her primary staff not to mention Edwards's use of the state helicopter while he was a state official, nor could they refer to the convict pardons he had approved as former governor Kean's legal counsel.

Meanwhile, the voters were still uncertain about who Whitman was. And the attacks by Edwards and Wallwork were taking center stage. "The vacuum is being filled by dogs nipping at her ankles," Stephen Salmore, a Republican consultant working for Edwards, told the *Star-Ledger.* "They become the story."

When Whitman did go on the attack, in one of six radio ads aired in April, she stumbled again. The ads made vague promises about ending wasteful government spending, curbing unnecessary state regulations, and promoting business growth in New Jersey. Three of them failed to even mention that she was running for governor. All of them ended with the slogan: "Christie Whitman. Common sense. Uncommon leadership." The only ad that gained any real attention charged that taxpayers were spending $1 million a year on the office of First Lady Lucinda Florio. When the ad came under immediate fire from the Democrats, the Whitman campaign acknowledged using a "guesstimate" on the costs of the office. It quickly became clear that the amount was far too high, as Florio's office claimed it was closer to $200,000. The campaign was forced to pull the ad.

At the end of April when gubernatorial candidates file their financial disclosure statements, Wallwork and Edwards used Whitman's disclosures to resume attacks on her wealth. Whitman's financial statement showed that she and John, now a private investment counselor, had earned $3.7 million in 1992. Trying to force Whitman to release her income tax returns, which would have revealed more details of her wealth, Edwards released eleven years of his income tax returns. Whitman disclosed only a summary of her 1992 tax statements because she had filed for an extension on the filing date.

In reality, none of the Republican primary candidates could legitimately claim a modest background. Edwards and his wife had earned $387,835 in 1992, down from $592,514 in 1991. They paid $89,791 in income taxes and $57,827 in state taxes. Wallwork and his wife reported an income of $209,413 in 1992. However, Edwards billed himself as a self-made man whose income had grown from $65,306 in 1982 to $387,835 in 1992. His campaign pointed out that over the eleven years he had earned less than $2.2 million, 40 percent of the Whitmans' earnings in 1992 alone.

On April 28, with just over a month remaining in the primary race, the candidates held their first broadcast debate on New Jersey 101.5. Edwards focused on Whitman's lack of experience in state government. "This is serious business, a life and death business, not a job for amateurs." Whitman shot back with a reference to Edwards's ties to the establishment in Trenton: "There's no school where you go to learn how to be governor. I've been spending the last two years listening and talking to the people of New Jersey, so I'm not coming into office with a set of IOUs, a set notion that things have to be done in a certain way."

Meanwhile, Louisiana consultant James Carville, who earned the title of the "Ragin' Cajun" with his in-your-face campaign style, gave an early indication during a press conference on April 29 of the issue that would be central to the Florio attack on Whitman. Carville criticized Whitman for not releasing her tax returns, for backing away from her pledge to repeal Florio's tax increases, and for airing the radio ad on the office of the First Lady. However, his real focus was on the comment, "As funny as it seems, $500 is a lot [of money]," which Whitman had made when asked about the possibility of curtailing the state's $500 property-tax rebates.

Dubbing the wealthy Whitman a "let 'em eat oat bran" candidate, Carville said she was out of touch with New Jersey's hard-working citizens. "It sounds pretty reasonable to me that $500 is a lot of money. She thinks it sounds funny." Ironically, when the *Atlantic City Press* took a close look at contributions to the Whitman and Florio primary campaigns, the newspaper found that while Florio liked to emphasize his blue-collar roots, his contributors tended to be more "blue chip." Although accused of being out of touch with the common folk, Whitman was the one receiving small, grass-roots donations. Florio's average donation was $839 with 75 percent of the money he raised coming from contributions of at least $1,000. In contrast, Whitman's average contribution was $296, and at least half of her donations were for $100 or less.

Early in May, Whitman was the subject of more negative newspaper reports when reporters discovered that on April 20, the day she released her blueprint for state education policies, she failed to go to the polls in Tewksbury township, where Oldwick is located, and vote on her local school board's budget. In a stroke of bad luck for Whitman, her vote did matter. Because of a 207-207 tie, the $4 million school budget was defeated and died. (In New Jersey, if voters do not approve a school board's budget by a majority vote, it must be redrafted by municipal officials.) Reacting to reporters' questions on the missed vote, Whitman made the situation worse by issuing conflicting excuses. At first, a Whitman aide maintained that she had voted in the election. Later, after being confronted with election records, he said she had not.

When initially questioned by a *Burlington County Times* reporter about the vote, Whitman replied: "I didn't have children in those schools, and I don't think I ought to be telling them how to run those schools." (Taylor, fourteen, was attending the Far Hills Country Day School, and Kate, sixteen, was attending Deerfield Academy in Deerfield, Massachusetts.) The next day, Whitman backtracked on her statement to the *Burlington County Times* by saying that she had not been referring to the Tewksbury vote, but to her previous voting record on school budgets in Far Hills where she had resided prior to 1992.

She issued an eight-point statement which said, in part: "I absolutely intended to vote in the April 20 school board election and made that intention known to my campaign staff. A notation to arrive in Tewksbury by 9 P.M. [when the polls closed] was placed on my schedule." Whitman's arrival at the polls was delayed by a candidates' forum forty-six miles from Tewksbury where she was scheduled to participate until 8:45 P.M. She departed from the forum at 8:25 P.M., arriving in Tewksbury at 9:09 P.M., nine minutes after the polls closed. Edwards charged that the eight-point clarification to address a simple issue "clearly indicated the Whitman candidacy was in serious, serious trouble." Whitman's blueprint for New Jersey's educational system stressed the importance of public involvement in the schools, and Edwards charged that she had not taken the time to live up to the standards she called for in her own plan.

However, Whitman enjoyed some luck, as newspaper coverage of the school vote ended abruptly on May 4, when New Jersey newspapers reported that Gov. Florio's Chief of Staff Joe Salema was at the center of a federal investigation into whether improper influence had been used to direct billions of dollars in state bond business to certain Wall Street firms. (Salema was charged in February 1995 for an incident related to a municipal bond deal and eventually pleaded guilty to securities fraud.) Before the end of May, Salema, while maintaining his innocence, resigned as chief of staff in order to distance himself from Florio's reelection efforts.

The revelation of the federal probe into Salema's activities proved to be bad timing for Gov. Florio, as it sullied the announcement that he was the winner of the 1993 John F. Kennedy Profile in Courage Award for his gun control and education initiatives. On May 10, as Whitman unveiled her own anticrime plan, she accused the Florio administration of being soft on white-collar crime and called for Salema to resign. "The tone for law enforcement is set by the governor. It starts with a scandal-free administration that truly sets the highest of ethical standards." Whitman's crime plan called for broadening the death penalty to include persons who order or direct a murder, imposing stiffer penalties for child abuse or murder, requiring inmates to pay for healthcare services, and supplying those convicted of drunken driving with a special license plate for traveling to their jobs. (The suggestion for the special license plate would later be used by Florio to portray Whitman as soft on crime.) During the primary, Whitman also supported a constitutional amendment to ban one-shot budget gimmicks and called for the establishment of a bond review board to consider the cumulative effect of bonded indebtedness on the taxpayer. (Those two proposals would come back to haunt her, not so much during the race for governor, but during her first two years in office as she grappled with state spending and budget deficits.)

In statements to the *Record* of Hackensack, Whitman was critical of Florio's refinancing of the state debt without a voter referendum and of his administration's use of gimmicks, such as the state's sale of a major roadway to the turnpike authority in order to balance the 1992 budget. "We've got to stop the one-time gimmicks to close the budget gap because that's a lousy way to do any kind of financial planning." Ironically, Whitman said she was not prepared to cut the state income tax. "We've looked at all of those. But I haven't been satisfied with the numbers on the economic impact of doing away with those taxes to be able to justify the cut, given the need to have a balanced budget."

Whitman said she did not know how she would pay for the tax breaks she favored to stimulate private-sector businesses. She said that that decision would have to wait until she was elected and able to audit every department of state government. "You don't know, until you get in, how much is going to come from budget cutting and how much from stimulating the economy." In early May a poll published by the *Record* of Hackensack showed Whitman leading in the Republican primary race by 27 percentage points. Of those polled, 41 percent said they would vote for Whitman, 14 percent for Edwards, and 8 percent for Wallwork. Thirty-seven percent remained undecided.

With the first of three televised debates in the Republican primary race scheduled for May 11, Ed Rollins and Whitman's brother Dan Todd prepared her for what was expected to be a bruising night. Hoping to narrow Whitman's lead, Wallwork and Edwards went on the attack, criticizing her stand on taxes and her record as a Somerset County freeholder. Edwards called for an immediate $500 million reduction in taxes, and when Christie talked about improving the economy, he asked: "Christie, if you feel that way, why don't you support a tax cut right now?"

Whitman fought back, accusing Edwards of putting words in her mouth. Holding to her previous statements, she said her "goal" was to reduce taxes by cutting government spending and stimulating the private sector. Wallwork attacked Whitman's record as a freeholder by pointing out that during her tenure county spending soared.

When Whitman countered by saying that the tax rate actually went down, Wallwork, a Somerset County resident, contended that wasn't the case with his tax bill. He said that he, unlike Whitman, didn't have a farmland assessment to lower his taxes. Whitman returned the fire with a claim that Wallwork, as a state senator, had voted to raise taxes six times in a two-year period. And she cut off an anticipated attack by Edwards on the crime issue by charging that violent crime increased by 9 percent in New Jersey while Edwards served as attorney general. The day after the debate, the *Philadelphia Inquirer* reported that Whitman had easily deflected the criticism of Edwards and Wallwork and had added some barbs of her own in order to remain the frontrunner.

On May 22, seventeen days before the primary election, the second televised debate was held in Trenton, and once again the underdogs were on the attack. Preempting the charge that she didn't have enough government experience to be governor, Whitman took some potshots at her Republican opponents: "I admit I'm not a lawyer. I did not serve in the legislature, and I did not run for governor and get defeated." Then she turned the statement on her upcoming opponent with the kicker: "Jim Florio was all of those things." However, Edwards landed a salvo on Whitman for promising to roll back Florio's taxes and then later saying the rollback was only a goal. "She seems to have more twists and turns than Michael Jordan," Edwards charged in a reference to the Chicago Bulls' basketball great. "We are still trying to find out where she stands on a lot of issues."

Once again Whitman came under fire for flip-flopping on an issue. This time it was sports betting. In January Whitman indicated that she would support a ballot question asking voters whether they wanted to legalize sports betting in Atlantic City. Yet a few days before the second primary debate, she issued a statement calling for the legislature to reject the proposal. After the debate, she backtracked on that statement by saying that while she was opposed to sports betting, she was not opposed to placing the question on the ballot for voters to decide.

During the final month of the primary race, Edwards and Wallwork tried to narrow Whitman's lead with negative television ads. As newspapers reported that he was spending nearly $1 million on air time, Edwards attacked Whitman for failing to vote on her school budget and for supporting state funding to help students in Jersey City attend private schools. He accused her of wanting to take homestead rebates (property tax relief) away from senior citizens, questioned the tax breaks she received from the farmland assessment on Pontefract, and criticized her failure to file a 1992 tax return. On the school budget vote and her numerous excuses for having missed it, Edwards accused her of "saying one thing then doing another." The ad showed Whitman with a cartoon bubble above her head. The bubble said, "We send our children to private schools," and the ad ended with the question, "Christine Todd Whitman? Can we afford the risk?"

Edwards pointed out that Whitman had paid only $47 in taxes for fifty acres at her former home in Far Hills. (He failed to say that she paid an additional $9,310 in taxes on the house and the remainder of the property.) And an Edwards flier portrayed Whitman as an insensitive multimillionaire by quoting her as saying, "As funny as it seems, $500 is a lot [of money]." The flier stated: "Five hundred dollars may be funny to millionaires like Christine Todd Whitman, but to New Jersey seniors, $500 is not a joke." Wallwork aired commercials that labeled Whitman a "liberal" and reminded voters that she had hired illegal aliens. In the final days, he aired an ad stating that Whitman had voted seventeen times to raise taxes and four times to increase her own salary as a freeholder.

The attacks by Wallwork and Edwards were so harsh that Republican leaders feared that Whitman would emerge from the GOP fray permanently tarnished for the run against Florio. Edwards's attacks on Whitman's wealth were laying the groundwork for Florio's fall campaign, even as some Republicans contended she was a "Teflon candidate" who couldn't be touched. Whitman's ads continued to portray her as the candidate for change without attacking Edwards or Wallwork. "She's a mother. She has children. She understands what we're going through," a woman carrying a baby said in one of the Whitman ads.

As election day approached, the state Republican party and all the gubernatorial candidates, including Florio, began airing ads focusing, not on the upcoming primary, but on the fall election. "Fed up with Florio?" the GOP ad asked. It told those angry at Florio to call 1-800-BURY JIM to volunteer help and money. Florio's ad showed him working out with a punching bag and billed him as a former boxer who had made some tough decisions and took some punches. "Jim Florio. Strong principles. Tough decisions." Failing to mention his $2.8 billion tax increase, the ad contended that Florio had tightened welfare rules, strengthened the death penalty, and taken on the gun lobby to ban semi-automatic weapons in New Jersey.

Whitman's ad hammered Florio on the tax issue: "Three years ago, Jim Florio raised taxes over $2 billion. I said it was wrong then, and I campaigned against it. . . . Now I'm running for governor, and I'm still campaigning against higher taxes."

In Edwards's ad, Florio's face was transformed into the Joker character in the *Batman* movie. "Jim Florio said he wouldn't raise taxes. Then he gave us the largest tax increase in history. . . . Let's put a stop to the Joker."

On May 26, the GOP candidates for governor participated in their third and final debate. One newspaper described it as a "verbal brawl." By asking the candidates what they would do about unemployment, a jobless woman set off an exchange of barbed attacks. Whitman responded to the woman's question by talking about her "economic revival blueprint" and by calling for the state to put its "fiscal house in order." Edwards cut her off: "Christie, you don't understand, the girl doesn't have a job, today."

Whitman: "Can you offer her one?"

Edwards: "At least I have had a job in my life."

Whitman: "I would ask for an apology for that, Cary, but I think that you owe an apology to every woman for saying last weekend that you resent having to run against a woman."

Edwards: "I'm not apologizing to you for anything. I haven't done anything to you. You have made more mistakes and flip-flops than Slick Willie's White House."

The exchange ended when Wallwork spoke up, telling his fellow Republicans to calm down. With his comment questioning whether Whitman had ever had a job, Edwards continued his efforts to point out Whitman's wealth and to paint her as out of touch with the average voter. Whitman, after the debate, told the *Asbury Park Press* that the remark was sexist and that Edwards would never have accused a man who had worked for the Republican National Committee, the U.S. Office of Economic Opportunity, and who had served as freeholder and president of the state Board of Public Utilities of never having held a job. Edwards explained later that he meant a private-sector job not obtained through political connections. He also insisted that his comment about being resentful over running against a woman was taken out of context. (On a New York news program, Edwards had said, "I sit here a little resentful having to run against a woman when I have that kind of experience and real background in real life, both personally and in government.")

After the debate, Edwards's staff handed out a five-page document titled "Whitman Wiggles," which claimed to outline her "lame excuses, flip-flops, half-truths, and double-talk" on fourteen issues, including school vouchers, assault weapons, and taxes.

On the same day the debate was held, eleven GOP county chairmen, all Whitman supporters, called on Edwards to stop running his commercials attacking Whitman because they were bad for the party. In a letter to Edwards, the party leaders stated that former Gov. Thomas Kean "knew that negative campaigning among Republicans only served to tear our party down, not build it up." The chairmen called Edwards's ads attacking Whitman's failure to vote on her local school budget "politics-as-usual in its crassest form." The day after the debate, Edwards added a new allegation to his attacks on Whitman. He charged that in her final days as president of the state Board of Public Utilities, Whitman had approved the development of watershed land in Bergen County without following the necessary state rules and that a court had later overturned the decision. Whitman responded by saying that the issue had undergone public review and hearings.

On June 2, six days before the election, a few New Jersey newspapers also carried stories that a blind trust, which Whitman had set up when she became president of the BPU in 1988, was managed by the Somerset Trust Company at a time Whitman was on the bank's board of directors and her uncle, Reeve Schley, Jr., was bank chairman. In addition, the bank had been founded by Whitman's grandfather, Reeve Schley, and its officials included relatives, political allies, and people Whitman had appointed to public office while a Somerset County freeholder. The trust was approved by the Executive Commission on Ethical Standards, but Whitman was called a hypocrite by critics like Democratic State Sen. John Lynch because when questions were raised about Chief of Staff Joe Salema's blind trust, she had called for tougher ethical standards and said blind trusts for officials should be managed by an absolutely independent trustee.

With less than a week remaining in the race for the GOP nomination, Whitman—who throughout the race had refused to be provoked by Edwards's and Wallwork's negative attacks—decided to strike back. A Whitman television ad, showing alternating pictures of Edwards and Florio, said that Edwards, as a top aide to Republican Gov. Kean, had drafted four state budgets that increased government spending by $3.3 billion and raised taxes. "Florio—he raised your sales and income taxes. Edwards—he wrote sales and income tax hikes costing us $700 million," the ad said. Its conclusion, as pictures of both Edwards and Florio flashed on the screen: "Florio. Edwards. Not a dime's worth of difference."

Whitman had grown tired of being a punching bag for her GOP opponents. "We consider this ad an object lesson for Jim Florio and James Carville," Whitman's campaign manager, David Murray, told the *Star-Ledger.* "It shows, when faced with slash-and-burn campaign tactics, Christie will respond in kind."

Some GOP leaders felt Whitman had waited far too long to strike back. She had used the typical strategy of a frontrunner perhaps for too long, limiting her public appearances and staying positive. Edwards, however, charged that Whitman was running the ad because he had narrowed her lead.

Former Gov. Tom Kean, the popular two-term Republican who had stayed neutral during the primary, publicly criticized the negative tactics of all three GOP candidates and called Whitman's ad particularly unfair to Edwards's record as Kean's chief counsel. Kean said the tax increases Whitman described in the ad were the fault of Democrats who controlled the legislature at the time. Kean was so miffed that he allowed Edwards to re-air the ad that the former governor had made for Edwards when he ran in the 1989 gubernatorial primary. In the ad, Kean stated: "No one has worked closer with me than Cary Edwards. And there's no one I trust more or in whom I have more confidence."

A KYW-TV poll, released from Philadelphia on June 3, five days before the primary election, showed Whitman still ahead with 37 percent of those polled saying they would vote for her and 23 percent saying they would vote for Edwards. Eighteen percent said they would cast their ballots for Wallwork, while 20 percent were still undecided. Whitman still enjoyed a fourteen-point lead, but the poll revealed that her two challengers had put a deep dent in the twenty-seven-point advantage she had enjoyed a month earlier, cutting it in half.

In the final days of the primary race, all three candidates crisscrossed New Jersey, each claiming to be the savior of New Jersey's economy and the best candidate to beat Jim Florio. A poll, published by the *Asbury Park Press/Home News* two days before the election, showed that wasn't the case. The poll indicated that in head-to-head contests with each of the three Republican candidates, Florio would win, and the closest race would be between Florio and Edwards, not Florio and Whitman. Whitman attributed the numbers to the negative campaigning by her opponents and Florio's ability, as the lone contender in the Democratic primary, to spend up to $2.6 million in publicly financed campaign money on self-promotion. The Democrats had successfully deflected an attempt by John Budzash, a former leader of Hands Across New Jersey, to enter the Democratic primary. After the Democrats filed a court challenge, a judge ruled that Budzash had not collected enough valid signatures on his nominating petitions.

"I've been beaten up on," Whitman told the *New York Times*. "Both Cary and Jim Wallwork have been throwing everything they can against us."

The day before the election, the *Inquirer* described Whitman as "buoyant" and reported that she "was greeted like a celebrity everywhere she went." (A similar reaction to Whitman would occur in the final days of the general election against Florio.) Whitman's handlers told reporters that her private tracking polls showed her ten points ahead of Edwards and seventeen points ahead of Wallwork. As Republicans went to the polls on June 8, more than 20 percent were uncertain about how they would cast their ballots. With turnout expected to be low, all the candidates initiated major get-out-the-vote efforts. Whitman's own statewide organization and GOP operations in ten counties worked to bring voters to the polls for her.

On June 8, Whitman fended off the challenge by Edwards and Wallwork to win the Republican gubernatorial nomination. She defeated Edwards by only 7 percentage points, indicating that the primary race had taken its toll. It set the stage for a difficult, no-holds-barred showdown against Gov. Florio. With 399,825 Republicans casting ballots in the race, Whitman had captured 40 percent of the vote (159,765) to Edwards's 33 percent (131,578). Wallwork earned 24 percent (96,034) of the ballots. Winning in fifteen of twenty-one counties, Whitman had captured all but the northern counties of Sussex, Morris, and Bergen and the southern counties of Atlantic, Burlington, and Cumberland.

After Edwards conceded, Whitman was greeted by hundreds of supporters waving a sea of red, white, and blue pompons and dancing to "Celebrate" as she stepped forward to claim her victory at about 11 P.M. in the ballroom of the East Brunswick Ramada Renaissance. Balloons fell from huge overhead nets and colored confetti was tossed everywhere, covering the clothing of the celebrators and coating the ballroom floor. The well-dressed Republican crowd, drinking white and red wine, was jubilant and determined to celebrate after the bruising primary their candidate had endured.

Signs bearing the name of Hands Across New Jersey were waving in the throbbing throng as the victory crowned Whitman the first woman candidate in New Jersey history to carry the banner of a major party into a gubernatorial election. Bobbie Horowitz, cochairwoman of Hands Across New Jersey, told the *Asbury Park Press*: "It's those who oppose her who made me realize that she's our candidate. It was the good old boys, the ones opposed to I & R [initiative and referendum], the ones opposed to term limits, the ones who don't want change in government who didn't want her. I really believe that this candidate, Christine Whitman, is the one who's going to deliver government reform to the people."

Other women candidates for New Jersey governor had been bumped out in primary contests. The late Barbara Boggs Sigmund finished second in a field of three candidates in 1989, losing the Democratic nomination to Florio, and the late Ann Klein finished second to Brendan Byrne in the 1973 Democratic primary.

In the end, Edwards's staff conceded that Whitman's two-year head start had allowed her to build a lead that their candidate just could not overcome. In his concession speech, Edwards congratulated Whitman for a "very, very well-run" race. Whitman talked tough in her acceptance speech on primary night. Her face revealed the relief she felt. The brutal primary campaign was over. "The strategy is going to be to take it right to Florio on the issues. Jim Florio is going to find out it's a very different world when he has an opponent after him every day."

Declaring that Republicans would be united despite the brutal primary battle, Whitman summoned her primary opponents and the state's GOP leaders to a "unity" breakfast the following day. "This is going to be a united Republican party."

Borrowing the slogan used by New Jersey's gun advocates who would work as hard as Whitman to unseat Florio, she promised, "We're going to be Florio-free in November." Whitman supporters responded with chants of "Jim must go."

Congressman Dick Zimmer, Whitman's campaign cochairperson, predicted the task ahead for both candidates: "Jim Florio's job is to change the subject any way he can and draw attention away from his record of tax hikes and scandals. Whitman's job is to keep him from changing the subject." Even though he had no primary opponent, Florio celebrated his uncontested win in New Brunswick. "We've taken a lot of lumps over the last three years, but now, ladies and gentlemen, it's our turn at bat." Florio declared.

Democratic consultant Steve DeMicco promised that Florio, a one-time Navy boxer, would come out swinging. There was little doubt that Florio would try to paint Whitman as a friend of the powerful National Rifle Association. DeMicco also warned that Florio was poised to badger Whitman for specifics on her proposals. "Tell us what you're going to do and how you're going to do it," DeMicco said. "It's easy to go around preaching change—but change to what?"

Whitman campaign manager Dave Murray did some tough talking of his own on primary election night. He said Whitman would remind voters that Florio had lied to the New Jersey electorate during the 1989 race for governor by promising not to raise taxes and then pushing his $2.8 billion tax increase through the state legislature six months after taking office. "We aren't going to sit still for negative attacks," Murray vowed. "We'll respond in kind."

However, Whitman indicated that she intended to follow the same strategy that had cost her ground in the primary. She intended to take the aristocratic high road. "We're going to do it, but we're going to do it based on issues, by appealing to people that it's time for a change, that it's time for jobs, and it's time to bring people into the process. And we'll do it together."

8

The Stumbling Race

"Luckily, the election isn't going to be held today. . . . I think you are going to see people change their minds."

Christie Whitman (September 27, 1993)
one month before election day

As Christie Whitman formally began her race for the powerful governorship of New Jersey, she made what Republican leaders and longtime political observers in Trenton believed to be several major campaign errors. The day after the primary election, she kicked off her campaign with a GOP unity brunch at a posh Princeton hotel where more than two dozen gourmet breakfast items graced the brunch menu, including baked salmon en croute and blintzes with strawberry sauce—not exactly the image the wealthy "candidate for the people" should have been projecting.

Her poor judgment on the location and menu paled in comparison to the statements she made about another Republican proposal to cut taxes in New Jersey. Apparently unaware of GOP support for the proposal, which Gov. Jim Florio also was backing, Whitman said, "Common sense, by the way, suggests very strongly that, in an election year, the governor should resist the cynical call to promise tax cuts for the purposes of reelection when the money isn't there."

149

It was obvious to most people that Whitman, now running against Gov. Jim Florio, who had become one of the most hated governors in New Jersey because of his tax increases, should have favored any proposal to cut taxes. Instead she had managed, at the very start of her campaign, to anger Republican leaders in the legislature, some of whom weren't her fans anyway, and to confuse the electorate with regard to her position on taxes. On the same day she held the brunch to kick-off her campaign, Whitman made another decision that many consider the most critical, and near fatal, mistake of her race for the governor's seat: She placed her brother, Webster "Dan" Todd, Jr., in charge of the campaign. Dave Murray, the Princeton media consultant who had run her primary campaign, was quickly pushed aside. Dan Todd, who had helped with the primary campaign, was named campaign manager for the general election. When asked why his sister picked him to run the campaign, Todd, a self-styled Montana rancher, said, "I sort of got stuck with the buffalo chip."

During interviews with the press, Dan Todd, who wears a moustache and glasses, promoted his "man of the West" image by using his thumbnail to strike matches for his cigars. In addition, he came to work at his campaign office in Clark, New Jersey, wearing a western bandanna twisted beneath his collar and sporting a pair of fence-mending pliers on his wide leather belt, held together by a silver belt buckle shaped like an oversized fishhook. Tacked to the wall of his office was a sweatshirt with "Will Rogers never met Jim Florio" across the front.

However, cracks were evident in Todd's Marlboro-man image. Instead of western shirts, he would wear striped broadcloth, and he often could be found in popular boat moccasins instead of boots. Even though he was reared in the wealthy, politically connected Todd family in northwestern New Jersey and educated at Princeton University, homespun phrases were sprinkled throughout his conversations. Yet, whenever he forgot to compare politics to cutting out calves for branding, he could be found using such terms as "eclectic electorate" to describe the New Jersey voters. A number of Republican eyebrows were raised when Whitman announced that her brother would run her campaign, as party members wondered aloud whether Todd had the background to handle a major gubernatorial race. His most recent political experience was helping his friend Lew Fleege, a fertilizer salesman in Winifred, win an election for fire chief in the area surrounding the town of one hundred fifty people in central Montana.

Fleege told the *Trentonian* that Todd helped him develop the strategy that won the election, a proposal to scatter the fire company's four fire vehicles throughout the district, rather than keep them centrally located. "He overcome the odds real good," Fleege said of Todd's ability as a campaign manager. "He ran a hard, clean campaign." Before helping with Whitman's primary race, Todd had been out of active politics for twenty years, and his resume gave him the appearance of a rich dilettante, flitting from one enterprise to another and eventually ending up as a rancher.

Born in New York City in 1938, Dan Todd was eight years older than Christie, but still the closest in age of her three siblings and the only brother remaining after John Todd died in 1988. Dan was someone she had always relied on and trusted. He was close to her emotionally, acting as a friend as well as a brother. Todd earned a bachelor's degree in geology from Princeton University in 1961 and then attended Stanford Law School for a year before deciding he didn't want to become a lawyer. Like Christie, his involvement in political campaigns started early. Todd said he learned about "shoe-leather campaigns" in 1949 when he was eleven and selling hot dogs at rallies during New Jersey Gov. Alfred Driscoll's successful reelection campaign. He worked on President Eisenhower's 1956 campaign in New Jersey, served in Malcolm Forbes's 1957 campaign for governor and Robert Kean's 1958 U.S. Senate race, and then helped in New Jersey with Richard Nixon's unsuccessful bid for the presidency in 1960. Todd was elected to the New Jersey Assembly in 1967, but withdrew as a candidate for reelection in 1969 (the year Nixon became president) to accept a position in Washington, D.C., as special assistant to the chairman of the Civil Aeronautics Board. During his brief stint in the state assembly, Todd is best remembered for making a critical statement about the lower house, which was controlled by his own party. He told a wire-service reporter, before departing from the position, that the assembly was no different from a "monkey house in the Bronx Zoo."

Todd stayed in Washington until 1977, serving in a series of positions with long, bureaucratic titles: executive director of the White House Conference on Aging in 1971; director of the Older Americans Division of Nixon's infamous Committee to Reelect the President in 1972; director of the special interest group division for the 1973 Presidential Inaugural; deputy special assistant to the president for personnel; assistant secretary of state; and chairman of the National Transportation Safety Board.

In 1977, Todd moved to Denver to become the public affairs vice president for Frontier Airlines. A flight instructor who had logged in more than 8,000 hours of flying time, he also served as senior vice president for government and technical affairs for the Aircraft Owners and Pilots Association and held the McConnell chair in Aviation at Ohio State University in Columbus. Todd served as transportation group director of Democratic Gov. Dick Lamm's Front Range Project, a nonpartisan group charged with coming up with solutions to problems on Colorado's front range. Todd was the land manager of the PN Ranch, where winter wheat, alfalfa, and cows were raised, before he joined the Whitman campaign.

When Todd was hired, Washington-based GOP consultant David Welch quoted an old political saying on the subject of placing a family member in charge of a political campaign: "You never hire someone you can't fire." Todd was miffed when he learned of Welch's comment. "There is a consultant who doesn't know my sister from a fire plug," he said, and then boasted: "This is a nontenured position." Whitman spokesman Carl Golden likened Dan's hiring to President Kennedy hiring his inexperienced brother Robert as attorney general.

Under Todd's leadership, the campaign put aside the fiery election-night comments of David Murray, who was ready to enter the ring with the scrappy former boxer, Jim Florio. The campaign took on a more genteel, we'll-take-the-high-road attitude, as Whitman set out to define her campaign in what was described as a "positive, leadership-oriented" way. In the few days following the primary, the campaign quickly put together an ineffective television spot in which Whitman, speaking from a formal office setting in a voice that lacked animation, introduced herself to New Jersey citizens. Scaring Republican party strategists even more, Whitman disappeared from the state's political radar screen for six weeks. She was busy visiting street fairs and mingling with small groups of voters, but she failed to make any major policy statements or to attract much-needed, positive media attention.

Meanwhile, Florio's game plan was to ride to reelection on the semi-automatic weapons ban he had pushed through the legislature in 1990. In June, Whitman gave him the perfect chance to attack her on the issue when she visited one of New Jersey's largest gun dealers. A local reporter for the *Jersey Journal* reported Whitman's trip to Caso's Gun-a-Rama in

Jersey City and quoted her as saying to the dealer, Frank Caso: "I think the legislation on the ban should be cleaned up a bit. I think the concern of the bill should focus more on the people who commit the crimes. There are also several weapons that shouldn't be included in the law."

Whitman's concerns about certain provisions of the law opened the door for Florio to paint her as a friend of the National Rifle Association and someone who favored the maiming of children by gun-wielding drug dealers. Even as she declared that she favored the ban on assault weapons and was opposed to efforts to repeal it, Florio would continue to twist her statements throughout the campaign.

When Whitman wasn't unintentionally stirring the waters on the gun issue, her campaign was quiet, and the downtime was deadly for her campaign. Fellow Republicans warned that if she sat back during the summer months and allowed Florio to define her image, she would remain on the defensive throughout the campaign. Behind the scenes, Republicans were telling her to attack Florio on the tax issue and clarify her own position on taxes. What troubled Republicans even more, however, was that when Whitman did begin to campaign, she repeatedly stumbled over herself. During the third week of July, Whitman scheduled a fourteen-stop bus tour of northern New Jersey. It was her busiest day since the primary, and a media bus had been chartered to encourage generous, positive news coverage. But instead of getting positive newspaper and television coverage, Whitman spent the day defending a decision made twenty-four hours earlier to hire controversial media consultant Larry McCarthy. McCarthy, working for a political action committee in 1988, had produced the Willie Horton ad, which had been labeled racist during George Bush's presidential campaign against Massachusetts Gov. Michael Dukakis.

Keith Jones, state president of the National Association for the Advancement of Colored People, reacted by sending Whitman a letter calling McCarthy "one of the most deplorable figures in American politics" and labeling his hiring "unconscionable." When television crews showed up at the campaign stops, their questions were about McCarthy and the NAACP, not the issues Whitman had planned to focus on during the tour. Before the day was over, McCarthy had officially resigned to avoid becoming what he described as a "distraction" to the campaign. Insiders, however, say he was fired once the Whitman campaign realized that his hiring had created a firestorm of criticism. Dan Todd, in an interview with New Jersey Network, called McCarthy's departure a "mutual professional agreement."

The most startling part of the incident, however, was that no one in the Whitman camp could explain why the campaign was unprepared for the controversy the hiring would create. Nor could they clarify the issue of why he was hired the day before her planned media tour. Whitman further inflamed the situation and angered a high-powered Republican consultant with comments she made on the issue to New Jersey Network. In numerous interviews on the decision to hire McCarthy, Whitman made it clear that she was aware that he had created the Horton ad and defended him as a technician, who would have followed her instructions. She told the Associated Press that no matter whom she hired as a media consultant, her campaign would not produce racist ads. "As far as I'm concerned, nobody in my campaign does an ad that isn't sanctioned by me, and I don't sanction those types of things. There's absolutely nothing about my campaign that is racist. They [NAACP leaders] know one of my campaign chairmen [Lonna Hooks] is a minority."

However, in an interview with New Jersey Network, Whitman was quoted as saying that it was her understanding that Roger Ailes, George Bush's 1988 political adviser, was more responsible for the Willie Horton ad than McCarthy. A furious Ailes lashed out at Whitman, saying that she was trying to cover up McCarthy's involvement in the Horton ads. Ailes criticized not just Whitman's misstatement on the Willie Horton ads, but issued a sweeping statement about the fumbling nature of the campaign and what the consequences could be. "I'm sad, really sad, to say that Christie Whitman is going to hand Florio a victory if she keeps confusing and alienating people with her misstatements and misjudgments," Ailes said in a statement distributed to the New Jersey media.

Whitman spokesman Carl Golden explained that when Whitman made the statement about Ailes she was referring to an earlier time when, like many others, Whitman believed Ailes was responsible for the ads. The campaign ran into more trouble when it was slow to issue a correction that would satisfy Ailes. At first, Golden balked at making any kind of correction, and GOP state party chief, Virginia Littell, issued a statement criticizing Ailes for "shooting from the lip." Later, when a correction was issued, campaign staff blamed the delay on their difficulty in reaching Whitman because she was on vacation.

Shortly after McCarthy tendered his resignation, Whitman departed with her family on a one-week vacation to the Sun Valley in Idaho. The trail-bike trip, coming at a time when her campaign was in trouble, raised questions about her commitment to winning and gave the Florio campaign an issue that it could seize on to paint Whitman as a wealthy socialite merely dabbling in politics. When she arrived back at the Newark airport, reporters were waiting. While reporters fired questions at Whitman about McCarthy and Ailes and questioned her delay in issuing a correction on the Ailes statement, as well as the timing of her vacation, Kate cried. Even with her campaign appearing to fall apart, Whitman defended her decision to vacation with her family, although she later would describe the incident as one of the lowest points in her campaign for governor.

It was clear now that the campaign was in serious trouble. A cover story in the *Trentonian* declared on Sunday, July 25, just before Whitman returned from Idaho: "Christie's campaign stuttering and stumbling."

New Jersey Republicans were growing fearful that she would squander what once appeared to be a clear shot at the governor's office. Analysts like Cliff Zukin of Rutgers University's Eagleton Institute of Politics began to openly say that if Whitman waited too long to get started, Gov. Florio and James Carville, who had saved President Clinton from several scandals, were likely to put Whitman on the defensive, hindering her attacks on Florio's record. "She has not progressed from the primary. You can't sit back. You have got to be aggressive."

Statewide public opinion polls showed Florio and Whitman running almost even, with each of them having support from slightly more than 35 percent of the New Jersey voters. The polls showed that Whitman suffered from poor name recognition throughout the state, despite having run a near-winning campaign against the popular U.S. Sen. Bill Bradley in 1990. Whitman was still failing to attack Florio in the areas he was considered most vulnerable, high taxes and a weak state economy. She refused to call for a rollback of the $2.2 billion in Florio tax increases that remained in effect. She continued to maintain that tax cuts were a goal, not a promise, and she rejected the private advice of former Gov. Tom Kean, who told her to endorse an across-the-board income-tax cut.

"She will not make the George Bush, read-my-lips, no-new-taxes promise," Dan Todd predicted as I sat across from him during an interview in his campaign office in July. "That is irresponsible." Using his homespun style, Todd indicated that the New Jersey economy would remain the focus of the campaign. "When you get done peeling the onion, the single most important thing in this campaign is the state of the economy." But Whitman couldn't even get that point across without stumbling.

When she announced her Council for Economic Recovery, tapping grade schoolmate and New York publisher Malcolm S. Forbes, Jr., and economist Lawrence Kudlow as cochairmen, Florio's camp quickly belittled the appointments by asking whether the well-to-do members were "blue ribbon or blue blood." Ironically, the two well-qualified advisers would become key players in the development of a plan that salvaged Whitman's campaign.

Whitman made another false step when she held a news conference in front of an empty building in Hoboken, which had once housed a Maxwell House factory, to criticize Florio's handling of the state's economy. Her staff had failed to do its homework regarding the site, and the campaign was embarrassed when Florio pointed out that a new business had already decided to occupy the building. The Florio campaign was quick to take credit for the redevelopment effort and to point out that Whitman, and her campaign, were "out to lunch" on the issues.

As the race began to take on national implications, Republicans in Washington started to get nervous about the outcome. If Whitman's campaign was so poorly run that she lost to the unpopular Florio, Republican consultant David Welch predicted that it would be a "monumental embarrassment for Republicans" nationally. Because only Virginia and New Jersey held governor's races that year, the eyes of the nation were focused on both as referenda on President Clinton's policies.

Florio went into the campaign after having received some of the lowest popularity ratings in the state's history with only 18 percent of New Jersey voters believing he was doing a good job in September of 1990. His record tax hike in 1990 spawned a tax revolt of unprecedented proportions, and the state's economy was deflated with a loss of 300,000 jobs during his tenure in office. Florio clearly would have to rely on policy, not personality, to make a comeback. Even his supporters couldn't make the claim that people would vote for him because they liked him. A *Wall Street Journal* report described him as having the polarizing charm of a velociraptor, a cunning and vicious creature featured in the movie *Jurassic Park.*

A Whitman loss would be seen as more than just a referendum on how New Jersey should be governed. President Clinton, who the previous year had become the first Democratic presidential candidate since 1964 to win in New Jersey, was pointing to Florio as an example of a politician who had made some hard choices, even if it meant raising taxes. Clinton referred to Florio as "the Resurrection Kid," and the president's top campaign strategist, Jim Carville, as well as Democratic aides who helped Clinton put together his New Jersey win, were working hard on Florio's reelection. A Florio win would be portrayed by Democrats as an endorsement of Clinton's policies. A Whitman victory would allow Republicans nationally to point to higher taxes and Clinton's economic program as failed strategy.

Whitman's campaign strategists explained that she was waiting until Labor Day to get started because New Jersey caps gubernatorial campaign spending (which is partially funded by the taxpayers) at $5.9 million. They said a late start would assure that Whitman wouldn't run out of money by late October, when costly television ads would be key to a victory. "We have to talk to people when they are prepared to listen," said David Murray, who was still with the Whitman campaign as a consultant. "People aren't ready to listen while the weather's hot and they are at the beach or chilling out in their back yards."

According to Dan Todd, Whitman was still getting acquainted with the New Jersey electorate and getting organized for the post Labor Day campaign. Her strategists believed that it wasn't necessary to attack Florio so early in the campaign. "Mr. Florio is known by every New Jerseyan," Murray said. "Right now, it is the responsibility of this campaign to talk about Christie Whitman and the direction she plans to take the state and the type of person she is."

Meanwhile, Florio and the Democrats were trying to draw Whitman into a more active contest. Privately calling her a "Jim Courter"* in pearls, the opposition believed that the more active Whitman was, the more likely she would be to continue to stumble and hurt herself. "As long as she stays on the sidelines and refuses to be specific and interact with voters, her ability to do that later becomes compromised," warned Democratic consultant Steve DeMicco. "If she lets the summer go by and thinks this can be a post Labor Day campaign, she is mistaken."

---

*Courter was the GOP candidate who lost to Florio in 1989.

The Whitman campaign, however, refused to be drawn into a confrontation with Florio. "What the governor and his people are trying to do is roll a different tar baby through the door every week to see if we are going to stick our foot in it," Todd contended. The poor campaign strategy that nearly cost Whitman the race can be blamed on those who ran the campaign. It was a close-knit group of three: Christie, her husband, and her brother. The campaign's Washington consultant, Ed Rollins, had the most influence on the small, elite leadership. Spokesman Carl Golden, the campaign's lawyer Peter Verniero, and Whitman's longtime friend and campaign cochairwoman Hazel Gluck also had some say in how things were done. However, even those inside the campaign described it as a "family operation."

On a day-to-day basis, Dan Todd was in charge, and his attitude was: "Do it, and do it this way." There was little discussion with those who disagreed. Whitman basically took the summer off because that's the way things were done in the 1960s, the last time Dan Todd was involved in New Jersey campaigns. But things had changed in New Jersey politics. Summer campaigns had begun to determine the outcome of elections, and the old-fashioned strategy nearly cost Whitman the governorship.

Florio, in the meantime, was taking full advantage of his office to promote his candidacy. He spent his days cutting ribbons for state-funded seniors centers and announcing funding for new programs, such as the revitalization of Camden. "The governor is doing what he does best, going out and promoting economic development," declared Ray Lesniak, chairman of the Democratic State Committee.

Cliff Zukin of Rutgers' Institute of Politics likened the campaign at that point to a game of chicken. "If Florio initiates and she responds, she is, in effect, letting him define her." What worried many Republicans was the strategy Carville had used the last time he ran a campaign in New Jersey. In 1988 when Democratic U.S. Sen. Frank Lautenberg defeated the pre-campaign favorite, Republican Pete Dawkins, Carville's strategy of launching an unexpected summer attack on Dawkins was key to the victory. Dawkins, who Lautenberg hit hard and early, was never able to recover. Zukin recalled Carville saying after the race that he didn't want to let Pete Dawkins get established, that he wanted to cut him off at the knees.

Carville was known for his in-your-face-with-his-fist kind of campaigning. Most Republicans knew he wouldn't hold his punches much longer. Florio, even without the help of Carville, had used a similar strategy in the 1989 gubernatorial race when he hammered Republican Jim Courter with negative attacks throughout the summer. After Courter stumbled through the summer and then tried to flip-flop on his anti-abortion stance, his campaign was virtually over before the race formally began in the fall.

By the end of July, Whitman's poorly run campaign had begun to affect the flow of campaign contributions, and she significantly trailed the fundraising efforts of Gov. Florio. Whitman's contributions totaled $515,542, a third of Florio's $1.5 million.

With funds for the race capped at $5.9 million, each candidate was required to raise about $2 million to get $3.9 million in matching public funds. Whitman campaign officials defended the sluggish fundraising by saying they planned to log in the contributions in phases. But the campaign's failure to raise money early hurt Whitman later because she had to continue to devote time to fundraising when she should have been concentrating solely on campaigning. In an effort to bring in more money, the Whitman campaign arranged for Kansas Sen. Bob Dole, who raised $2 million at a $1,000-a-plate dinner, and former Secretary of Housing and Urban Development Jack Kemp to appear at New Jersey fundraisers. While the events boosted Whitman's war chest, when Kemp came for a cocktail party and fundraiser in Princeton, it was obvious that Republicans were miffed at Whitman's disorganized and error-filled campaign. They gave her a low-keyed reception.

During the summer, Whitman tried to capitalize on her status as a woman. Women's organizations held a fundraiser for her and she gained the "recommendation" of the National Organization for Women of New Jersey. Both candidates met NOW's standards by supporting a woman's right to chose abortion, the Equal Rights Amendment, and lesbian/gay rights. Florio, however, failed to get any support from NOW because of his strong position in favor of welfare reform. Whitman lost the organization's full endorsement because she supported the reforms, but was willing to look at alternatives.

Once the campaign was engaged from both sides, Florio was expected to try to turn the race into class warfare, portraying himself as representing the work ethic of the middle class against the upper-class values of Whitman, a woman born into a wealthy and politically connected family.

Florio was born in the Red Hook section of Brooklyn in 1937. His father, Vincenzo "Jim" Florio, painted ships in the Brooklyn Navy Yard. At seventeen, the future governor dropped out of high school to join the Navy. A light middleweight boxer in the Navy, one of his cheek bones was slightly pushed in during a boxing match. Leaving the Navy after three years, Florio used the GI Bill to attended Trenton State College and later received a law degree from Rutgers University. He served six years in the New Jersey Assembly before being elected to Congress in 1974 where he served until becoming governor in 1989. He had unsuccessfully run for governor in 1977 and 1981.

As the Florio campaign prepared to raise the issue of Whitman's wealth, an incident in mid-August at Whitman's estate drew media attention. Planning to air an ad focusing on the tax breaks Whitman was afforded because her 232-acre estate was also a working farm, Florio's media consultant sent a film crew to the Oldwick property. When the film crew pulled onto her family farm, Whitman tried to corner them, and her husband called township police to report the trespassers. The incident began at 9 A.M. when a van pulled to the side of a road on Whitman's property. As a man with a camera got out, a campaign aide and Whitman hopped into a car and went after the strangers. As they approached, the man jumped back into the van and sped away, but not before Whitman was able to get the license plate number, which was traced to the film crew. "You just don't come on property," an angry Whitman contended in an interview with the *Trentonian*. "We've got kids. You just don't do that."

In what was to become a daily dose of sarcasm from the Florio campaign, his spokeswoman Jo Glading, referring to the tax breaks afforded to the property, said, "Since taxpayers provided a significant subsidy, we wanted to take a few pictures of it." No charges were filed over the incident, but the perception in political circles was that Whitman had overreacted and had come off looking like a privileged landholder protecting her multimillion-dollar estate. Her statement that she feared for her children's safety appeared ludicrous because the van was not even near the Whitman home, and her children were sixteen and fourteen years old at the time of the incident.

To add fuel to the issue of her wealth, shortly after the filming incident, the Whitmans filed their 1992 tax returns, confirming that they had earned

$3.7 million that year. The only portion of the income contributed by Whitman, other than income from investments, was $32,000 in executor's fees for the management of her deceased mother's estate. The forms showed her husband's salary contribution of $1.8 million was from Citicorp Capital Investors of New York and from his work as a private financial consultant.

The remainder of the Whitmans' income was from investments. They received money from royalties, commissions, profit-sharing rents, dividends, interest, parternships, and securities sales, with most of the money coming from profit-sharing in Prudential Insurance Company of American and Citicorp Capital Investors Limited. Unearned income was reported from stock holdings in Texas Utilities, Norfolk Southern, American Electric Power, First Fidelity, GTE, Ford Motor Company, AT&T, Kodak, IBM, Monsanto, General Electric, Texaco, Upjohn, Exxon, DuPont, and Mobil. Income also was listed from the sale of stock in Summit Bancorp, Arco, Exxon, Mobil, Bell Atlantic, Bell South, Texaco, Dr. Pepper, Reliance Electric, Wilson Bottling Company, and Specialty Packaging Incorporated. Dividend income was reported from Prudential-Bache Capital Partners and the Prudential Moneymart Asset Fund.

The filings indicated that the Whitmans paid $918,395 in federal taxes, $236,588 in New Jersey taxes, and $21,200 in nonresident New York taxes. They gave $102,867 to charity, including a donation of $3,500 in clothing to the Far Hills Country Day School. Gov. Florio's tax returns, in turn, showed that he and his wife, Lucinda, earned $162,593 in 1992. They paid $30,160 in federal taxes and $10,837 in state and local taxes. Their contributions to charity totaled $1,123.

In August, the Whitman campaign bore the brunt of more negative publicity when Roger Stone, a Washington-based Republican strategist who helped former Gov. Tom Kean in his successful bids for governor in 1981 and 1985, wrote a scathing internal memo to Whitman, which was obtained by and printed in the *Trentonian*. Stone, a political enemy of Whitman campaign adviser Ed Rollins, suggested that Whitman fire Rollins for his failure to foresee the firestorm created by the hiring of Larry McCarthy. Stone also advised Whitman to put forward a proposal for tax cuts and to seize on the federal probe that led to Chief of Staff Joe Salema's resignation as a way to paint the Florio administration as corrupt.

Ironically, Rollins didn't dispute any of the advice, except his own firing. He said Stone's advice was "similar to what Tom Kean told us."

At the same time, the executive editor of the *National Review,* Geoffrey Morris, warned Whitman in an editorial that if she stayed on the defensive, she was in danger of losing the race. Morris said the populist message could be Whitman's if she wanted it: "Whitman must remind the voters of Florio's tax and spend history while offering clear and explicit alternatives to stimulate New Jersey's failing economy. If she preaches caution and a nuanced approach to cutting taxes, she will appear savvy to some, but others will see her as deceptive: just another rich Republican hoping to ride voter discontent into office and then do nothing."

Under fire on several fronts and in the wake of the poor handling of the trespassing incident at Pontefract, the Whitman camp held a three-day strategy session in Princeton to try to put the campaign on back track. Attending the mid-August session were former Gov. Tom Kean and Congressman Dick Zimmer (R-New Jersey). "It doesn't take a rocket scientist to figure out Christie Whitman will win if voters are thinking about Jim Florio and the state of the economy," Zimmer said after the session. "Christie's chief task is to stay on message. It is in Florio's best interest to keep distracting us." Trying to take the offensive on the issues of her wealth and the tax breaks afforded to her estate, Whitman held a news conference at Pontefract on August 16. Dressed in blue jeans and a pink crew shirt, she proved the estate was also a working farm by showing reporters the cows, sheep, pigs, and chickens, and by feeding reporters the farm's products: hamburgers, lamb, potato salad, and deviled eggs. While the approach showed that Whitman's spokesman Carl Golden was having some impact on the campaign strategy, it was not a total success, as reporters noted that no one was allowed near the Whitman home, pool, or tennis courts during the press event. And Whitman made another gaffe when asked by a reporter whether everyone should take advantage of tax loopholes. "That's why they pay accountants," Whitman said, in a remark that stung the millions of New Jersey voters who couldn't afford an accountant to prepare their taxes.

Meanwhile, Florio's strategy, which appeared to be working, was to keep raising questions about Whitman's ability to govern. GOP consultant David Welch said: "The only hope Jim Florio has is to convince voters she is even worse than he is." Democrats were already beginning to worry about the urban vote. They feared that city Democrats—blacks and Hispanics—might stay home rather than vote for a governor with a weak employment and economic record. Two Democratic strongholds were at risk. In Jersey City, Bret Schundler, the first Republican in seventy-five years to be elected mayor, had the old Democratic machine working for Whitman. In northern Essex County, county executive Thomas D'Alessio had been indicted, and the Democratic party was fractured. Though they had made inroads, Republicans conceded one certainty: Jim Florio was a fighter, and he would never give up, no matter what the odds.

Despite the advice from Stone and Kean, there was little movement in the Whitman campaign for the remainder of the summer. Whitman did make one significant decision in August when she hired Washington, D.C.-based advertising man Mike Murphy of the Murphy, Pintak, Gautier Agency as Larry McCarthy's replacement. In the end, the decision would prove a crucial factor in her narrow win over Florio. Murphy, when allowed to work his magic, wins campaigns. He helped U.S. Senators Dirk Kempthorne of Idaho and Paul Coverdell of Georgia win in 1992; his ads were an important factor in Michigan Gov. John Engler's 1990 victory; and in 1991, he helped direct an independent citizens' campaign to defeat former Ku Klux Klan leader David Duke's bid for governor of Louisiana.

Dirk Kempthorne, a Republican underdog for the Idaho seat, beat Congressman Richard Stallings with ads that showed Kempthorne in front of the U.S. Capitol talking about the perks of office and waste in government. In one ad, he decried manned elevators that took people only a few floors. "He [Murphy] took a candidate that was essentially behind, packaged him, and won by a wide margin over one of the best candidates we have had in a decade," said Alan Minskoff, executive director of the Idaho State Democratic Party. Minskoff warned: "If I were Florio, I would be careful."

The key to how much help Murphy would be to Whitman depended on how much of a free hand he would be given in a campaign that was being tightly controlled by Dan Todd. "If they let Mike Murphy play a real, integral role in the campaign, and not just treat him as a television producer, he will help bring a real focus to the message of the Whitman campaign," GOP consultant David Welch said of Murphy's hiring. It took the Whitman campaign almost too long to find that out.

While Whitman sat back and waited, the ominous predictions and warnings of her fellow Republicans came true. Florio began portraying Whitman in a negative way, putting her on the defensive. In campaign appearances and news conferences, Florio painted her as insensitive to the fears and demands of suburban, middle-class New Jersey. His campaign organization seemed smooth, strong, and tough. Hers appeared disorganized and bumbling. As his standing in the various polls rose, hers slipped.

For Florio, the election would be the final determination of whether he could ram a tax hike through the legislature during his first six months in office, sink to one of the lowest approval ratings of any governor in the state's history, and survive to win reelection. For Whitman, the election would decide whether she and the Republican party would be able to hold on to what appeared to be a piece-of-cake gubernatorial race or whether too many gaffes and Whitman's weak campaign organization would allow Florio to squeak to victory.

As the official and final phase of the race began on Labor Day, Florio and Whitman stood in a virtual dead heat with just under 40 percent of the voters supporting each candidate. An unusually large portion of the electorate, 22 percent, was still undecided. For Florio supporters, it was beyond their wildest dreams that their candidate would be within an easy shot of Whitman at this point in the race.

Whitman's task still appeared an easy one. Polls showed 60 percent of the voters didn't want to put Florio back in office. All she had to do was present herself to the New Jersey electorate as a viable, reasonable alternative. So far, she had not been equal to the task. "She needs to convey and command a confidence that she can run the state," said Cliff Zukin. "But there has not been anything in her campaign to indicate that she can do that." Failing to take the fight to Florio early, Whitman remained on the defensive, slow to define her position on taxes. "Florio should be on the defensive," Zukin said. "Yet, it seems the roles are reversed."

Those close to Whitman were whispering that she was now considering proposing a tax cut. The Democrats were licking their chops, preparing to attack the proposal as having no credibility because it was coming so late in the campaign. Republican political analysts warned that the proposal had better be credible or Whitman would be in trouble with cynical voters who felt burned by earlier no-tax promises from Jim Florio, Bill

Clinton, and George Bush. The first television ads of the campaign were produced by the Republican and Democratic parties early in September. In their opening shot at Whitman, the Democrats focused on the one issue they hoped, in the end, would put Florio over the top. Public opinion polls showed that the ban on semiautomatic weapons, which Florio had pushed through the state legislature immediately after taking office in 1990, was most often cited by New Jersey residents as the thing they liked about the unpopular governor.

The Democratic ad—without ever mentioning Florio or the Republicans—showed a man pulling a semiautomatic weapon out of his coat and firing it at the camera, while a young, blond girl stood in the background. "Weapons like these have one purpose—to kill people—often children are in the crossfire." The television spot asked voters to stand up for the Democrats, who "stood up" for them against the National Rifle Association, as Florio seized on the gun issue to portray himself as a strong leader who had challenged the NRA and won.

Because of the powerful nature of the ad, ABC balked at running it until Democratic party chief Sen. Raymond Lesniak agreed to change the sponsor from the Democratic State Committee to his own campaign for re-election. In New Jersey, ads for specific candidates are more difficult for stations to refuse to air and are afforded more protection from lawsuits. John Pollock, assistant professor of communications at Trenton State College, said Florio, in a creative approach, was transforming his battle with the NRA into almost the New Jersey equivalent of the Cold War.

Fearful that the NRA would retaliate with personal attacks, Florio's chief counsel penned a letter to television outlets in New York and Pennsylvania threatening legal action if they broadcast political advertisements that the governor believed infringed on his privacy rights, the *Trentonian* reported. Republicans immediately accused the Democrats of using the gun issue to divert attention from the subject that polls showed New Jersey residents cared the most about—the economy. The Republican ads showed New Jersey residents complaining about the lack of jobs and the state's high taxes. The GOP's hope was that Whitman would win because of New Jersey's sagging economy and the anger that remained over Florio's tax increase.

After Labor Day both candidates began stumping full-time. While Whitman tried to zero in on the economy, Florio managed to dictate the focus of the campaign by attacking her ability to govern and by raising questions about her ability to relate to the working-class people of the state. Florio was positioning himself to attract white, suburban voters and managed to make himself appear more conservative than Whitman on social issues, such as welfare reform and crime. He managed to avert much of the campaign's attention from taxes and the economy in favor of gun control and a proposal to tighten the rules for welfare payments.

Trying to usurp a traditionally Republican issue and appeal to middle-class suburban voters and blue-collar Democrats disenchanted with traditional Democratic social programs, Florio proposed requiring welfare mothers to identify the fathers of their children before receiving benefits. As the Florio proposal received significant coverage from several of the state's major newspapers and the Associated Press, Whitman overreacted in her attack on the plan:

> The governor's proposal to deny benefits to welfare mothers who are unable to identify the father of their child or children cannot be defended on humanitarian, moral, or public policy grounds. What is the governor's next idea in his headlong rush to embrace extreme, right-wing radicalism? A program of tattoos for welfare mothers? A badge sewn onto their clothing identifying them as welfare recipients? How about an involuntary relocation program into camps?

Whitman found herself accused of being insulting to victims of the Holocaust, as a rabbi and two other people criticized Whitman for comparing Florio's proposal to Nazi tactics during World War II. When she suggested that some women cannot identify the fathers of their children because they are promiscuous or will not because their children are products of incest, she was attacked by several black leaders who criticized her for stereotyping low-income women. Whitman allowed the welfare-reform issue to dominate press conferences and the campaign rhetoric for weeks as she continued to lose ground and failed to turn the focus of the race back to the issue of Florio and his tax increase.

Meanwhile, the depth of the national Democratic party's commitment to Florio became apparent when Attorney General Janet Reno and Secretary of Health and Human Services Donna Shalala made appearances in New Jersey. While even naive observers believed that the Clinton cabinet members were stumping for Florio, the Democrats maintained that the timing of their visits was a mere coincidence. It was clear, however, that the Democrats believed that a win for Florio would reflect positively on President Clinton.

Whitman's people began to fear that she was losing the election, and there were signs that she was gearing up to try to seize the reins of the campaign from Florio. Early in September, when she publicly announced that she was preparing to unveil several tax cut proposals, Florio responded with a personal attack. Raising an old issue from the primary race, he criticized Whitman for hiring illegal aliens to care for her children. While the purpose of Florio's attack was to focus on Whitman's wealth, it ignored a similar hiring by one of his top aides. Trying to make her own appeal to traditionally Republican business leaders, Whitman promised to reign in the state Department of Environmental Protection by getting rid of unnecessary regulations and red tape for businesses. Industry leaders, frustrated with expensive fines and permit costs, were giving Whitman more than lip service, as checks were written for her campaign. But during a discussion open to reporters, Dale Chaote, the refinery manager at Mobil Oil Corporation in Paulsboro, expressed the frustration of those who wanted to see Florio's tenure as governor end. He told Whitman that his employees had been asking: "When are you going to slug it out with the governor?"

In mid-September, the candidates started to vie for endorsements from the state's unions. Florio came out on top when they both tried to woo the state's firefighters at a meeting of the New Jersey State Firemen's Mutual Benevolent Association in Atlantic City. Whitman, who stumbled over some of her words and read portions of her speech to the firefighters, ducked some pointed questions. Florio, visiting the convention later that day, clinched the endorsement by announcing that additional state funding would be made available for firefighter testing. Yet Whitman made some inroads with the traditionally Democratic labor unions because of their disenchantment with Florio. After union leaders supported Florio's candidacy in 1989, he had turned his back on them in 1990 by trying to break New Jersey's contracts with the state's union workers in order to balance his budget.

At a luncheon for members of Local 1037 of the Communications Workers of America on September 14, a table full of state clerical workers, most of them black, fawned over Whitman. They had worked for

Whitman when she was president of the state Board of Public Utilities, and they were breaking ranks with the CWA's Democratic tradition to support her. For the first time in their lives, they would go into the polling booth and pull the lever for a member of the Republican party. "She was fair," Najm Mahammad explained. To get the unprecedented endorsement from the union local, Whitman had promised union members only one thing: if she became governor, they would sit at the table when decisions affecting them were made.

But some of the most powerful labor unions in the state were not about to turn their backs on the Democratic party. The same evening, Whitman received a different reception when she addressed Teamster leaders, who were packed into a small hotel conference room in central Jersey. Looking straight into the crowd of husky men, Whitman, dressed in a crisp, navy blue suit, said she had no intention of lying to them: she was opposed to closed, or all-union, shops. The union leaders, uncomfortable with her honesty, shuffled in their seats, cast their eyes to the floor, and later that evening, in a private session, voted to endorse Florio.

During a September 16 address in Atlantic City to 300 members of the powerful state AFL-CIO, Florio made the first major blunder of his re-election campaign. His well-oiled research team failed him, and he mistakenly identified Whitman's agricultural adviser as a farmer who had been cited for environmental violations. Whitman had named William S. Haines, Jr., a prominent cranberry farmer, to her Economic Advisory Council, but the environmental case Florio was referring to was against Larchmont Farms, owned by peach farmer and State Sen. C. William Haines, Jr.

Thinking she had finally found an issue she could get some positive news coverage on, an indignant Whitman called a press conference at the statehouse to blast Florio. "The governor, in his haste to attack me, has now gone over the line," Whitman told an unsympathetic statehouse press corps. The Florio campaign had already issued a statement from Jo Glading saying: "It was an honest error. We regret it, and we apologize." And reporters were more anxious to continue to question Whitman about Florio's welfare reform proposal than to report on an error made in an Atlantic City speech.

Working the campaign circuit, Florio continued to attack Whitman's wealth. He touted his childhood in Brooklyn and reminded voters of his working-class past while alluding to Whitman's wealth. "There is not a lot of blue blood in Red Hook," he quipped. Meanwhile, speaking to government accountants and builders organizations, Whitman vowed to end Gov. Florio's "tax and spend" policies and to begin a new era of "cut and save." She promised audits of all of the state's departments and called for an end to the hiring of state employees for purely political reasons.

By mid-September, a public opinion poll published in the *Record* indicated that Whitman and Florio were still running neck and neck. Forty-three percent of those polled backed each candidate, with 13 percent undecided and one percent supporting neither candidate. The poll also showed that Florio's supporters were less likely to go to the polls on election day, meaning Whitman could win in a close race. Whitman advisers said they were encouraged that Florio had been unable to move past Whitman in the polls despite the aggressiveness of his campaign. However, four days later, a poll conducted by the *Star-Ledger*/Eagleton gave Florio a nine-point lead with 47 percent of the New Jersey voters polled saying they would support the governor and 38 percent backing Whitman. The second poll was conducted just as the Florio campaign began running television ads distorting Whitman's positions on drunken drivers, mandatory sentencing for carjackers, and assault weapons. The ads told viewers that Whitman favored the release of drunken drivers and carjackers and painted her as a tool of the National Rifle Association.

The second poll also showed that support for Florio was not very firm. Of the voters who said they were firmly supporting a candidate, Florio and Whitman were still in a dead heat with 26 percent each. According to Eagleton polling, Florio's support had increased by 4 percentage points since June while support declined for Whitman during the summer among independent voters who switched to the undecided column. Florio also had widened his lead among women voters and received his strongest support from the elderly. Janice Ballou, director of polling for Eagleton, attributed Florio's upswing to his focus on welfare reform and crime, which was having an impact among independents. In a statement issued with the poll results, she cautioned that it was far too early to declare a winner. "With only half of the voters committed to a candidate, there are plenty of opportunities for both candidates. These uncommitted voters are critical to the candidate who wants to win this election. They are the group that is most likely to be influenced by the October debates and the candidates' advertisements."

Six weeks before election day, in a move Christie Whitman hoped would save her failing bid for the New Jersey statehouse, she unveiled a bold plan to cut New Jersey taxes. Her pledge was to cut income taxes for most New Jersey residents by 30 percent over three years. Florio had so dominated the fall campaign for governor that Whitman's only hope of winning was to bring the focus back to taxes and the economy. The tax proposal fulfilled that goal by shifting the focus of the campaign back to the issues that could produce a win for Whitman.

The tax plan was hammered out at four informal planning sessions around the dining room table at Whitman's estate in Oldwick. Those working on the tax proposal with Whitman included Wall Street economist Lawrence Kudlow; New York editor Malcolm S. Forbes, Jr.; John Whitman; Dan Todd; ad man Mike Murphy; Ed Rollins; Carl Golden; David Sackett of the Tarrance Group, her Washington, D.C., pollster; and Lyn Nofziger, former Reagan adviser and longtime friend of the Todd family.

John Whitman was her closest counsel, but the final decisions were made by Christie Whitman herself. Whitman locked into the idea of an income-tax cut to spur the economy after learning that a federal luxury tax on boat building had devastated the industry in New Jersey and that once the tax was repealed by President Clinton, the industry came back to life. While even some skeptics inside the campaign questioned whether the bold tax cut she would propose could fly politically, Whitman's position was that the tax cuts were what New Jersey's economy needed. She decided that she wanted a mandate for the sweeping tax cuts she was about to propose to a skeptical audience, or she didn't want to be governor.

Whitman made the announcement on September 21 to newspaper and television reporters who filled a small conference room at the Ramada Hotel in Clark near her campaign headquarters. Appearing nervous, Whitman delivered a strongly worded speech with little animation, as she stumbled, on occasion, over her words. But there was little doubt that what she had to say was heard across the state:

> Jim Florio deceived New Jersey. He promised to hold the line on taxes, then raised them nearly $3 billion. Overnight, we went from a low tax state to the second highest taxed state in America. Jim Florio may be a former boxer, but when he made that promise, he threw a sucker punch

at the people of New Jersey. And now the Clinton tax increases will hit us again, when we're already down.

On November 2, New Jersey can send a message to Bill Clinton and Jim Florio. New Jersey is not a punching bag. And, we're ready to punch back. We won't answer with an echo, but with a roar. Because, while Jim Florio enacted the biggest tax increase in our history, I will enact the biggest tax cut. Jim Florio rolled the people of New Jersey with high taxes. I'm going to roll those taxes back. His faith is in more dollars for Trenton. Mine is in people, in farmers, shopkeepers, teachers, truck drivers, homemakers, and entrepreneurs, from the Palisades to the Pinelands. So this program is about giving the future of New Jersey back to the people of New Jersey, with tax reductions to create jobs and rejuvenate the economy; budget savings and executive leadership to control government's growth and power; regulatory reforms to make New Jersey business-friendly once again; and new ideas and initiatives to revive our urban areas. I am proposing a 30 percent tax rate reduction in state income taxes—10 percent per year for three consecutive years—for every taxpayer with taxable income up to $80,000.

Whitman said the 30 percent income tax cut would affect 60 percent of the state's residents, those filing joint income tax returns and earning up to $80,000 and those filing individually and earning up to $40,000. Under the plan, a single taxpayer earning $40,000 would save $308 a year; a couple earning $50,000, $345; a couple earning $80,000, $705.

Forty percent of the New Jersey taxpayers would see a smaller cut in their taxes. She promised a 25 percent tax reduction for individuals earning $40,000 to $75,000 and for couples earning between $80,000 and $150,000. Those earning more would have their income taxes cut 20 percent. Whitman also proposed to take 350,000 people off the New Jersey tax rolls by raising from $3,000 to $7,500 the amount of income a resident had to earn before paying income taxes.

Whitman also pledged to repeal a sales tax on telephone calls, a surcharge on the corporate income tax, and a truckers' motor-fuels tax. Whitman gave broad-brush guidelines on how, during the first eighteen months of her administration, she would cut government by the $900 million needed to make up the money lost as a result of the tax cuts. The total cost of the tax reduction was estimated at between $1.4 billion and $1.5 billion.

To get the money needed, Whitman said she would reduce the state work force through voluntary furloughs, attrition, and a hiring freeze. In addition, she would have private industry take over some government services. She promised to limit the growth of government to 3 percent and use the governor's authority to impound funds to end government waste. She promised to sell the governor's helicopter, cut the governor's staff by 20 percent, and reduce the number of patronage employees in the state work force. She pledged to stop the practice of three residences for the governor and chauffeur-driven cars for thirty-five state officials while promising to end a practice that mandated the purchase of art works for public buildings.

Whitman said the budget cuts needed to fund the tax decrease during her first eighteen months in office would amount to less than 5 percent of the $14 billion state budget over the next year and a half. "In other words, we will restrain the budget by five cents on every taxpayers' dollar."

She promised that her strong leadership could accomplish the task, but, at the same time, she promised to give New Jersey residents a greater say in how their government operated. "I propose the opportunity for the people of New Jersey to take back control over their lives, their state, and their future. I can think of no better way to start than with a peaceful revolt on November 2, a Trenton tea party to throw the rascals out, to throw their oppressive taxes overboard, and together, begin a new day for our children, our future, and our state." While making the announcement, Whitman was flanked by the popular former Gov. Tom Kean, Speaker of the State Assembly Garabed "Chuck" Haytaian, and Senate President Donald DiFrancesco. Kean and Haytaian gave the plan a polite public endorsement. "You can do it, but it's tough," Kean said. "You've got to have courage." DiFrancesco, who had privately backed the plan when briefed by the Whitman campaign, hesitated in his endorsement, which surprised and angered the Whitman camp.

After making the public and the press wait months for her plan to spur the economy, Whitman's proposal was summarized for reporters on two sheets of paper, placed in a glossy white folder with tax charts and colored graphics depicting economic trends in New Jersey. The first sheet listed budget savings that totaled $1.2 billion, while the second sheet listed the cost of the tax cuts at $1.4 billion—a discrepancy reporters wanted justified. In addition, the press immediately noticed that a list of state-government reforms, which were supposed to total $500 million, actually added up to savings of only $430 million.

It was obvious that cutting such items as the governor's helicopter and staff would be a very small start toward reducing state government by the amount of money Whitman would need to fund the tax reductions. When reporters pressed her for more specifics on how she would come up with the $1.4 billion needed to fund the tax cuts, Whitman said she could offer no further details on what would be cut from the state budget. "Until you get in there, until you have control and can do your performance audit, you don't have all those answers."

"Suppose it doesn't work?" one reporter asked. "It's going to work," she quickly shot back. Whitman promised that the tax cuts would promote economic growth and would result in the recovery of the jobs lost during Florio's tenure as governor, which the Whitman campaign overestimated at 450,000. "I can tell you, there will be growth. And I hope we can, and I believe we will, have those 450,000 jobs."

While those close to Whitman knew that they would have to defend the tax plan to a skeptical public and critical opponents, they never planned for the firestorm that occurred.

The Florio campaign quickly labeled the tax-cut plan a political ploy that Whitman had resorted to only when she found her campaign in serious trouble. A Florio press release charged: "One of the big problems in evaluating this plan is that Mrs. Whitman won't even say how she's going to pay for this." Using Whitman's own charts, the Florio campaign also charged the her plan was "welfare for the rich" because someone earning $300,000 a year would have a tax cut of $4,000 while a middle-class family earning $50,000 would get a tax cut of $345. On the campaign trail the next day, Gov. Florio took the two-page proposal from his jacket pocket, waved it at reporters, and labeled the plan "voodoo redo," a reference to Ronald Reagan's supply-side economics. "Mrs. Whitman owes the people of New Jersey more than two pages with numbers that don't add up. She owes specifics. How do you cut taxes for the rich without hurting schools, throwing open the doors of jails, taking cops off the street?"

Florio offered little in the way of an alternative to Whitman's plan, but he had no shortage of colorful phrases to attack it. "This year the voters will elect a governor of New Jersey, not fantasyland."

Within two days, the Florio campaign had produced a television ad using a statement Whitman made in February about a legislative proposal to cut taxes: "It insults the intelligence of New Jerseyans and shows contempt for their finances to dangle election-year handouts before the voters." The ad concluded: "You got that right, Christie."

The Whitman campaign objected, saying the February comment was being taken out of context because it referred to one-time tax cuts during an election year. Whitman responded to Florio's accusations with this barb: "Gov. Florio had three-and-a-half years to put his economic proposals together, and they cost the state dearly in a loss of jobs, loss of revenues, loss of homes, loss of people. My question to him is 'What's his plan to reverse that?' "

Economic experts criticized the plan almost from the minute it was unveiled. In interviews with the *Trentonian,* Princeton University economics professor Gilbert Metcalf labeled the tax cuts "quite specific" and the means to pay for them "vague." Herbert Gishlick, professor of economics at Rider College, said that it could take up to six years for the tax cuts to affect the state's economy.

From the beginning, critics contended that by cutting income taxes, Whitman would be cutting funding to local municipalities for schools and other services, thereby increasing property taxes. When asked whether Whitman was planning some kind of property-tax reduction, Lawrence Kudlow told the *Philadelphia Inquirer,* "She doesn't want to look at that. We have not examined in any particular detail or analytical framework the issue of property tax." Eagleton's Cliff Zukin went the full step, telling the *Trentonian* that Whitman had made a tactical error because the tax-cut plan was more risk than she needed to take. "When you have an unpopular governor, you just need a reasonable plan. She left the door open for people to call it unreasonable. With a plan that can be attacked as not credible, Whitman allowed Florio to keep her on the defensive. I think this race was hers to lose, and so far, she has been doing a good job of that."

With few exceptions, New Jersey, New York, and Pennsylvania newspapers covering the race attacked the plan in their editorials. The *Wall Street Journal,* one of the few exceptions, ran a lead editorial applauding Whitman's proposal and indicating that it was exactly what New Jersey needed.

A Whitman victory on a platform of tax cuts would send heavy waves down the Jersey Turnpike to the Beltway and other citadels of what has made the 1990s the slow-growth decade of envy. Ms. Whitman will also face the hostility of some New Jersey elites, especially the state press partisans and perhaps even some big business types who prefer direct government subsidies. Against that, Ms. Whitman has an optimistic, lift-all-boats message, which, as we've often noted, won three presidential elections the past twelve years. The national political establishment had hoped this platform was buried because it transfers control over resources and economic decisions away from them and toward the electorate.

Cliff Zukin said the election would now turn on how well Whitman could sell the proposal to voters. However, while Florio, the Democrats, newspaper editorials, and economic experts were criticizing the plan, Whitman made the critical campaign error of failing to sell it. In addition, the campaign stuck to its decision not to detail the budget cuts that would fund her tax cut. "Everything is on the table," was the stock answer to what would be cut. According to Forbes, it was a conscious decision not to muddy the waters by allowing Florio to focus on specific program cuts.

Rather than focusing on the tax-cut plan and holding press conferences so that key Republicans and special interests could endorse it, Whitman resumed her normal campaign visits to a wide variety of voter groups. A television ad did little to boost voter confidence in the plan, as the commercial showed a low-keyed Whitman, in a studio setting with piano music in the background, assuring viewers that she would fix the economy by cutting taxes. "I'm not in charge of her campaign, but I would certainly have asked for a more vigorous follow-up," Assemblyman Rodney Frelinghuysen, assembly budget chief and childhood friend of Whitman, told the *New York Times*.

In lieu of selling her tax plan, Whitman spent the day after her announcement picking up an endorsement from controversial talk-show host Howard Stern, who announced over the air that he would endorse the first gubernatorial candidate who called in, and Whitman responded first. In 1989, GOP gubernatorial candidate Jim Courter had gotten himself in trouble by responding to the same offer. When Courter was asked if he would name a New Jersey Turnpike rest stop after Stern in return for the endorsement, Courter, apparently unfamiliar with the practice, said he didn't think they were named after people. Whitman, however, struck the agreement with Stern and used the air time to debunk the television ads Florio was using to paint her as a gun-toting supporter of carjackers and drunken drivers. The only additional request Stern had of Whitman was that she wear a G-string to the inaugural ball.

Speaking to the Mercer County Chamber of Commerce just outside Trenton on September 23, Whitman, with a determined set to her jaw, told the businessmen that people had been approaching her with one question: "Why should I believe what you tell me?" The answer, she declared: "I am committed totally to my economic plan because I am committed totally to the health and well-being of New Jersey."

Whitman explained why she wanted to be governor:

> I am not running for governor to put initials in front of my name. I am running for governor to put our people back to work, to put money back in the pockets of people who are overtaxed, and to put government back on its proper track. . . . I feel strongly and so deeply about New Jersey and about the serious economic condition it is in that I felt a bold and dramatic step was essential. To the skeptics and the cynics I can only say: you have heard my program, you have heard my commitment to it, and you have heard my commitment to enacting it. We have seen for the past few years what does not work. I have a commitment to what I feel will work. So, if there is skepticism and if there is cynicism, I will work as hard as I can to enact my programs and, at the same time, restore public confidence and faith in what our candidates and our elected officials say and do.

The race for governor of New Jersey hinged on whether voters believed Whitman when she said she would cut their taxes 30 percent or whether they believed Gov. Florio when he labeled her program "voodoo redo." As I interviewed people on the campaign trail, some were skeptical of her plan, while others praised it. "I think she needs to explain the details a lot more," said Jim Clingham, vice president at the David Sarnoff Research Center in Princeton. John Brian, a retired general manager from the General Motors plant outside Trenton, where 1,400 jobs were at risk unless a buyer could be found for the plant, said Whitman's plan was the way to get New Jersey's economy back on its feet. "I would support it very much."

C. J. Kielbus, seventy-six, one of three hundred seniors at a Whitman campaign stop in Elizabeth, said, "That's a sugar-coated deal. If she's going to give these people a tax break, where is this money going to come from?"

Whitman spent the Saturday after the tax-plan announcement, her forty-seventh birthday, defending the plan in front of television cameras and trying to shore up support from her own party. When only about forty people showed up for a Republican club rally in Collings Lake along the Jersey shore, organizers attributed the low attendance to the morning rain. But it was clear that the tax-cut plan had generated little excitement, even among Republicans. GOP leaders were complaining that they were never consulted about the plan. The Republican bigwigs believed that the Whitman campaign was listening to too many Wall Street advisers who weren't street-smart politicians, and therefore was losing touch with the average New Jerseyan. An income-tax cut wouldn't help people if they didn't have jobs.

The few supporters gathered at Collings Lake, members of the Folsom Republican Club who would stay loyal to Whitman throughout the campaign, gave her a birthday present of red and white boxing gloves. They said it was to help in her slugfest with Gov. Florio, a former boxer. "Knock out Florio," Jim Kaczmarski, the club president, told Whitman.

On Monday, October 27, six days after she announced her plan, Whitman finally began to sell it by holding a press conference where small business owners gave the tax cuts their endorsement. But it was too late. On Monday evening, lightning struck the Whitman campaign with the release of a *New York Times*/CBS poll showing Gov. Florio with a twenty-one-point lead in the race for governor. Of those polled during the week after Whitman announced her tax plan, 51 percent said they would vote for Florio while only 30 percent said they favored Whitman.

However, there were immediate questions raised about the way the poll was conducted. The *New York Times* had polled 804 registered voters for most of the questions, and then polled an additional 206 unregistered voters for at least one additional question. Also, the week-long polling, which was supposed to have a margin of error of 3 to 4 percent, had been interrupted for a Jewish holiday. But it didn't matter whether questions were raised about the poll's accuracy. It had a devastating effect on the Whitman campaign because of the prestigious positions of the news organizations that had conducted it.

The poll showed that Whitman's economic plan had failed with a significant number of New Jersey voters. Only 10 percent of those polled thought Whitman would lower taxes as she had promised. Yet Whitman remained firmly committed to her plan: "Luckily, the election isn't going to be held today. Polls are a snapshot in time. I think you are going to see people change their minds."

Florio reacted the way he always did to polls: "I never paid attention to polls in the past, and I am not paying attention to them now." It was an ironic statement for a man who was basing his entire campaign for reelection on polling that showed the gun issue as his best possible chance for winning the race. The *Times*/CBS poll showed 45 percent of the people believed Florio did the wrong thing when he raised taxes by $2.8 billion in 1990, but 45 percent now thought he did the right thing. Of those polled, 47 percent approved of the way Florio had handled the job of governor and only 38 percent disapproved.

In an apparent backlash to Whitman's proposal to cut taxes, voters gave her a low rating on honesty and integrity. While 61 percent of the voters said that Florio had the honesty and integrity needed to be governor, only 35 percent said Whitman had those qualities. Florio received that vote of confidence despite having made statements in 1989 that he saw no reason to raise taxes. Only 35 percent of those polled said Whitman had enough experience to be governor, and only 30 percent thought she understood their needs. "So much for the race for governor," a *Trentonian* editorial said the day after the poll was released. "This is the fault of Whitman and her campaign geniuses, who have run the most inept race possible against Florio."

The misgauging of public reaction to the tax plan appeared to be the most serious in a series of missteps by the Whitman campaign. "Credibility, like virginity, is very hard to get back once you give it up," said Eagleton's Cliff Zukin. "It may well be over for her."

9

The Final Victory

"We are going to give everyone a future."
Christie Whitman (November 2, 1993)
during her acceptance speech on election night.

Christie Whitman was devastated by the *New York Times*/CBS poll showing her twenty-one points behind in the race for governor with just a month remaining before election day. She had believed that her tax plan, and the accompanying television ads, would turn the race around. Her own pollsters had been telling her that the campaign was progressing far better than it appeared. The *Times* poll dashed that illusion. The night the poll was released, Whitman was visiting her sister, Kate, in Washington, D.C. It was one of the rare times that friends and family can recall Whitman being disheartened. Nancy Risque Rohrbach said, "Christie had lost heart a little bit."

Christie asked Rohrbach, who resides in Washington, and her sister to join her on the campaign trail in New Jersey for support.

However, with her campaign in shambles, Whitman was forced to do more than rally loyal family members and friends to her side. Two days after the *New York Times* poll was released, under tremendous pressure from New Jersey Republicans, she removed her brother as campaign manager and moved Ed Rollins into the top campaign position. Fearful that a devastating loss by Whitman would cost the Republicans control of the state legislature, state GOP leaders were up in arms. Campaign insiders actually believed the poll saved Whitman from a defeat because it was the only thing potent enough to force her to remove Dan from the campaign's leadership. "It was the only way of pushing the brother aside," a campaign source stated. "It was because the pressure on her was so tremendous."

The decision to remove Dan from the top of the campaign hurt Christie, who had a deep sense of loyalty to her family and an emotional attachment to her brother. However, it was obvious even to loyal Republicans that Florio was going to win if the reins of the campaign weren't taken out of Dan's hands. A member of the campaign team, who asked to remain anonymous, attributed Whitman's campaign woes to Todd's know-it-all management style. "He is virtually a dictator. He thinks he knows everything, and he does not know that much about New Jersey politics. In addition, as Christie's brother, he has carte blanche to run roughshod over people. Close friends were shut out of the campaign because he wanted control."

From the beginning, Republicans questioned whether Todd had the background to handle a major campaign because of his very limited political experience. When questions were raised in July about Whitman hiring a family member for such a key slot, Dan Todd bragged that Christie would not hesitate to fire him if she thought it necessary. Publicly, Whitman fudged on the firing. She told the press that her brother was not demoted and that she had always planned to have Ed Rollins take over during the final weeks of her campaign. "It was always a part of what we planned to have happen," a poised Whitman said at a Jersey City news conference where she revealed none of the painful emotions she was experiencing behind the scenes.

Whitman had kept her brother at the helm of the campaign, leaving the public with the perception that she was unable to learn from her repeated mistakes, because of her fierce loyalty to family, friends, and employees. Backing away from her commitment to her brother, who qualified as all three, was extremely difficult for her. She was able to hide those feelings from the public by drawing on the poise and political composure she had learned from her parents.

Todd's version of what had occurred differed from his sister's. He said that while the campaign had always planned to have Rollins come on board full-time at the end, the original plan did not include Rollins taking over the day-to-day operations which had been Dan's responsibility. "I think there are a lot of people delighted that I'm not the campaign manager, and I'm one of them." When asked to explain the change of plans, Todd replied: "That part, you have to ask my sister. She made this decision." Todd denied having run the campaign with a dictator-like management style and said he never ran roughshod over people.

For critics and supporters alike, the signs of a poorly run campaign were there for all New Jerseyans to see. The Whitman campaign had been on the defensive ever since Dan Todd was brought on board. Gov. Florio's strategy to discredit Whitman's tax plan and to smear her by distorting her positions on crime was working; and at this stage of the campaign, she had lost any advantage she may have had over the unpopular governor.

While there was dissension among a demoralized Whitman staff, there was still a sense of hope that, with Rollins at the helm, Whitman might become more aggressive. However, Dan Todd blamed his sister for the campaign's soft-handed approach. He said Whitman had made the decision herself not to run a negative campaign. Those people inside the campaign who had hoped for a more aggressive style remained uncertain about whether the addition of Rollins to the tiny inner circle that controlled the campaign could change Whitman's strategy. "It is unclear whether she has the will to do what needs to be done," one campaign source said. As he took control of the campaign, Rollins, a gray-haired, bearded man who liked to talk about his political expertise, promised a more aggressive strategy focusing on Florio's record. Negative ads were being produced, a tougher-talking Whitman released a crime-fighting plan, and the campaign stepped up its schedule of events amidst the controversy over her brother's firing.

With four weeks remaining in the campaign, people were already asking whether Whitman was finished and whether the offensive was too little and too late. Analysts interviewed by *Trentonian* reporters were hard pressed to identify anything that Whitman had done right. "They are headed on a downward spiral," Cliff Zukin said.

"The whole campaign has been characterized by one mistake after the other," added Neil Upmeyer of the Center for Analysis of Public Issues, a Princeton-based independent policy research organization.

Many believed Whitman had waited far too late in the campaign to announce her proposal to cut state income taxes by 30 percent. By the time she made the announcement, voters had grown skeptical of politicians' promises, and newspaper editorials hammered it as being long on rhetoric and short on specifics. The plan had given Florio just one more opportunity to portray her as a lightweight. In addition, Florio's television ads managed to keep the focus of the campaign off the economy and taxes by reminding voters of his tough gun-control law and by portraying Whitman as wealthy, out of touch with most of the state's residents, and soft on crime. He criticized her for taking tax breaks on her family farm and for hiring illegal aliens for domestic chores.

Using her proposal to give first-time offenders in drunken-driving cases special license plates, Florio's television ad showed a drunken driver, swerving in a car, and then claimed that Whitman favored releasing drunken drivers onto the streets. Florio's ad also claimed that she favored assault weapons that kill and maim children, and that she was ready to release carjackers onto the streets. The ad opened with a photograph of Whitman in front of a National Rifle Association seal while an assault weapon fired in the background. With Whitman's face still on the screen, the scene changed to the swerving, skidding car and then to an assailant grabbing a young pony-tailed woman in a parking lot. "Assault weapons. Weaker drunk-driving laws. No mandatory sentences for carjackers. Does Whitman even understand?"

During the first week of October, Whitman tried to counter Florio with the campaign tactics she should have employed months earlier. On October 4, she held a news conference at the statehouse and attacked Gov. Florio's record multibillion tax increase by refuting the statements he had made during a July 27 interview on New Jersey Network. Whitman was accurate in challenging Florio's contention that the state had a $3 billion debt when he came into office, and she accurately pointed out that state budgets grew under his tenure. But coming so long after Florio had made his statements, the challenges did not give Whitman the powerful punch she needed. And pressed by reporters for a promise not to raise taxes if she were elected, Whitman still refused to make the ironclad pledge that would have helped her credibility.

Criticized by political observers for failing to sell her tax-cut plan, two weeks after she announced the proposal, Whitman trotted out four Republican congressmen who praised her tax initiative at a Newark press conference. Whitman said GOP support for the plan was slow in coming because no one knew the plan's details in advance. "We didn't talk to anybody about it before it came out, other than those who were actually involved in developing it. It is very difficult to muster support for something like this if people don't know ahead of time what it is." Whitman said that while the plan had gotten negative reviews from editorial writers and Democrats, her internal polling showed 57 percent of the public believed that income taxes could be cut over time.

After the Newark press conference, she defended her decision not to get input from her own party before announcing the plan: "I wouldn't change it. This is the right plan for the state of New Jersey." Even skepticism voiced by some of her own advisers, who believed the plan to be too bold, had not deterred her. "If you look at the fiscal state of New Jersey, you just can't tinker around the edges. You have to do something meaningful."

On October 6, while still trying to build momentum for her campaign, Whitman encountered a hurdle from her past when the *Courier-News* reported that as a Somerset County freeholder, she had voted to deposit millions of dollars of county taxpayers' money into the Somerset Trust Company in which she held stock. However, working to Whitman's advantage was the fact that only a few newspapers showed an interest in the story when it broke as she was preparing for her first debate with Florio.

On the eve of their first debate a new poll conducted by the *Record* of Hackensack reaffirmed Florio's commanding lead by showing him thirteen percentage points ahead of Whitman. Fifty percent of those polled said they would vote for Florio, compared to 37 percent for Whitman. The poll showed a considerable decline from the twenty-one-point lead Florio had in the *New York Times* poll, but the consensus among New Jersey's political observers was that it was a more accurate portrayal of the status of the race and that it was more in line with the private polling being done by both candidates.

On the down side for Whitman, the *Record* survey revealed that support for Florio had increased among both Republican and Democratic voters while support for Whitman had decreased with both groups. Even as Whitman received an endorsement from the Women's Political Caucus of New Jersey, the poll revealed a softening of support for Whitman among women, a decline that analysts attributed to Florio's television ads portraying her as soft on crime. Support for Whitman among women slipped from 39 percent to 33 percent while Florio's support among female voters increased from 43 percent to 53 percent. The *Record* poll also showed that 70 percent of New Jersey voters thought it was unlikely that Whitman would be able to cut income taxes by 30 percent.

The first debate, on October 7, was billed as Whitman's last chance to reverse the momentum Florio had gained and to salvage a poorly run campaign. It was uncertain how well the inexperienced Whitman would fare against Florio, a seasoned politician who had been given added confidence by the latest polls. Florio was known as a master at using detailed information, even if it was incorrect, to make a point. Whitman, in turn, had spoken only in generalities about how she would accomplish her tax cut. If Florio could gain the advantage with detailed facts, Whitman ran the risk of appearing as if she lacked the knowledge needed to run the state. "Florio, like him or not, he's a gut fighter," said David Welch, a Washington, D.C.-based GOP consultant. "He is a former boxer, and he carries that whole mentality into the debating ring."

At the cost of $600 an hour Florio had been visiting a New York speech coach for more than a year in an effort to improve his harsh demeanor and to smooth out his staccato speech patterns. He was being coached for the debate by his prestigious Washington consultant James Carville and Carville's partner Paul Begala. It was reported that Florio was practicing for the debate with a woman stand-in for Whitman. Whitman believed she could win the advantage in the debate if she could force Florio to lose his temper and become abusive or if she could present a reasonable contrast to his stiff persona. "My job is to convince the voters that I care, that I understand, and that my policies are real," Whitman told reporters at the statehouse. "I just have to be me."

The consensus among the statehouse press corps: she was going to get eaten alive. To the surprise of nearly every official observer of the race, that's not what happened. In fact, Whitman bested Florio. She appeared relaxed, confident, and in command of the facts needed to buttress her points. Florio, on the other hand, appeared stiff, nervous, and at times, shrill and strident in his responses. The tenor of the debate was set even before the arguing began. When Whitman arrived at the WPVI-TV studio in Trenton, she was asked how she felt. "Great, nice and relaxed," she said. However, Florio appeared serious and said to the woman fitting his microphone, "You are making me nervous."

During the debate, Whitman looked directly at Florio when she asked him questions. Florio, on the other hand, avoided eye-contact with her, as they sparred over the economy, jobs, school funding, ethics, and gun control. The most powerful moment of the debate came when Whitman challenged Florio on the $1.5 billion his administration had spent on a state educational system that had failed to cure the inequities between New Jersey's rich and poor school districts. "Jim, where did the money go? The people have a right to know where the money went."

Florio was at his best when he took Whitman's two-page tax plan out of his pocket and waved it in front of the cameras. "It's promising people pie in the sky without telling people where the dough is coming from," Florio charged.

However, Whitman defended her ability to cut state government by the nearly $1.5 billion needed to fund her income tax reductions. She said there were plenty of ways to cut the waste in state government. She surprised everyone by charging that the Florio administration had wasted tens of thousands of dollars by purchasing expensive Adidas® sneakers for state prisoners. Without directly answering the charge, Florio shot back: "One point five billion in Adidas® sneakers is a lot of sneakers."

In what some considered the knock-out punch of the debate, Whitman asked Florio another question he chose to ignore. Taking the initiative, she challenged him to abandon his negative ads and run a campaign based on the issues. "It's become very clear that we need to change the way we govern and the way we campaign. I propose that starting next week, we ban all negative ads; that from now on it's you talking about your record and what you are going to do for the future and me talking about my economic program for the state of New Jersey."

Ignoring the proposal, Florio talked about his favorite issues: his ban on semiautomatic weapons and his proposal to cut welfare benefits for mothers who fail to identify the father of their children. Florio charged that Whitman had termed his ban on semiautomatic weapons a "lousy law." Whitman countered by saying, "Contrary to what the governor has been saying in his ads, I oppose assault weapons."

While saying that he welcomed a federal investigation focusing on his former chief of staff, Joe Salema, Florio attacked Whitman for voting to approve pay increases for herself when she was a Somerset County freeholder and for voting to deposit county funds into a bank that she and family owned shares in. Whitman countered: "I'm glad the governor welcomes investigations. He's sure got enough of them going right now."

At a point when most observers in Trenton were poised to write her political obituary, Whitman had kept her campaign alive with the strong debate performance. "One thing is very clear. She is still in the race," said Janice Ballou, director of polling at Rutgers University's Eagleton Institute of Politics.

Alan Rosenthal, political science professor at Rutgers, agreed that Whitman's performance helped her campaign. "By coming off well, I think she made a marked gain. She had been discredited by the inside-baseball people and the public, and she did better than the campaign up to this point predicted."

Nearly one million households, one-third of the households in New Jersey, watched the first debate, and during a call-in poll, viewers overwhelmingly picked Whitman as the winner. The pollsters, the CIT Group, said of the 3,011 calls made to an 800 number, 73 percent said Whitman won, compared to 25 percent who gave the win to Florio. The question now was whether Whitman could use the debate performance to build some momentum.

While the Democrats were charging that the lift to her campaign was only momentary and were greeting President Clinton on a well-timed visit to New Jersey, the Whitman campaign stumbled the day after the debate in its first effort to capitalize on post-debate enthusiasm. The campaign announced that a pep rally would be held at the statehouse, featuring former Gov. Tom Kean and Whitman's primary opponent, Cary Edwards. Apparently the event had been scheduled before confirming that the key players were available, and they failed to show.

Meanwhile, Clinton's visit managed to eclipse two events that under ordinary circumstances might have had a negative impact on Florio's campaign. Unemployment rose in New Jersey for the second month in a row, jumping from 7.1 percent to 7.7 percent. In addition, the *New York Times* reported that, partly as a result of the investigation centering on Joe Salema, nine prestigious bond firms had temporarily banned political contributions to public officials. "Florio will continue to lead," predicted state Democratic party chief Ray Lesniak. "The key is where people stand on the issues, and Christie Todd Whitman has come up short."

Democratic consultant Steve DeMicco said the campaign's outcome depended on one thing: "What does she do now to convince voters that her plan is anything other than a fraud? She needs to do something she has failed to do—get voters to believe she is a credible alternative."

While the Whitman campaign did some things right in the week following the debate, for the most part she failed to gain any immediate momentum from her solid debate performance. On Monday, October 11, Whitman tried to bring the focus of the campaign back to jobs and the economy with a campaign stop at a small Newark appliance factory whose business had been hurt by Gov. Florio's huge tax increase. When Florio was elected in 1989, the factory had four basement assembly lines operating; now it had two, and three southern states were trying to encourage the troubled company to leave New Jersey and relocate in the South. Company president Ted Pearlman said Florio's one cent increase in the sales tax hurt appliance sales and his income tax increase hurt small business owners.

While Whitman was trying to point out that 79,000 jobs had left the state during the summer of 1993, Florio and newspaper reporters were nagging her about the charge she had made during the debate that the state was spending tens of thousands of dollars on Adidas® sneakers. Florio, dangling a pair of Adidas® sneakers, attacked Whitman's credibility by saying prisoners were never supplied with Adidas® sneakers. Because the information Whitman had used about the sneakers had come from the state legislature and apparently was inaccurate, she found herself responding to questions about sneakers instead of focusing on the economy.

To make matters worse, the campaign was uncoordinated and inept at handling the apparent mistake. After the state Department of Corrections said it supplied only generic sneakers to inmates, Whitman began dancing around the word "Adidas®" without actually admitting an error. "Whether the brand name was Adidas, or not, may have been a mistake," Whitman hedged. The *New York Times* quoted Whitman spokesman Carl Golden as saying that the campaign had been given faulty information about the sneakers by lawmakers, but Golden later said he had been misquoted.

(Sources inside the campaign confirmed that the information had come from a high-level legislative staffer.)

Trying to gain ground on the issue of taxes, the Whitman campaign began to air a new television ad contrasting her tax plan with Florio's tax increase. "Christie Whitman wants to cut state spending. Jim Florio increased spending by $3 billion." For the first time, a Whitman ad attacked Florio's ethics by mentioning that his administration was the target of two grand jury investigations, one focusing on Joe Salema and the other on the questionable allocation of school aid to a north Jersey school district. "Jim Florio—rising unemployment, corruption, and high taxes. We can't afford more." Meanwhile, Florio previewed a radio ad for reporters without scheduling the ad to go on the air, fueling speculation that he was running low on campaign funding. Florio's counterattack focused on Whitman's tax plan, as he charged that it would never create the 450,000 jobs she claimed.

Whitman went on the offensive again by filing a formal complaint with the state Election Law Enforcement Commission charging that Florio had an illegal head start in the governor's race by spending more than $200,000 on his general election campaign prior to the legal starting date of the June 8 primary. "I have never seen anyone try to steal a campaign two months before it begins," Ed Rollins charged at a news conference in the statehouse. In an attempt to distance herself from the negative attacks on Florio, Whitman was on the campaign trail when the charges were levied.

The complaint filed with the election board was based on Florio's own campaign reports that listed fifteen expenditures prior to the June 8 starting date for the campaign. The Florio campaign defended the payments as legal by contending that they were payments made for fundraising events or for services that were to be delivered after the primary. In New Jersey's publicly financed gubernatorial races, every dollar a gubernatorial candidate raises is matched with $2 from the state, with each candidate's spending capped at $5.9 million. The Whitman complaint sought to have the Florio campaign return $450,000 to the state—the matching money for the more than $200,000 that she charged had been spent illegally.

The Republican complaint also contended that the Florio campaign should pay travel expenses related to the visits to New Jersey by President Clinton and his cabinet members. The Whitman campaign charged that the visits were political even though the Florio campaign maintained that they were official government visits to New Jersey. As a result of the complaint, the state Election Law Enforcement Commission fined Florio's campaign $2,500 for spending its general election money too early, but the Whitman campaign was unsuccessful at its attempt to have the visits by Clinton officials declared campaign stops.

Later in the week of October 10, Whitman opened herself to more attacks by Florio when she traveled to north Jersey to receive an endorsement from Bergen County executive Pat Schuber, a Republican who had openly criticized Whitman's performance as president of the Board of Public Utilities in 1990. During the news conference announcing the endorsement, workers from the Democratic State Committee held up a sign showing a 1990 newspaper article in which Schuber termed Whitman's decision to allow the sale of protected watershed land "an absolute outrage."

While Whitman refused to answer reporters' questions about the watershed sale, the Democrats distributed packets detailing the controversial incident. The following day, newspaper accounts outlined how in the final day of former Gov. Tom Kean's administration, Whitman presided over last-minute meetings that granted the exemption for the sale of the protected land.

Any positive campaign energy that Whitman had generated from her debate was further dissipated when she allowed the Florio campaign to focus on her failure to release her 1990 income tax records. Even Republicans, who gave her high marks for her debate performance the previous week, wondered why she allowed what should have been a nonissue to snowball out of control.

Whitman had released her 1989, 1991, and 1992 tax returns, but she had refused to give reporters access to the 1990 return. Even though she was a candidate for the U.S. Senate in 1990, Whitman maintained that she was a private citizen in 1991 when the forms were filed.

On October 12, when Florio's campaign adviser Jim Carville attacked Whitman in a radio tirade heard throughout a major portion of the state for not releasing her 1990 tax returns, Whitman balked one more time and then finally agreed to make the returns public by week's end. "Where are her 1990 tax returns?" Carville asked thirteen times in his thick, Cajun drawl during two morning telephone calls to radio show host Jim Gearhart on New Jersey 101.5. Taking center stage for the first time in the campaign,

Carville said Whitman's 1991 return showed that she received a $276,000 tax refund in 1990. Carville's logic was that a mistake on Whitman's part in estimating her 1990 taxes would call into question her ability to manage state finances. Interviewed at a morning campaign stop about an hour after Carville's first telephone call to the station, Whitman, obviously frustrated with the situation, continued to maintain that she wouldn't release the tax forms. "This is just a never-ending game they have been playing, and I am not going to be suckered into it," she said. But by early afternoon, the Whitman campaign had changed its mind.

"The governor's whole history is nitpicking to avoid having to discuss his record," said Whitman spokesman Carl Golden. "If he's that boiling with curiosity, fine, we'll release them by the end of the week. This may serve to get him back to discussing the issues."

The campaign released the forms, in part, because Florio was preparing a television ad in which he would continue to attack Whitman on the issue. "There was never anything here that we were attempting to hide," Golden stated to reporters when the forms were released. "He [Florio] became obsessed to the point of lust at getting this thing. He is going to be terribly disappointed when he gets these." In spite of Whitman's decision to finally release the forms, Florio continued with plans for a vaudeville-style press conference that day. He mocked Whitman by emulating talk-show host David Letterman's notorious "Top 10" list. Ten cards were propped on an easel, each with a different reason why Whitman would not release her returns. As Florio read from the cards, an aide flipped each one and threw it to the floor. Carville emerged from the wings to call attention to an additional card that quoted Whitman's statements in support of full financial disclosure for candidates. The controversy over the 1990 returns was one more indication of the indecision that had plagued the Whitman campaign, as issues that should have been dispensed with quickly were allowed to drag on and hurt the candidate. The tax return incident was reminiscent of the campaign's waiting until Roger Ailes issued his scathing public statement before giving him the correction he demanded. In July, Whitman had wrongly identified Ailes as the creator of the controversial Willie Horton ad.

When the tax returns were finally released, they made the Whitman campaign appear even more inept because there was nothing in them that would have warranted Whitman withholding the documents for so many months and allowing Florio to turn them into such a hot campaign issue. "Once again, she played into Florio's hands," Neil Upmeyer of the Center for Analysis of Public Issues told the *Trentonian.* "She allowed him yet another issue by not having resolved the question months ago."

The 1990 tax returns confirmed Whitman's wealth, which was no surprise to anyone. The tax forms showed that Christie and John earned $4 million in 1990 and paid $1.2 million in taxes. The salary portion of the earnings included $2.5 million earned by John Whitman while he was employed by Prudential-Bache Securities, and $23,279 earned by Whitman for the portion of the year she served as president of the state Board of Public Utilities. The tax refund Carville had harped on resulted from an overly large tax payment being withheld initially from the $2.5 million bonus Prudential-Bache Securities paid to John Whitman.

Florio had clearly maneuvered the tax return issue to his advantage, but some observers, noting Carville's radio tirade and Florio's staged press conference, said the governor was approaching the point where his own antics and negative attacks on Whitman could make him appear arrogant and cocky, an image many already had of him. By the weekend of October 17—just two weeks before election day—Republicans were reporting that their private polling showed the race had tightened and Florio's lead had been reduced to eight percentage points.

Whitman spent most of that critical weekend campaigning in Middlesex County, an area located in the central portion of the state where the election's bloodiest battlefields were located. On Saturday, Whitman went door-to-door seeking residents' support. She chatted with senior citizens at a community center and shook hands at a flea market.

On Sunday, she dressed in a royal blue Giants sweatshirt and stumped at tailgate parties outside Giants Stadium in the Meadowlands where the fans greeted her with a warmth that even surprised her aides. Later in the day, Whitman raised eyebrows when she arrived at a formal luncheon, hosted by the New Jersey Federation of Republican Women, still wearing her sweatshirt. A Whitman aide joked privately that she had earned the right to wear whatever she wanted to the event because her mother and grandmother had both chaired the organization.

Still campaigning in Middlesex County, Whitman, who normally does not eat at campaign stops, shoveled in a plateful of kielbasa at the South River Polish American Club. Members of the club explained that no candidate who had come to eat the polish sausage, potatoes, and sauerkraut during a campaign had lost, so Whitman ate the ethnic mixture. "This will do it," Whitman, smiling and obviously enjoying herself, predicted. After eating the kielbasa during his first successful race for the presidency, George Bush failed to return to the New Jersey spot during his second, unsuccessful bid in 1992, club organizers pointed out.

In a new speech style developed after Rollins took over the campaign, Whitman told the Polish-American crowd that her candidacy symbolized a return to the optimism New Jersey residents had enjoyed in the 1950s. The speech was reminiscent of President Ronald Reagan's 1984 appeal to old-fashioned patriotism in his successful reelection campaign, also directed by Rollins.

By mid-October, the official *Star-Ledger*/Eagleton poll showed Whitman trailing Florio by 12 percentage points. Of those polled, 52 percent said they would vote for Florio while 40 percent said they would cast their ballots for Whitman. The good news for Whitman was that 34 percent of the New Jersey voters had not yet committed to a candidate. "There is definitely room for Whitman to make some inroads," said Eagleton polling director Janice Ballou. Even Democrats, like consultant Steve DeMicco, admitted Whitman still had the opportunity to overtake Florio and win. Whitman had gained significantly (11 percentage points) among independent voters to pull into a dead heat with Florio among those with no party affiliation. In addition, Florio's negative rating—those believing he was doing a poor job as governor—jumped from 19 percent to 31 percent. In the first official indication of the movement toward Whitman, it was apparent that Florio was doing something wrong and Whitman was gaining ground.

On October 18, after it had appeared that Florio had bested Whitman on the sneaker issue, a state auditor's report surfaced indicating that the state had purchased L.A. Gear® sneakers for prisoners, an even more expensive brand than Adidas®. Auditor Richard Fair said that between July 1989 and March 1991, the state spent $50,000 on sneakers, boots, and arch supports for inmates, and state auditors, checking one of the shipments, had found L.A. Gear® sneakers. Even though Whitman proved her point in the end, Florio, once again, had been able to use an issue to divert attention away from the New Jersey economy during a critical time in the campaign.

The next issue was whether Whitman would be able to keep her campaign alive with another good debate performance on October 19. "She's far enough behind that she really needs to find something that will resonate and work," Cliff Zukin said.

Democrats billed the second debate as a "do or die" situation for Whitman. Whitman prepared for the debate by relaxing and biking at Pontefract. Florio, in turn, said he was taking his wife Lucinda's advice to "lighten up" during the second debate. "I'm walking around smiling," Florio told reporters on the campaign trail. "I'm practicing lightening up." When asked whether he would like to tell a joke, just for practice, Florio revealed the difficulty of the task. In a deadpan voice, he said, "Well, uh, no."

In the second debate, Whitman repeated her confident performance, but failed to drop a bombshell or turn in the extraordinary performance needed to win. More animated and relaxed than during the first debate, Florio held his ground and strengthened his position with a solid performance. Both candidates were cautious, neither of them wanting to make a serious misstep, but because of her caution, Whitman was neither as sharp nor as challenging as she had been in the first debate.

The high point for Whitman came as Florio bragged about cutting state government by $2 billion. (The $2 billion was really the amount he cut from spending requests made by state departments that always have oversized wish lists.) Whitman turned the tables on Florio by using his point to defend her plan to cut government by $1.5 billion in order to finance her tax cut. "If you can cut $2 billion, why are you worrying about my being able to cut $1.5 billion?" Whitman asked Florio.

Whitman pointed to the governor's helicopter as a way to trim the waste in government. "We don't need to have a helicopter with a wet bar and leather seats." Striking back, Florio said, "We don't even have the foggiest notion what programs she will be cutting."

Florio criticized a Whitman campaign brochure that told voters that they would see a $1,000 savings from her tax plan. (The figure was far too high for the average New Jersey resident.) "Next, we are talking about timeshare condos and Ginsu knives," Florio quipped. Florio also attacked the budgets Whitman voted for as a Somerset County freeholder and her decision to sell wetlands while head of the state Board of Public Utilities. Whitman retaliated by contrasting her record with questions that had been raised about corruption in the Florio administration. "Nothing has risen to the level of grand jury investigations and subpoenas." Florio countered by saying, "I am more than happy to match ethical levels with anyone in this room."

Whitman hammered Florio on his $2.8 billion tax increase, the state's loss of jobs, and its sagging economy. In his response, Florio denied promising not to raise taxes in 1989. (On the campaign trail, he said he saw no need to raise taxes.) On the tax increase itself, he said, "I take full responsibility. We made the tough decisions."

Carville declared the debate a win for Florio. Rollins claimed it for Whitman: "From our perspective, she did exactly what she had to do. She connected with the voters." However, it was clear that Florio had done nothing during the debate to jeopardize his position as the frontrunner. After the debate, he once again received help from Washington, as Hillary Clinton arrived to stump on his behalf. As late as October 20, Republicans were saying Whitman still faced the same problem that had plagued her campaign from the start. "She has thirteen days to do what should have been done last summer—show that she is competent enough to do the job," said Republican consultant Stephen Salmore. "By running an awful campaign, she has allowed Gov. Florio to portray her as 'out to lunch.' "

Polls were showing that a significant number of Republicans—23 percent—had left the fold and were likely to vote for Florio. "If you are asking me if the election is over, it's not," said Eagleton's Cliff Zukin. "The question is, can she get the Republicans to come home."

The door was clearly open for Whitman, as a *New York Times* poll showed that among those supporting Florio, 51 percent said they might change their minds. But even GOP supporters shuddered when Golden explained what the campaign had planned for the final weeks: "Exactly what she has been doing."

Zukin and others told the *Trentonian* that Whitman's strategy was doomed without specifics to give voters more confidence in her economic plan. "She needs to do something in the last two weeks of the campaign to make herself more credible. She needs to convince people she can run the state."

On October 20, Christie Whitman began that task. She kicked off an intense, three-day bus tour, the first leg of a campaign effort that would take her throughout New Jersey during the final days of the campaign when undecided voters where trying to make up their minds. In a bus dubbed the "Wheels of Change," the Whitman tour headed north, south, and then into the central section of New Jersey, covering fourteen of the twenty-one counties. "I intend to bring my campaign and my message of economic recovery to as many people as possible over the next three days," Whitman said in a statement announcing the tour. "I will listen to the concerns of the people. I will discuss those concerns, and I will seek their support based on my proposals to get New Jersey moving ahead and to restore our state to the position of economic prominence it held during the 1980s."

At the same time Whitman was making the bus tour, she launched a series of television ads attacking Florio's record and defending herself against Florio's portrayal of her as "out to lunch" on state issues and soft on crime. Her television ads termed the Florio attacks "cheap shots" at the same time a radio ad by Kate decried Florio's "nasty" attacks.

Dressed in blue jeans, a pink shirt, and sneakers, Whitman traveled into south Jersey on the second day of her tour and stumped at diners, stores, farms, and businesses. When asked why she was campaigning for governor in a pair of blue jeans, she said, "I'm more comfortable in this kind of clothing." She said the tour would allow the residents of New Jersey to see her as she really was, rather than the way Florio had portrayed her in his ads. She encouraged those she met to ask questions that would clear up some of the concerns they had because of the Florio ads. At the Atlantic Electric Company in Pleasantville, workers asked her to explain her positions on gun control and drunken drivers, and Whitman assured the audience of 100 that she supported the New Jersey ban on semiautomatic weapons and that as governor no one would be tougher on drunken drivers than she would be.

At another campaign stop, Camden County farmers, angry over an increase in the state's minimum wage, gathered at Donio Farms and greeted Whitman as one of their own. "As farmer to farmer, I wish you the best of luck," said an overall-clad peach farmer, Joe Battaglia. "We need you bad." Whitman fell short of promising to lower the minimum wage, but she promised to support other tax breaks for farmers. Discounting Florio's attacks on Whitman because she received tax breaks for Pontefract, Dennis Donio said, "She has land, and she is entitled to the farmland assessment."

Whitman, who was known for her campaign antics during the 1990 Senate race, was less lively during the grueling 1993 campaign. Yet one day on the bus tour, she ended up behind the wheel of the bus as it made its way out of a rest stop along the New Jersey Turnpike. She only drove about 100 yards in the parking area before the bus driver took over, but her staff said the short, rough ride was enough. Even when there was only a handful of supporters on the bus, those on board the "Wheels of Change" behaved like it was loaded with fans, and the bus often left its destination to the tune of Willie Nelson's "On the Road Again."

Meanwhile, Florio's campaign appeared desperate. Mindful of the 1981 gubernatorial race when Florio wasted a lead in the final days of the campaign and lost by 1,797 votes to Republican Tom Kean, the Florio campaign was nervous. In October 1981 with less than two weeks remaining in the race, polls had showed Florio leading Kean by eight percentage points, yet Florio had lost the contest. He was determined not to let that happen again in 1993. Even after a state judge ruled that senior citizens in subsidized housing were ineligible for the state's homestead rebate checks, the Florio administration sent the rebates to the elderly residents anyway in what Republicans saw as a bid to secure votes.

Florio continued to hammer Whitman on the gun issue because his private polling showed that that was his best chance of winning. To call attention to Florio's ban on semiautomatic weapons, the Democrats brought in Republican James Brady, who was shot in the head during a 1981 assassination attempt on President Reagan. And Florio used photographs, taken of Whitman shooting at a firing range during the 1990 race against U.S. Sen. Bill Bradley, in a campaign ad that portrayed her as a friend not only of the National Rifle Association, but of gun-toting criminals. Also airing a television ad touting his record of balancing budgets (something mandated by state law) and of refusing pay raises, Florio charged that Whitman's income tax cut would result in higher property taxes.

As Florio and Whitman prepared to go head-to-head in a third and final debate on October 24, an independent newspaper poll showed Florio was leading the race by only five percentage points. Of those polled, 45 percent said they would vote for Florio with 40 percent favoring Whitman. Fourteen percent of the voters said they were still undecided. Whitman's performance in the debates, her television ads clarifying the positions Florio had used against her, and her stumping throughout the state had cut Florio's lead in half.

The third debate gave Whitman another opportunity to counter the image that Florio had painted of her. "When she is one-on-one with him, she does really well and looks like a person who could be governor," Ballou said. While Florio was painting Whitman as a candidate who was "out to lunch," those meeting Whitman during her campaign tour and those watching the debates saw her as a viable candidate. By discrediting Florio's charges against her, Whitman was reminding voters that Florio was someone who could not be trusted. She was, in turn, successful at reviving the old anger over Florio's tax increases. The Whitman campaign maintained: he had lied about taxes, and now he was lying about Whitman.

Whitman held her own during the third, hour-long debate hosted by Gabe Pressman at Channel 4 studios in New York. Political analysts called it a draw. Even though Whitman failed to aggressively attack Florio on his weakest points—the New Jersey economy and his record tax hike—she still gave viewers the chance to see her as a credible candidate. She turned questions into opportunities to clarify her positions on drunk drivers and welfare reform.

Appearing strident at times, Florio was helped by questions on his favorite topics of crime and gun control. At one point in the debate, he managed to back Whitman into a corner by holding up a picture of a .22-caliber semiautomatic gun that he said had been used to shoot an East Orange child. "She's talked about putting more weapons back into circulation," Florio charged.

Meanwhile, Whitman remained unable to clarify her statements about the need to remove some weapons from the list of banned guns. In addition, she missed a major opportunity to attack Florio on the corruption issues that had plagued his administration. When asked about the importance of character, rather than zeroing in on the Florio administration's negatives, Whitman replied: "I think character is definitely an issue in the sense that it translates into your ability to handle government." However, Florio scored points with his answer: "Character also manifests itself in terms of who is willing to make the tough decisions." It was one more opportunity for Florio to defend his tax increase and subsequent decline in popularity by maintaining that he had made the tough decisions that were best for New Jersey.

Florio charged that Whitman's plan to cut income taxes would result in higher property taxes. "Everyone is arriving at the conclusion that what this plan really is, is a shell game." Whitman fired back that when Florio raised taxes by $2.8 billion, it did not result in lower property taxes.

By October 25, several polls were showing that Whitman had narrowed the race to a statistical dead heat. While an independent newspaper poll showed Whitman trailing by 5 percentage points, Whitman's private polling showed her behind by only 3 percent. According to Democratic sources, even Florio's private polling showed Whitman behind by only 4 percentage points. From October 20 to election day, Whitman continued to narrow Florio's lead by touring the state in her "Wheels of Change" bus. Accompanied by John Whitman; her sister, Kate; friend Nancy Risque Rohrbach; and, in the end, her children, Kate and Taylor, Whitman explained her tax plan and continued to refute the "out-to-lunch" image Florio tried to give her.

Whitman said the race had narrowed because of her ability to explain to voters how cutting government by 5 percent would generate enough money to cut income taxes. She described the sentiment of the people she met on the campaign trail: "They've had to cut a lot more than five cents on the dollar and restrict themselves in their spending, and they want to see government start to do the same thing." Gaining confidence from the poll results and debate performances, Whitman gave one of her strongest campaign speeches of the race before an audience of five hundred American Telephone & Telegraph Company employees on October 25, in Basking Ridge, while an additional eight hundred employees watched the speech on the company's internal cable-television system. Under Rollins's direction, a confident Whitman had fine-tuned her plan for cutting taxes and state spending into a message about a better future for New Jersey. "You have to ask yourself this. Are you happy with the past four years, or do we dare to dream that we can be better and do better?" Unhappy with the sales tax Florio added to telephone calls in 1990, the AT&T workers gave Whitman a friendly reception. Women voters also began warming to the Whitman message. "I support her," said Sandra Coltelli, an executive secretary at AT&T. "She seems honest."

By October 26, one week before election day, Whitman's private tracking polls showed that victory was within her reach, as voters continued to move away from Florio and into her camp. There was a sense inside the campaign that her fortunes had turned at just the right time to capture the race.

Initiating a major mail blitz, the Republicans mailed 1.2 million four-page fliers to independent voters in key districts throughout New Jersey. One flier attacked Florio's most vulnerable point—his tax increases. "The Big Lie!" screamed red letters across the first page of the flier. "How could we ever forget?" the mailing continued. "Candidate Florio said he would not raise taxes. Gov. Florio raised taxes $2.8 billion, and he did it with glee!" In a live interview on CNN's "Inside Politics," Whitman continued the theme by saying that people were having trouble believing in her plan to cut income taxes because of Florio's broken promises. She said voters were skeptical because "they have been lied to so much, particularly by this administration." Meanwhile, the Democratic State Committee tried to attract conservative, middle-class voters by mailing fliers about Florio's welfare-reform plan to voters in key districts. The flier said, "On election day, New Jersey could end welfare as we know it."

When Whitman visited Trenton's downtown on October 26, it became apparent that people on the street had developed a keen interest in her candidacy. In the predominantly Democratic district where voters generally give Republican candidates a chilly reception, people approached Whitman on the street to ask her questions. After talking with Whitman on the Trenton Commons, Joe Giardino, a state maintenance worker, said he was convinced that she would keep her promise to cut taxes. "She seems like she is speaking the truth," Giardino said.

However, the Whitman campaign made a final misstep before heading to the finish line. Waiting until the last week of the race to formally attack Gov. Florio on ethics, the campaign stumbled in the effort. After Whitman's people announced that Ed Rollins would host a news conference at the statehouse on "ethical standards," he failed to show. In Rollins's stead, David Norcross, an attorney for the Republican National Committee, conducted the news conference while Whitman campaigned in north Jersey. Asked why Whitman wasn't launching the attack herself, Norcross said: "It's too late to send her to Trenton to do this. She needs to be out and about campaigning."

With public opinion polls still showing Florio leading among women voters, on the Thursday before the election, Whitman rallied with more than four hundred Republican women at the East Brunswick Hilton in an effort to try to swing the tide the other way. Three months earlier, when the campaign held its last rally for women, her private polling had shown Whitman running ahead of Florio among working women. Now, less than a week before the election, a poll conducted by KYW-TV in Philadelphia showed Whitman significantly trailing Florio among women. Florio's television ads portraying Whitman as soft on crime had turned women away from Whitman, and the GOP wanted to bring them back into the fold.

The goal of the last-minute rally was to energize Whitman's female supporters for the final days of the campaign. Flanked by Congresswomen Marge Roukema of New Jersey and Susan Molinari of New York, Whitman was greeted by chants of "Christie, Christie." The rally was billed as a way to set the record straight. Trying to get her message out to female voters, Whitman told the crowd that she was against drunk drivers and semiautomatic weapons. Turning next to the campaign theme of jobs and the economy, she told the hundreds of women who jammed the room, "Under Jim Florio's policies, more than 280,000 people have lost their jobs here in New Jersey. This is most devastating to women, who are often the last in and the first out of any position."

John Whitman was one of the few men in attendance. When the rally ended, I heard him tell Christie that he would head home first to start preparing dinner.

Star-Ledger/Eagleton polling showed that Whitman's efforts to win back a significant number of female voters was successful. In mid-October, Florio led among women by a thirty-point margin, 61 percent to Whitman's 31 percent. By the end of the month, Whitman was trailing Florio among female voters by only sixteen points—51 percent to 35 percent. Between October 14 and October 30, Whitman's support among Republican women grew from 60 percent to 77 percent while Florio's support among Democratic women fell from 82 percent to 73 percent.

Meanwhile, a battle among politically active women had erupted over the governor's race. The Whitman campaign had sent out a flier for the women's rally which stated: "Florio believes a woman's place is in the home . . . on election day!" Florio's female cabinet members immediately attacked Whitman for the comment. In response, Hazel Gluck, cochairperson of the Whitman campaign, dredged up a 1992 *Gentleman's Quarterly* article that attributed a sexually offensive remark to Jim Carville. The Republicans also distributed a two-decade-old *Courier Post* article by Dennis Culnan, who later became a Florio aide, in which Culnan wrote, "Jim Florio says he believes in the old family philosophy that the man goes out and earns a living while the wife stays home having and raising children."

In the final days of the campaign, Whitman received endorsements from two black organizations. Black businessmen in Newark gathered at a press conference in Ruben's Restaurant, the first black-owned restaurant and supper club in Newark, to praise Whitman's plan to cut income taxes. Then on the Friday before the election, in an unprecedented break with the Democratic party, a coalition of black employees from six state authorities endorsed Whitman for governor. "This is a very big step for African Americans in an urban city to say they support a Republican governor," said Kevin Ali, a coalition official. Coalition representatives said Florio had not put enough blacks on authority boards and had failed to settle job-related grievances filed by black employees. "The Democratic hierarchy has taken the black vote for granted," said Leroy Robinson, an engineer with the New Jersey Highway Authority.

Later in the day, Whitman also got an enthusiastic response from two hundred business people at a meeting of the New Jersey branch of the National Federation of Independent Businesses. "Save us," one businessman shouted from the crowd when Whitman went to the lectern to give her stump speech.

With forty-eight hours remaining in the race, public opinion polls were contradicting each other on their predictions about who would win. A poll by the *Asbury Park Press* showed Whitman and Florio in a virtual dead heat, each with 38 percent of the vote while 22 percent of the voters remained undecided. The *Asbury Park Press* poll coincided with Whitman's private tracking polls, which also showed the two candidates even.

Nevertheless, two major newspaper polls showed Florio with a substantial lead. The *Record* of Hackensack reported that Whitman was trailing Florio by ten percentage points while the *Star-Ledger*/Eagleton poll had Whitman behind by nine points. Yet even the *Star-Ledger* poll showed that among those people who were most interested in the race, Florio had only a two-point lead.

As the race entered its final days, Whitman had three factors working in her favor: momentum, enthusiasm, and a television-ad blitz. "The bottom line is, it's an extremely close race," a tired Ed Rollins told me during a campaign stop in East Orange. "The momentum is coming to us and moving away from the governor. Any incumbent who has numbers like this can't win."

Florio was now in a position of having to fend off Whitman's last minute charge. "He threw everything he had at her, and she came back," said New Jersey Congressman Dick Zimmer, cochairperson of the Whitman campaign. "Now they are going to slug it out in the next few days. I think this may be decided in the voting booth when the electorate thinks about the consequences of what four more years of Jim Florio means."

Analysts were saying that the outcome of the race would be determined by whether or not Whitman could sway voters with her television ads. "She has got to get Republicans back and pull more independents, and she doesn't have a lot of time," Cliff Zukin told the *Trentonian*.

Purposely saving money for the end of the campaign, Whitman's strategists were poised to spend $1 million on television ads in the final ten days. Mike Murphy, Whitman's Washington-based ad man, said television station records showed Whitman would have 30 percent to 40 percent more air time than Florio in the final days, a claim disputed by state Democratic chairman Ray Lesniak.

Murphy produced seven new ads, whose style was a stark contrast to the early ads that had featured a stiff, formally attired Whitman in a studio setting. The new ads contained actions shots of Whitman on the campaign trail mingled with film footage of a relaxed and articulate Whitman explaining to New Jersey voters why it was time for a change, why they should not reelect Florio, and why they should discount the attacks Florio had launched against her. Some of the ads, showing unflattering photographs of the governor juxtaposed with negative newspaper headlines and shots of vacant warehouses, attacked Florio for raising taxes and for failing to keep jobs in New Jersey.

In one ad, Whitman told viewers that she wanted to be a "job-creating governor" in order to "end the hurting." The film ended with Whitman dressed in a T-shirt giving a young girl a hug on the Atlantic City boardwalk. In his best effort to counter Florio's attack ads, Murphy produced a television spot with Whitman, dressed in a blue blouse and cardigan sweater, talking directly into the camera with a garden setting as the backdrop. Pointing out her role as a mother of two teenagers, she raised questions about Florio's honesty. "As governor, nobody will be tougher than me [an obviously intentional grammatical error to make her appear more down-to-earth] on drunken drivers and criminals. If he [Florio] can't tell the truth about raising taxes, how can you trust him to tell the truth about me?"

Two days before the election, the Whitman campaign released an ad by the popular former Gov. Tom Kean, who told New Jersey residents that Whitman would restore pride and prosperity to New Jersey. "I'm voting for Christie," Kean said. "She'll make a great governor." Whitman, who had gained the endorsement of a number of Hispanic leaders in the state, aired some of the ads and distributed some of her brochures in Spanish.

In the last days, Florio, whose campaign had consisted principally of attacks on Whitman, changed his focus to positive ads about himself. Florio had been endorsed by most of the state's newspapers while only a handful of publications, including the *Trentonian* and the *Home News,* endorsed Whitman. Florio's last ad featured editorial endorsements in which he was praised for being a tough leader, for supporting the ban on semiautomatic weapons, and for protecting the state's environment.

In the final hours of the race, the unanswered question was whether Whitman could pull ahead of Florio before the polls closed on Tuesday, November 2. There was a sense that the election could turn on which candidate would do a better job of bringing out the troops on election day. Public-opinion surveys showed that about one-third of the voters were either undecided or showed weak support for the candidate they favored. "It is up to the candidates to get their folks out there, and that will make the difference," said Janice Ballou. Once again, Ballou said neither candidate was assured of a win. The candidates spent their final preelection hours trying to rally their supporters to a last-minute surge.

Hillary Clinton came into New Jersey for a "Women for Florio" rally on the Saturday before the election, as Florio, with Democratic female candidates from across the state at his side, made a final pitch to female voters. On Sunday, Florio, accompanied by U.S. Senators Frank Lautenberg and Bill Bradley, staged a "Democratic Rally for Victory." Florio's rally speech focused on the issues on which he had staked his reelection bid: gun control, crime, and welfare reform.

Bradley likened Florio's days as a boxer to his current fight with Whitman. "Remember, a couple of years ago, and a couple of months ago, he was knocked down. He was down for a seven, for an eight, for a nine," Bradley told the crowd. "And he got up, and he started to fight again. And Tuesday will be the knockout punch."

Traveling with U.S. Sen. Bob Dole on Sunday, Whitman held an emotionally charged rally at her last stop in Morris County, the Republican territory in northwest New Jersey where the GOP was hoping a large turnout would offset Democratic votes in the urban areas.

After campaigning with Whitman from dawn to dark, Dole told four hundred cheering party faithful in the Mountain Lakes High School gym: "I can smell victory in the air."

Whitman confidently predicted: "We are going to send a message, not just throughout New Jersey, but throughout the nation, that voters aren't dumb. You can't tax them and drive out jobs and cost them their livelihood, and cost them their homes, and expect them to forget." When the rally ended, the phenomenon that had been occurring over the last days of the campaign was evident, as well-wishers gathered around Whitman. They wanted to talk with her, to have her autograph whatever they had in hand, to touch her, to wish her good luck.

Mercer County executive Bob Prunetti, a street-smart politician, was among those finding it hard to equate the reception Whitman was getting on the campaign trail with the two prominent newspaper polls showing her trailing Florio by about ten percentage points. "My sense has been that she has generated a tremendous amount of momentum," Prunetti said. "The feeling on the street is that it looks very, very good. I don't know how to reconcile that with the polls."

The secretary of state was predicting that no more than 57 percent of the state's 3.9 million registered voters—about 2.3 million people—would go to the polls on November 2. To make a gain of one percent, Whitman or Florio would have to change the minds of 23,000 people. Adding to the uncertainty of the outcome of the race was the large percentage of people who had not yet made up their minds. In addition, New Jersey voters—half of them not formally registered with either party—were known to be volatile, sometimes changing their minds at the last minute.

The race for governor would likely be defined by key suburban areas, which in recent years had replaced the cities as the political subdivisions that decided New Jersey's statewide elections. Whitman would need to do well in her home base of northwestern New Jersey. Florio, in turn, would need to draw significant votes in his old congressional stronghold of Camden County and other south Jersey areas, as well as in the state's northern cities.

However, both sides agreed that the win would be clinched in northern, suburban Bergen County and the counties that make up the center of the New Jersey map, including Middlesex and Mercer Counties, where a large number of independent voters generally vote Republican. In addition, Whitman would need to do well among seniors in the shore counties of Monmouth and Ocean.

Whitman barnstormed in Ocean County on the day before the election, visiting a seniors' center, a housing project, and a food store. She ended the day in the blue-collar community of Hamilton Township, the highly populated suburban area just outside of Trenton that would prove key to the race.

Florio crisscrossed the state from Camden County to Bergen County. He encouraged factory workers and seniors to go to the polls and tried to shore up support among laborers in Newark, the state's largest city.

Several factors were working to counteract the Democrats' get-out-the-vote efforts. Bret Schundler, the first Republican mayor of Jersey City in seventy-five years, had endorsed Whitman and promised to deliver the city for her. In addition, an already fractured Democratic party in Essex County might fail to bring voters to the polls for Florio because officials feared that Florio intended to order a takeover of the Newark schools if he were reelected. Also, some traditionally Democratic groups like black businessmen in Newark and Hispanic leader Pedro Medina in Mercer County said the Democrats were taking them for granted. They, too, had endorsed Whitman.

In an odd portent of events to come, mock elections by students in several urban schools gave Whitman the nod for governor. "It's a nail-biter," predicted Congressman Dick Zimmer.

On election day morning, Christie and John Whitman rode their mountain bikes to the Lutheran Christian Education building in Tewksbury Township to cast their votes. Photographers captured her in her bike helmet, sweatshirt, and athletic pants. On election night, Whitman and her supporters gathered at the Princeton Marriott to await the returns. Early in the evening, the subdued faithful huddled in small groups inside the Marriott's ballroom. They knew the major newspaper polls were still showing Florio with a substantial lead that could produce an easy win for the governor. Sitting across from me at one of the tables in the Marriott's ballroom were Whitman's ad man, Mike Murphy, and her pollster, David Sackett, who came the closest to predicting the outcome of the presidential election in 1992.

Before the polls even closed, Sackett was predicting that Whitman would win by one percentage point. He said Whitman had been trailing Florio throughout the race until early in the last week of October when she pulled even with Florio and stayed there for the entire week. On the Sunday before Tuesday's election, Sackett's polling showed Whitman pulling ahead by three percentage points. She maintained the lead on Monday, the day before the election, with a two-point edge. According to Sackett, "We saw it turn around on Saturday and Sunday when independent and women voters started coming back. We always thought it would turn around. We needed to make sure people focused on Jim Florio at the end, and then it would move toward us."

Murphy predicted that the campaign's plan to save its money for television ads in the final days would pull off the win: "As excellent as their tactics were, they are going to lose the war."

For the one thousand Whitman supporters, it was a night of highs and lows, of raging cheers and hushed silences. The subdued crowd showed its first signs of euphoria halfway through the night when, with 10 percent of the votes counted, Whitman took a 2 to 3 percent lead. Growing more confident, they cheered to the results and swayed to the band's pop music, as votes were reported from throughout the state. Later, with 70 percent of the vote counted, Florio began gaining ground. The race was a dead heat. The celebrators grew silent. Worry lines appeared on faces in the crowd. Despite the efforts of a Republican booster at the microphone, the party remained subdued.

At midnight, an eerie sense of uncertainty gripped those in the Marriott ballroom. The crowd knew the election scales were tipping toward one candidate. There were whispers that the north Jersey votes, counted last, could give Florio the win. Then at 12:10 P.M., as the latest returns showed Whitman with a slight edge, the seesawing emotions of the evening gave way to a final explosion of joy. With 99 percent of the votes reported, Whitman believed she had won by a narrow 2 percent. Florio had not yet conceded, but Whitman and her key aides, watching the returns from her hotel room, decided she would declare victory anyway, forcing Florio to demand a recount if he did not like the close election results. As they were leaving the room, Florio called to concede, just after 12:15 A.M.

In a stunning, come-from-behind victory, Whitman had become the first woman to be elected governor of New Jersey. The ballroom crowd erupted in pandemonium when she appeared on stage at 12:20. Surrounded by her husband and her children, Whitman, wearing a red suit with a colorful African-style scarf around her neck, threw her arms in the air and gave the crowd a thumbs-up sign. The campaign's "People for Whitman" slogan had been reversed on the huge banner behind the governor-elect, and the words "Whitman for People" served as the backdrop for the victory scene.

The people of New Jersey had spoken. They had chosen the woman who would lead their government for the next four years. "We did it," Whitman declared to the stamping, cheering crowd. "I want to tell you that I do understand what it means to be the first woman governor in the state of New Jersey." Standing on a chair with me in order to see Whitman above the crowd, Mary Ann Campbell, a Whitman supporter from Riverton, New Jersey, yelled, "Do us proud."

Whitman pledged to bring jobs back to the state and to give its children the education they deserve. "We're going to give everyone a future."

As hundreds of red, white, and blue balloons drifted down from the ceiling nets, the crowd started to shout, "Florio-free in '93," the battle cry of the campaign, the slogan it had borrowed from the gun advocates. "We are home free, 100 percent," said Deb Smarth of Monmouth County. "She's a winner." Dennis Knight of Newark predicted: "It feels like something new is happening, something new is beginning."

Florio's watch party was a solemn contrast to the Whitman celebration. During the evening when exit polls showed the race too close to call, the confidence of the supporters at the Florio party in East Brunswick had given way to somber uncertainty and sadness. In conceding defeat, Florio said, "I've won elections and I've lost elections. Winning is infinitely better, but I think it's also important to know that there are things more important than the outcome . . . like the well-being of the people of the state of New Jersey."

Jim Carville, wearing a "Clinton Democrats" jean jacket and a five o'clock shadow, had little to say about the upset. "We lost," he told *Trentonian* reporter Phyllis Plitch. "The voters have spoken." When the official vote count was completed, Whitman had won by only 26,093 votes, or one percent. She had captured 49 percent of the vote to Florio's 48 percent, the second closest election in state history. The closest election was Florio's 1,797-vote loss to Tom Kean in 1981.

Left alone in the polling booth, New Jersey's volatile electorate had decided to seek revenge for Florio's record tax increase. Exit polls showed that for many voters, Florio's taxes were the most important issue of the campaign. In the words of Mercer County freeholder Calvin Iszard, a celebrator at Whitman's victory party, "I think there's a message here that is going to go all the way to the White House: if you promise change, you'd better deliver."

10

A Challenge

"It did not happen. It's not only illegal, it's immoral, and I do not play the game that way."

Christie Whitman (November 10, 1993)
during a news conference in Trenton.

Christie Whitman captured her narrow victory over Gov. Jim Florio by winning big in her suburban home base. Florio, in turn, lost the election by failing to capture the plurality he needed in the state's traditionally Democratic urban counties and South Jersey. "We cut Florio's margin in Hudson and Essex counties," Whitman's spokesman Carl Golden said on election night just after Whitman had declared victory. He finished the explanation with a statement that would later come back to haunt the campaign: "Sometimes vote suppression is as important in this business as vote getting."

Whitman won in twelve of New Jersey's twenty-one counties, including the five northwestern counties of Morris, Sussex, Warren, Somerset, and Hunterdon. Her plurality in those five counties, where her hometown of Oldwick and the political base that had nurtured her were located, was 96,494. In the northeast corner of the state, an area critical to the election's outcome, she won both Passaic and Bergen counties by 10,000 votes.

In the central part of the state, Whitman won along the shore in Monmouth and Ocean counties, captured Mercer County where Trenton is located, and defeated Florio by a narrow 665-vote margin in Burlington County. The only southern area that Whitman was able to capture was Salem County, located in the southwestern corner of New Jersey. Florio won in the traditionally Democratic urban counties of northeastern New Jersey, including Essex, Hudson, and Union, but not by the margins Democratic candidates normally enjoy and not by enough votes to overtake Whitman. He captured the important central New Jersey county of Middlesex by only 1,298 votes. In his South Jersey home base of Camden, where he had served as congressman, Florio carried the counties of Camden, Gloucester, Cumberland, Atlantic, and Cape May by a plurality of 68,972. This was 27,000 votes less than Whitman's plurality in her five-county home base.

With the margin of victory so narrow, everyone had a theory on exactly what tipped the election in Whitman's favor. Claiming her victory at a statehouse press conference the day after the election, a smiling, assured Whitman attributed her win to an electorate that wanted change. "From this point forward, we go forward as a united New Jersey." She was a governor-elect awash in the glow of victory.

Whitman said voters had recognized Florio's attacks on her for what they were, a smoke screen for his failures. And she renewed her promise to cut taxes, going so far as to promise not to run for reelection if she failed to deliver.

When the votes were analyzed, it was clear that Whitman had made inroads into the Democrats' political base. Whitman had eaten away at Florio's support in the black communities of north Jersey. "The Democrats in Newark sat on their hands because they were not content with Florio," said Lonna Hooks, the black attorney who along with several others cochaired Whitman's campaign, on election night.

But beyond that, Whitman had captured the state's blue-collar, traditionally Democratic white voters who wanted less government spending and lower taxes. It was no coincidence that the day after the election, Whitman, after renewing her pledge to cut taxes, boarded her campaign bus and went to Fred & Pete's Deli in Hamilton, the heavily populated township bordering Trenton for the first stop on a brief "thank you" tour of the state. The politically active, blue-collar community, known for voting its conscience and swinging back and forth between Democratic and Republican candidates, had thrown its support to Whitman and proved key to her win.

In private, Florio placed the blame for his loss on the gun advocates, headed by Richard Miller of the Coalition of New Jersey Sportsmen. While not formally aligning itself with Whitman, the coalition worked day and night for her victory and for Florio's defeat. Afire with a zeal for their cause and their hatred of the man they believed had turned them into criminals by including guns already legally owned in the ban on semiautomatic weapons, Miller and key members of his organization of hundreds of thousands of members never rested until after the votes were counted on election day. (In June 1995 during an emotional address to New Jersey Democrats, President Clinton was still blaming Florio's defeat on his ban on semiautomatic weapons. "Jim Florio gave his governorship for it," Clinton said.)

Without giving voters his own vision for New Jersey's future, Florio had tried to win the race on the gun issue and on campaign tactics that portrayed Whitman as unfit to serve as governor. But it had not been enough to counter voter anger over his record tax increase. At a postelection press conference, Florio attributed Whitman's win to her tax-cut proposal. "If asked what made people decide in the twelfth hour, it was almost exclusively the 30 percent tax cut." Promising to cooperate with Whitman during the transition period, Florio said, "I don't regard this election as an overwhelming mandate of repudiation for the things we have done, only because of the closeness of the election."

Associated Press reports noted that the election, which had been billed as a contest between top political consultants Jim Carville for Florio and Ed Rollins for Whitman, had left the big-time Democratic consultant on the losing end. "Carville cowed as Rollins reclaims bragging rights," a *Trentonian* headline said on Thursday, November 4, 1993.

On the Thursday after the election, Rollins was present, but Carville was conspicuously absent, when key players in the campaign gathered for the traditional postelection analysis at Princeton University's Woodrow Wilson School of Public and International Affairs. In the final analysis, both sides said it was Whitman's spirit and resiliency that allowed her to beat Florio. "The beating she took, the vast majority of candidates would be under the bed saying, 'Please stop it. Please stop it,' " Rollins boasted. He said the campaign broke new ground in political campaigning since Florio did not soften his attacks because he was running against a woman. "She got treated like one of the boys." Florio's campaign manager, Jim Andrews, said, "We put Mrs. Whitman through the grinder. . . . Mrs. Whitman was a survivor and came out with her head high." Andrews said he had cautioned others inside the campaign of her ability to bounce back. "She will never go away," he had warned them. Carville's partner, Paul Begala, said the message to incumbents was "Don't just sit there. Do something." Rollins admitted that the Whitman campaign made a mistake on the tax plan. The Washington consultant said that he had tried to get Whitman to put forward her tax plan far earlier in the campaign and that a year before, he had told her to pledge not to raise taxes. "There was a lot of cynicism that it was a 'Hail Mary' pass," Rollins admitted about the last-minute tax proposal.

Dan Todd said the bus tour and the television ads aired during the final days of the campaign propelled Whitman to the narrow victory. In a statement he would later be questioned about by a federal grand jury, Todd said: "The state of New Jersey is still a state that is very susceptible to a well-run shoe-leather campaign, and that is where our summer went, and that is where a lot of our effort went and a lot of our planning, getting out the vote on one side and voter sup. . . ." Halfway through the word, Todd interrupted himself and then continued, "And keeping the vote light in other areas." During the formal analysis, Todd tried to explain away his being fired as campaign manager by saying, "It was time to do something dramatic in the campaign, so I got shot."

Some of the postelection attention focused on the newspaper polls which had predicted Florio as a sure winner. A *Trentonian* analysis of the polls pointed out that one of the questions in the *New York Times*/CBS poll showing Whitman twenty-one points behind had an obvious bias because the pollster had included the Democrats' explanation for Gov. Florio's tax increase in the question. Question 34 of the poll asked, "When Jim Florio first took office as governor in 1990 he said he had to raise taxes in order to eliminate the state budget deficit and to provide aid required for schools. Looking back on Jim Florio's decision to raise taxes, do you think he did the right thing for New Jersey or the wrong thing for New Jersey?"

The *Record* poll, showing Florio ten points ahead, had calculated its results based on voter turnout patterns during the 1989 gubernatorial race. By deciding not to bias its sample in the same way, the *Asbury Park Press* poll, showing the candidates in a dead heat, accurately reflected the race. Janice Ballou, whose *Star-Ledger*/Eagleton poll showed Florio with a nine-point lead, told the *Trentonian* that last-minute decision making by undecided voters changed the complexion of the race and perhaps could have been given more emphasis.

After conducting a poll for Philadelphia's KYW-TV in which he found Florio leading forty-six to thirty-nine, with 14 percent of the voters undecided, Dell Ali of Political Media Research in Washington, D.C., said he had concluded that Florio was likely to lose. Ali knew that any incumbent with less than 50 percentage points, accompanied by a substantial bloc of undecided voters that close to election day, was in serious trouble. Yet, when Channel 3 aired the poll on October 28, its staff focused on Florio's lead, not Ali's prediction. In the Whitman-Florio race, the signs of victory could be picked up on the street, not from the state's traditional public opinion polls. The *Trentonian* pointed to Michael Wheeler's conclusion in his book, *Lies, Damn Lies, and Statistics, The Manipulation of Public Opinion in America*: "Read the polls, eavesdrop on conversations in coffee shops, scan a variety of newspapers, put a finger in the wind, then forget about the polls."

A week after the election, the Whitman camp was busy enjoying the spoils of victory, putting together a transition team, and planning the inauguration ceremony. On Tuesday, November, 9, 1993, while Whitman was having a face-to-face meeting with outgoing Gov. Florio, Ed Rollins was breakfasting with a dozen Washington reporters at a Sperling breakfast, a meeting of reporters and newsmakers hosted by Godfrey Sperling of the *Christian Science Monitor.*

Putting his own spin on Whitman's victory, Rollins told the reporters that the Whitman campaign had spent a half million dollars dissuading black ministers from endorsing Florio and paying Democratic workers to stay home on election day. In remarks that would leave political observers across the nation aghast, Rollins said: "We went into black churches, and we basically said to ministers who had endorsed Florio, 'Do you have a special project?' And they said, 'We've already endorsed Florio.' We said, 'That's fine. Don't get up on the Sunday pulpit and preach. We know

you've endorsed him, but don't get up there and say it's your moral obligation that you go on Tuesday to vote for Jim Florio.'" Rollins did not name
the churches or the amounts paid, which he described as charity contributions whose size varied, depending on the size of the church. He said he did
not personally arrange any of the payments. "Those were our community
people who obviously knew what they needed to do and where they needed
to do it," he explained.

With those payments, the campaign intended to cut into Florio's margins in the cities. "What we did, I think, for the first time, is we played the
game the way the game is played in New Jersey or elsewhere," Rollins
bragged. "And I think, to a certain extent, our game plan was not to have
this intensified vote in the areas we couldn't obviously make up." Describing another shocking campaign strategy, Rollins said the campaign
also paid Democratic workers, who normally are paid by their own party
to get voters to the polls, to stay home on election day. "We said to some
of their key workers, 'How much have they paid you to do your normal
duty? Well, we'll match it. Go home, sit, and watch television.'" He did
not identify those who received the money.

The denials from the Whitman campaign and the statements of outrage
from the black community were simultaneous. Whitman spokesman Carl
Golden immediately denounced Rollins's statements as inaccurate. "We
have absolutely no knowledge of anything like this in the campaign." The
Democrats were quick to believe the statements, and as a result, they damaged their own relationship with the black community. Florio spokesman
Jon Shure responded: "It's a very cynical practice to scope out a plan that
says your chances of winning are enhanced if you can stop people from
voting." Taking the lead for the Democrats, state party chairman Raymond Lesniak called for a criminal investigation into the statements and
began talking about the possibility of voiding the election.

Paying money to stop someone from voting is illegal under the state's
elections laws and is punishable by jail time and fines. Rollins had described the money funneled to the churches and workers as "walking
around money," a term not normally used in New Jersey political circles.
What is commonly known in New Jersey as "street money" is legal. It is
money used on election day to pay workers, often college students, to "get
out the vote," not to keep voters home. Workers are paid for canvassing,

poll watching, telephone soliciting, and providing rides to the polls. In 1993, any expenditure of more than $25 had to be reported on an election expenditure form to the Election Law Enforcement Commission in Trenton. (Since the Rollins incident, all expenditures must be recorded on an election report and paid by check.)

Lending some credibility to Rollins's statements was the fact that Florio's margins in the urban areas, such as Essex and Hudson counties, and among blacks were narrower than in his previous two bids for governor. His total vote count in urban areas in the 1993 race was about 20,000 votes less than his 1989 showing against Republican Jim Courter. Exit polling conducted by Voter Research and Surveys showed that Florio received 75 percent of the black vote to Whitman's 25 percent. However, the size of the black vote was down to 8 percent of the total vote, compared with 12 percent in the 1989 governor's race, the *Wall Street Journal* reported.

When Rollins's statements were reported in the newspapers on Wednesday, November 10, 1993, a firestorm of national attention was focused on Trenton and Governor-elect Whitman.

However, Rollins recanted his remarks in a statement issued that day:

> This is the first time that my desire to put a spin on events has crossed the line from an honest discussion of my views to an exaggeration that turned out to be inaccurate. I went too far. My remarks left the impression of something that was not true and did not occur. I know that the Whitman campaign, which I managed, itself, in no way sponsored, funded, or sanctioned improper voter turnout activities. I have no knowledge that the party or any other entity connected to the campaign did so.

Armed with the retraction and flanked by two black ministers, Whitman held a press conference and adamantly denied the allegations that money was paid to discourage blacks from voting. "It did not happen," declared an angry Whitman, her face drawn and stern. "There was never any attempt by anyone to suppress the vote."

Calm, but obviously feeling the stress of having the glow of victory snuffed out so quickly, Whitman said she had called Rollins after reading the press accounts of his statements. "When I talked to him, he just apologized. Why it happened, I do not know. Why he said what he said, I can't possibly imagine. I've spent time in Washington. The air is a little rarefied, and I understand about egos, and I understand about wanting to put spins on things. But it flies in the face of reality, and it flies in the face of fact. You don't do that kind of thing. It's not only illegal, it's immoral, and I do not play the game that way. . . . I find this whole thing, everything that was alleged, degrading—degrading to the voters of New Jersey, to the African-American community, and, frankly, to me."

The ministers who appeared at Whitman's press conference scoffed at the idea of hundreds of thousands of dollars being paid in street money and at the allegation that black ministers would accept money to suppress the vote. "We are appalled in the black community that such a statement could be made," said Perry Simmons, of the Abyssinian Baptist Church in Newark. "In an area like Newark, if you've got $500,000 floating around, somebody would know about it. I don't know of any preacher who received any money from anybody."

The Rev. Reginald Jackson, pastor of St. Matthew African Methodist Episcopal Church in Orange, said low voter turnout in the urban areas resulted from lukewarm support for Florio, a weak get-out-the-vote effort by the Democrats, and the fear in Essex County that if Florio won, the state would take over Newark's troubled school system. However, in a moment of levity, Jackson said his telephone had been ringing nonstop. "All the preachers wanted to know where was this money," he quipped. "I guess they presumed that I had it."

Others failed to see the humor in the situation. Ten angry black ministers, attending a press conference in Newark, termed Rollins's remarks insulting and refused to accept his apology. "Five hundred thousand dollars is crumbs from Caesar's table. For us to sell out for half-a-million dollars is really a joke," complained the Rev. Raiford Wheeler, pastor of the Park Avenue Christian Church in East Orange. Meanwhile, the Democratic State Committee had filed a complaint with the U.S. Justice Department and was preparing to file a request in federal court to force Rollins to submit to a deposition. "I don't know whether he lied yesterday or he lied today," Lesniak told the *Trentonian*. "I think it's important he make his statement under oath. If this was as pervasive as Rollins said it was, it could be grounds for a new election. The court could order a new election."

The incident gained national attention, as President Clinton issued a statement and the Congressional Black Caucus asked Attorney General

Janet Reno to investigate. Clinton told reporters in Washington that if Rollins's original claims were true, it was "terribly wrong for anyone to give money to anybody else not to vote or to suppress voter turnout, and it was terribly wrong for anyone to accept that money."

Florio called for the facts in the matter to be uncovered. "The idea of paying money, in any way, to inhibit any group of people from voting or participating in democracy is very, very troubling. Mrs. Whitman's campaign manager describes this activity as 'The way the game is played in New Jersey.' Wrong. That is not correct and it is obscene to say that it is."

In light of Rollins's statements, New Jersey Democrats raised questions about Carl Golden's reference to voter suppression on election night. There was speculation that Dan Todd had stopped himself from using the term during the postelection analysis at Princeton University. And it was clear, from statements made by members of the black community, including Lonna Hooks, that efforts had been made to reduce support for Florio in the urban areas. But there was no indication that when Golden used the word "suppression," or when other references were made to narrowing the vote margin for Florio, that members of the Whitman campaign were referring to the payment of money or any other illegal activities to keep voters home. What they had appeared to be referring to was the campaign strategy of bringing out voters in their candidate's home base and keeping voter turnout and interest low in the areas where Florio was known to have strong support.

In addition, on the day before the election, Jersey City Mayor Bret Schundler told the *Trentonian* that the Whitman campaign's strict adherence to election regulations was hindering his get-out-the-vote effort for Whitman. Whitman also had gained unprecedented support from blacks in Newark and East Orange during the campaign. Vincent Dasilva, a black businessman and chairman of the East Orange Republican party, said phone banks helped to get the vote out for Whitman and in some cases, the Republicans ran low-key campaigns with few signs in order not to attract the interest of Democratic voters. Dasilva said it was not payoffs to black ministers that cost Florio a larger margin in urban areas, but the governor's failure to support blacks during his four years in office and his light campaigning in urban areas. Essex County Democratic Chairman Thomas Giblin said registration among Democrats had dropped by 17,000 in the city of Newark alone because of a weak voter-registration drive by the Florio team.

On Thursday, November 11, Carl Stern, a spokesman for the U.S. Justice Department, announced that federal investigators would first determine whether the actions described by Rollins were violations of federal law before the department launched an investigation. Meanwhile, there were rumors that some black clergy had contacted the Justice Department to report that they had been approached by Republican operatives during the campaign. The Whitman campaign declared that it welcomed the investigation while Jim Carville speculated to the *Wall Street Journal* that the election could be voided.

Under a consent agreement reached with the Republican National Committee after the 1981 gubernatorial campaign, the Democratic National Committee asked permission from the federal court to take depositions from Rollins and other Whitman campaign members. In the consent agreement, the GOP promised to refrain from ballot security activities and other practices that would turn away minority voters. The Republicans had been accused of intimidating black voters in New Jersey in 1981 by using ballot security guards, with armbands and signs, in black communities.

At a press conference in Newark on the morning of Friday, November 12, 1993, Ed Rollins's statements drew additional national attention as the Rev. Jesse Jackson, the Rev. Al Sharpton, and two dozen black ministers announced plans to file a class-action defamation lawsuit against Rollins, Whitman, and the New Jersey Republican party. In the afternoon, Jackson, Sharpton, and Newark Councilman Ralph Grant, Jr., traveled to Trenton to meet with Whitman in a closed-door session at her transition offices on West State Street. When they emerged from the session to face a mob of reporters, Jackson announced that while the group would continue to pursue the slander suit against Rollins and the state GOP, Whitman's name would be dropped from the legal action. In the first serious challenge to her administration, Whitman had prevailed. In the private session, she had convinced the angry black activists of her sincerity and of her determination to see the charges, which she maintained were false, put to rest.

Whitman, flanked by Jackson and Sharpton, joined the call for a federal probe into whether her campaign had paid money to keep black voters at home on election day. Whitman's announcement was made about an hour prior to an announcement by the U.S. Attorney's Office and the FBI that they were launching a probe into Rollins's statements. "I welcome that investigation," Whitman said. "There has to be an investigation. That is the only way to send a message, completely and thoroughly, that this did not occur."

The FBI announced a twenty-four-hour phone hotline for anyone having information on voter suppression during the campaign. "It's my expectation that we will get a lot of phone calls," James Esposito, head of the Newark office of the FBI, told reporters.

On another front, the Democratic National Committee and the state Democratic party filed a civil suit in U.S. District Court in Newark against Rollins, the state GOP, and Whitman. The lawsuit, alleging that there had been violations of the U.S. Constitution and the Voting Rights Act, sought to invalidate the election. In addition, acting State Attorney General Fred DeVesa named a special counsel to conduct a state investigation into the allegations, and the New Jersey Election Law Enforcement Commission began its own probe into possible violations of state election laws.

The strain that the accusations had placed on Whitman, once again, could be seen on her face. The laugh lines were gone. She was slightly ashen. But she appeared self-assured and in control of a situation that threatened to undo all that she had worked so hard to achieve. "This election was honestly won, and I will be governor of the state of New Jersey," she told reporters from across the nation. But she did not downplay the seriousness of the charges. She admitted, "I have put my credibility on the line."

While the campaign made no effort to get out the vote in areas where the campaign knew there was strong support for Florio, Whitman denied that there was any effort made to keep voters home in the black communities. "I cannot possibly explain to you why Mr. Rollins said what he said. He flat-out lied."

When reporters asked Rev. Jackson what question he would like to ask Rollins, the black minister drew chuckles when he said, "Was he drunk or sober?"

In an effort to discount Rollins's contention that the Whitman campaign spent $500,000 on "walking-around money," on Saturday, November 13, 1993, the Republican State Committee released preliminary campaign-finance reports indicating that the GOP spent less than $70,000 on election day "street" activities to "get out the vote." Ironically, it was not the Republicans, but the Democrats who spent $500,000 on election day get-out-the-vote efforts. The *Star-Ledger* reported that they paid about 20,000 people $25 each to assure that people voted for Florio.

With inauguration day two months away, the New Jersey branch of the National Association for the Advancement of Colored People (NAACP) urged Whitman not to take office until the allegations of black voter suppression were resolved. On Sunday, November 14, 1993, as black ministers throughout the state denounced Rollins and denied his statements from the pulpit, Christie and John Whitman, Herbert Tate (the black former Essex County prosecutor who ran Whitman's election-day operations in urban Essex County), and Lonna Hooks (Whitman's liaison with the black community during the campaign) attended church services at two black churches in an effort to smooth relations with the black community, the *Star-Ledger* reported. Whitman had little to say to reporters, except that she had come to pray and that she still planned to take office in January. Asked what Rollins should do, Whitman said, "Let his conscience dictate."

Whitman sat in the front pew at St. Matthew African Methodist Episcopal Church in Orange and listened quietly as the Rev. Reginald Jackson told the congregation that "much pain and suffering" has been inflicted upon the African-American church and community. "For it to be implied that the African-American community can be bought is repugnant and an affront." Jackson said his congregation believed that Whitman would have objected to any plan to fund suppression of the black vote. "I believe if she had known, she would have thrown the idea out and him [Rollins] with it." Even though he had supported Florio's reelection, Jackson told his congregation: "The election is over and I don't foresee anything happening to change the outcome of the election. She deserves the support of every citizen in New Jersey to make the state the best state it can be." At the First Baptist Church of Lincoln Gardens in Somerset, Pastor DeForest B. Soaries, Jr., told his congregation: "To attack and denigrate or undermine our church is to come against the most important thing in our lives. We cannot be borrowed, and by God we cannot be bought." When Whitman departed after the service, Soaries told her that the congregation would pray for her, the *Star-Ledger* reported.

On Monday, November 15, 1993, the Democratic party, as part of its civil action to invalidate the election, won permission from U.S. District Judge Dickinson Debevoise to question under oath Ed Rollins, Dan Todd, and John Carbone, an attorney for the Republican State Committee.

Todd was being called because of his statement at the Princeton post-election analysis in which he referred to the campaign's efforts to keep the vote light in areas where Whitman's support was weak. The Democrats wanted to depose Carbone because he had overseen the Republican "street money" for the campaign's get-out-the-vote effort. Carbone also had been a key player in the Republicans' 1981 ballot security task force that had resulted in legal action by the Democrats.

"The real question in this case is what happened," Theodore V. Wells, the attorney representing the Democratic State Committee, told the *Star-Ledger.* "I don't believe anybody believes Mr. Rollins made this up out of whole cloth. If it's true, the election is tainted. If he's lying, he has done a terrible disservice to African Americans, to Mrs. Whitman, and to the people of New Jersey."

On Tuesday, November 16, Whitman told reporters that U.S. Attorney Michael Chertoff had asked to question her about the voter suppression statements made by Rollins. Whitman admitted that the controversy over Rollins's statements had distracted her from the work she normally would have been doing with the transition team preparing her takeover of state government. She continued to maintain, however, that she would take office on schedule, January 18. Touring an agricultural facility outside Trenton on November 17, Whitman expressed her anger about unsubstantiated assertions by various Democratic officials. "If Democratic campaign workers were approached by the Whitman camp and offered money to suppress votes, you don't think the first place they would go is to the media and secondly to the authorities to blow my campaign out of the water?"

The fallout for Rollins's political career was immediate. He lost his job as commentator for the "Today" show. Pennsylvania Republican gubernatorial candidate Barbara Hafer asked him to withdraw as her campaign consultant. And New Jersey Assembly Speaker Garabed "Chuck" Haytaian announced that he would not be following through on plans to hire Rollins for his U.S. Senate race against Sen. Frank Lautenberg.

After being interviewed by the FBI, Rollins testified before a federal grand jury in Newark on Thursday, November 18, 1993. When he arrived at the federal courthouse in Newark, Rollins was greeted by a prayer vigil led by activist Rev. Al Sharpton. About a dozen Sharpton supporters formed a circle and bowed their heads in prayer at noon. "Wherever there's a rumor of Rollins, we intend to shadow him because he's cast a shadow on us."

As he entered the courthouse, Rollins said he was eager to "get this over with," and then added, "I wish I had eaten breakfast at home that morning." After the six-hour session before the grand jury, Rollins eluded the press by exiting the courthouse through a loading dock.

During the ten-day period after Rollins made his statements about voter suppression, not one member of the black clergy or any Democratic party worker stepped forward to admit taking money to suppress votes, and even some black leaders were beginning to get irritated with the Democrats' pursuit of the issue. "No one is going to step forward and say they got this money," said Newark Mayor Sharpe James, one of the highest ranking black officials in the state. "We should put this behind us and give Christine Todd Whitman a chance." Meanwhile, in a speech delivered in Atlantic City, Whitman promised to unify New Jersey. "We will revitalize the economy, but job 'A' is to see that the Jersey family is whole, that each person is invited to the table without regard to race, gender, or age, if they live in the suburbs or the cities, in the east or west, north or south." Of Rollins's testimony before the grand jury, she said, "I hope it's the truth, and the truth will show that there was nothing there. It did not happen."

On Friday, November 19, lawyers for the Democratic State Committee questioned Rollins for eight hours at a closed-door session in Washington, D.C. Citing the defendants' privacy rights, Judge Debevoise denied a motion by ten newspapers, the Associated Press, a radio station, three television networks, and Court TV to allow reporters to attend the civil depositions of both Rollins and Todd.

During his deposition, Rollins told the attorneys that he had fabricated the stories about voter suppression in order to "one-up" his archrival, Democratic consultant James Carville, Florio's campaign adviser.

After successfully guiding Bill Clinton through the 1992 presidential race, Carville was considered the top Democratic consultant in the country. Rollins, who had directed President Reagan's landslide victory in 1984 and had briefly worked for Ross Perot's independent candidacy for president in 1992, saw himself as Carville's Republican counterpart, although most political observers believed he had not risen to Carville's status. "I expected coming out of this breakfast, after I said this, that two or three reporters would call Carville, get him up from his fetal position, and say, 'Rollins kicked your ass . . . and here's how he did it.' That was my motivation. That was my game. I repeated rumors and innuendoes that I heard in the course of the campaign. It made for great stories, and it has damaged me in great places. . . . But the bottom line was this was an act of fiction."

In a statement read by his attorney Michael Carvin, Rollins apologized to Whitman, to the New Jersey black community, and to the voters of New Jersey. He said:

> I can never make up for what I have done in my actions of two minutes of pure unadulterated bullshit that I will pay a price for the rest of my life, and even that will not be sufficient to what I have done.
>
> Part of what I was doing here was playing a game with James Carville. My expectation was not that this was going to become a national story. Because obviously if I thought it was going to be a national story, I would not have taken a gun and put it to my head and blown my career apart, as I have done.

During the deposition, Rollins denied the suggestion that the Whitman campaign used the National Rifle Association or various GOP entities as a funnel for money to improperly influence voter turnout. Questioned about his statement that Democratic campaign workers were paid by Republicans to stay home on election day, he responded: "I had heard rumors from time to time that this was the way it was sort of done, that you could mess up the organization. . . . I'm sure since I had made the statement, there's been a lot of fingers pointed to a lot of ward leaders who didn't get their vote out, all being accused of being on the take. For that, I apologize. . . . I have absolutely no knowledge whatsoever of any payment by any Republican to any Democrat."

When questioned about his statements that black ministers were paid not to endorse Florio, he replied: "Did we make efforts, when . . . people [Democrats] were putting pressure on black ministers who were going to support us, to try and offset some of that pressure by having dialogue and conversations? Yes. Did we give anybody money for their charity before the election or after the election? I have no knowledge of that, and I don't think anybody else in our campaign has any knowledge of it." Lesniak denounced Rollins's explanations as "bizarre and unbelievable." The Democratic party chief admitted that Rollins's testimony had not produced a "smoking gun." Democrats did, however, label one of Rollins's statements a "smoldering gun." They were referring to Rollins's recounting of a conversation he had with campaign cochairperson Lonna Hooks, who came to Rollins for advice on the "terrible, terrible pressure" that Democrats were putting on black clergy. The Republicans believed that Florio was threatening to cut off state aid for drug-rehabilitation and daycare centers in urban areas if city voters supported Whitman.

Rollins testified that he told Lonna Hooks (who Whitman later appointed secretary of state): "Go back to these people and continue the dialogue and tell them, as far as we're concerned, we want to help them. Whatever their favorite charity may be, there are other ways of helping besides state funding that Florio has, or what have you, but I didn't authorize her to go commit resources, and she, as an attorney, wouldn't ask for that." He further testified: "All I did was give her [Hooks] some suggestions, and I said, tell them if they don't go up to the pulpit and preach against us on Sunday, we'd be way ahead of the game." Rollins testified that Lonna Hooks later reported that she had "talked to some people" and it "seemed to be helping somewhat."

During his deposition, Rollins confessed that the uproar over his statements had led him to thoughts of suicide: "I mean, it's to a point where I've . . . you know, I thought of putting a gun to my head."

After Rollins testified under oath, Republican party attorney John Lacey called for Lesniak to drop the civil suit. "The only thing that remains now is for this lawsuit to be dismissed," Lacey declared in a session with reporters. "It is the only remaining remnant of the cloud that is left to be lifted, and we recommend very strongly that Mr. Lesniak do the right thing for the African-American community, do the right thing for the people of New Jersey, and do the right thing for himself," the Star-Ledger reported.

While admitting that the suit had lost some of its thrust, Lesniak still wouldn't give up. "We have always said the chance of the election being overturned is slim. It still is. We have a very heavy burden to meet. We still hope to expose the whole Republican policy of suppressing minority votes."

Lesniak continued to claim that he had knowledge of several Democratic poll workers who had been approached by Republicans and offered incentives not to work on election day. But no one came forward, and the Whitman transition team was getting testy on the issue. "I'm getting sick and tired of Ray Lesniak being New Jersey's answer to Joe McCarthy," Carl Golden told the *Asbury Park Press.* "If he has something to contribute to this, let him contribute it. And if he doesn't, put a sock in it."

Democrats began to debate among themselves about whether or not the lawsuit should continue. Rev. Al Sharpton said that by admitting he lied, Rollins had only succeeded in further angering the black community. "His deposition in no way will impair our filing of a $500 million suit in federal court. It has intensified the reasons behind the tension."

Democratic state Sen. Richard Codey told the *New York Times* that he agreed with Lesniak's decision to continue with the case.

"I have never in my life heard the word 'suppression' used in any election talk in two decades. Independent of each other, Ed Rollins used the word; Carl Golden, her [Whitman's] press secretary, used the word; and the brother [Dan] starts to use the phrase and stops himself. Now if you don't think they had some kind of a meeting and talked about this, you and I are going to be under a chimney waiting for Santa to come down." Of the term "suppression," Codey stated, "They had an idea of doing this. When they used the word, they were not referencing stockbrokers in Somerset." United States Sen. Bill Bradley also was among those Democrats who thought the litigation against Rollins should continue. He said Rollins should be held accountable for his "besmirchment of African Americans."

But once again, in a statement to the *New York Times,* Newark Mayor Sharpe James told the Democrats to give up the lawsuit. "Did he [Rollins] lie the first time or did he lie the second time? This issue will never be resolved in the eyes of the public. I mean we lost, and to continue to go on and on, it serves no purpose."

Continuing to deal with the issue head-on, Whitman appeared on CNN's "Both Sides," hosted by Jesse Jackson, on November 20. She told Jackson that she had garnered 25 percent of the African-American vote in the election because her campaign "reflected their concerns and talked to the issues that they wanted to hear." Jackson, however, tried to tie Rollins's statements to the National Rifle Association. "The word is out that the National Rifle Association used some conduit to try to get to some people to either suppress or intimidate their vote," he charged. Whitman denied any affiliation with the NRA. "I was not endorsed by them, nor did I seek their endorsement or support. They, in fact, were not terribly happy with me because I did not call for the overthrow of the governor's gun ban."

By the third week of November, political advisers and pundits were giving Whitman kudos for her response to the Rollins crisis. Rather than hide in her transition office, Whitman continued an active schedule. Traveling throughout the state, she was hounded by reporters who were constantly questioning her about the Rollins affair. Her answer was always the same: "It did not happen." Her swift and straightforward response to Rollins's statements was a marked contrast to the way she had handled several crises during her campaign, when she would allow an issue to linger unresolved for days, sometimes weeks. During the campaign, she allowed Florio to harp about the property tax break she received for Pontefract before inviting reporters to see the farm for themselves; she allowed Carville to bait her on a radio program before releasing her 1990 tax forms; and she waited until consultant Roger Ailes blasted her in public before correcting a statement she made about him.

At the Republican Governors' Association meeting in Phoenix, Arizona, on November 21, Whitman, in a statement to reporters, personally called for the Democrats to drop their lawsuit and for the first time was critical of Gov. Florio's failure, as the unofficial head of the party, to end the challenge to her victory. "I hope the Democrats finally begin to recognize the damage they are doing to the state as a whole by keeping this issue alive and in front of the people. This election was fairly won. I will become governor of New Jersey on January 18. No one has come forward to change that. It has become abundantly clear: nothing happened." Ohio Gov. George Voinovich, chairman of the Republican Governors' Association, praised Whitman's handling of the Rollins controversy in statements to the *Star-Ledger.* "I admire the way she took control and took charge. She showed her stuff. She stood up rather than hiding in a corner. She got right out front, which is what you should do."

Toward the end of November, the Democrats' attempts to keep the lawsuit against Whitman alive began to fall apart, and even the federal judge began to lose patience with the case. On Monday, November 22, Judge Debevoise turned down a request by the Democrats to interview five more people under oath. The Democrats had already dropped their request to interview John Carbone, and Debevoise forced the Democrats to limit the scope of the case to one more sworn statement from Dan Todd. Even as members of his own party were beginning to say that the Democrats were starting to look like bad losers, Florio issued his strongest statements to date in support of the inquiries into the voter suppression allegations.

> I have said that I believe that any allegations of voter suppression are serious, that they send a distressing message about democracy in this country, and that they deserve to be fully investigated. I stand by that statement. I want what the people of New Jersey want, a clear and factual explanation of these serious allegations. In recent days, there have been news accounts of conflicting and contradictory statements that many people feel continue to raise questions. In the interest of fairness to the people of New Jersey, it is appropriate that the questions be answered—not for any partisan political aims, but for the integrity of the process.

Prominent members of Florio's own party disagreed and were starting to believe that state Democratic party chief Raymond Lesniak was out of control in his pursuit of the lawsuit and ought to be reined in. In an interview with the *Trentonian,* former Democratic Assembly Speaker Alan Karcher said the lawsuit never had a chance of overturning the election. "The suit is crazy. It's going nowhere. It had no prospects of going anywhere. I don't think the party, as a whole, has done itself proud by pursuing this. We are looking like very, very, very bad losers."

Karcher warned that if the controversy resulted in the passage of state legislation to curtail the use of legal "street money" to help get voters to the polls, Democrats, who rely heavily on such efforts, would find it difficult to win a statewide election. There were numerous prominent Democrats who echoed Karcher's sentiments in interviews with the *Trentonian.* "Why are they beating it to death?" asked State Sen. Raymond Zane. "It's time to fold the tents on this issue," stated Essex County Democratic party chief Thomas Giblin. "Put up or shut up," claimed Gloucester County Democratic party chairman John Maier. "Enough is enough," reported former Democratic State Committee chairman Phil Keegan. "Unless there is something I am not aware of . . . it's time to go forward," said Mercer County Sheriff Sam Plumeri.

On Tuesday, November 23, federal and state authorities announced that they would be coordinating their investigations into Rollins's claims of voter suppression. On Wednesday, November 24, Dan Todd and Whitman spokesman Carl Golden testified before the federal grand jury in Newark. Emerging from the Newark courthouse, Golden said, "As far as I'm concerned, it's pretty much behind us. There is not one shred of evidence anywhere to substantiate Ed Rollins's comments that morning in Washington." In the midst of the controversy that threatened her claim to the governorship, on Thanksgiving Day, November 25, Whitman took time from her busy transition schedule and the pressure of political events to spend time with her family. She personally cooked two turkeys and a ham for thirty family members and guests who were invited to Pontefract to celebrate the holiday.

The next day, after questioning Dan Todd, the attorneys for the Democratic party said they had learned nothing that would substantiate Rollins's initial claims that money had been paid to suppress black voting in the Whitman-Florio race. "I cannot say to you we have sufficient evidence to overturn this election," Gerald Krovatin, an attorney for the Democratic State Committee told the *Star-Ledger* during a briefing with reporters. "Mr. Todd had a surprising lack of knowledge about how street money was used or spent in the campaign he ran for so many months. We're not going to drag this out one day longer than necessary."

Todd testified: "Perhaps I can save time by saying that I have no knowledge of any monies being dispensed by anyone to discourage voters." He was asked repeatedly whether he was about to say "suppression" when he interrupted himself during the Princeton University postelection forum. "I'll be damned if I know," he said. "I looked at this tape four or five times, and I don't know what I didn't say. I know what I said."

Krovatin asked him: "Is it your testimony, then, that you, when you used the term 'voter sup,' you were not using the term 'voter suppression'?" Todd responded: "I don't know what I was using. If it said 'voter suppression,' I would still add, 'keeping the vote light.' . . . I'm not ashamed of 'voter suppression' as a term. It's not a normal term, but I'll tell you, I looked at that thing a half-dozen times since the fourth of November, and I don't know what I was going to say. I know what I did say."

Asked what he meant by "keeping the vote light," Todd said it meant, for example, trying to capitalize on the rift between Newark Mayor Sharpe James and Gov. Florio concerning a state takeover of the Newark school system. When some people advised Whitman to support Florio's fight with the Newark school district, Todd warned her to stay away from it. "That is the kind of thing that I might have had in mind when I used the phrase 'keeping the vote light in other areas,' " Todd explained.

Asked if he could remember any other examples, Todd responded, "It is—I am simply—I do not have the brain power or the retentive brain cells left to remember with specificity any of the things that we did in this campaign, other than the major ones that stand out in my mind."

On Monday, November 29, Lesniak announced that the Democrats could not find any evidence of wrongdoing, and the lawsuit against Whitman was dropped. Predicting that the federal and state investigations would "fall by the wayside too," Whitman held a press conference with a former governor from each party—Republican Tom Kean and Democrat Brendan Byrne. Kean criticized the Democrats for insulting the black community and for creating a national controversy. "I think it was an outrageous performance. They did it without one shred of evidence. It should have been dropped a long time ago. . . . I think they carried it too far." Asked whether the press had exaggerated the incident, Kean merely said that the story had three key ingredients of interest to the press—race, money, and politics. "It smelled like a very good story."

Rollins submitted a personal explanation to the *Washington Post*. His statement said, in part:

> I've watched many in this town get corrupted by power, money, or other tangible rewards. Most who fail, however, do so for the same reason I have failed: for the sin of arrogance. Succumbing to the vanity of thinking you are more important than others is usually what puts us all out of business and is now my own albatross.
>
> No one's been on a high like I was on three weeks ago when Christie Whitman won the governorship of New Jersey. No one's felt lower than I felt just one week later when my foolish words of bravado put a cloud over her victory and put me into the arms of lawyers, grand juries, and special investigators.
>
> Christie Whitman is an honorable person who deserved to win New Jersey's election. I may have thought I guided her over the finish line, but

in truth, she's the one who ran her heart out, who took the tough blows, who kept her chin up when the pundits counted her out. The legitimacy of her victory should not be tainted by my remarks seven days later. . . . I owe Christie, the ministers, and all the citizens of New Jersey an apology which I hope, over time, they will accept.

On January 12, 1994, six days before Whitman's inauguration, state and federal investigators announced that they could find no evidence that the Whitman campaign had suppressed black votes, and the investigations were closed. "No one is going to be charged with any violations of state or federal law," said U.S. Attorney Michael Chertoff.

The pending lawsuit by the Rev. Jesse Jackson's Rainbow Coalition was put on hold so that New Jersey ministers could take the lead in any legal action. After the announcement by Chertoff, the Rev. Reginald Jackson of the New Jersey Black Ministers' Council, which had threatened a lawsuit seeking $1 and an apology, said the group was hoping to reach a settlement with Rollins. (In October 1994, Rollins told the *Washington Post* that the lawsuits against him had been resolved. While it was believed by many that Rollins's political-consulting career was over, less than a year after making his comments on voter suppression, he was hired by some high-powered Republican candidates, who were willing to ignore the 1993 controversy.)

Whitman expressed relief when the ordeal was concluded: "I have been confident from the outset that this never occurred, so I knew what the end result had to be. But I'm obviously very pleased to finally have it . . . come to closure." Whitman had survived her first challenge, and she was ready to claim the office she had worked so hard to achieve.

11

The First Woman

"To those who question whether I am serious about bucking the special interests who hold so much quiet power in this city, let me be clear. I did not run for governor to conduct business as usual. It's going to be different around here."

Gov. Christie Whitman (January 18, 1994)
from her inaugural address.

On January 18, 1994, Christie Whitman's rough road to the statehouse ended at the War Memorial in Trenton when she was sworn in as New Jersey's fiftieth governor and the first woman to hold the office of what many believe to be one of the most powerful governorships in the nation.

Whitman took the fifty-three-word oath of office with her hand on the Whitman family Bible while cannons positioned along the Delaware River fired nineteen times in a salute to a woman most New Jersey residents thought would never achieve her goal. John; Kate, sixteen; and Taylor, fourteen, stood beside her and held the 141-year-old Bible, which had been used seventy-nine years before to swear in John Whitman's grandfather as governor of New York. As she took the solemn pledge, Christie Whitman became the thirteenth woman in United States history to hold the office of governor.

When Whitman went to the podium to deliver her inaugural address, the question in the minds of New Jersey voters was whether she would begin to back away from the tough promises she made on the campaign trail. After all, the public had been burned by Republican President George Bush, Democratic President Bill Clinton, and New Jersey Gov. Jim Florio; there was little reason to believe that Whitman would be any different. From the beginning, however, Whitman made one thing clear: "I have just taken the oath of this office you have entrusted me to. To me, this oath means one thing. I will not hedge. I will not backtrack. I will keep my promises to you, my friends, to the best of my ability, so help me God."

Whitman intended to keep her promise. Beyond that, she surprised everyone, including legislative leaders, by moving the date for the first proposed tax cut ahead by six months. A 5 percent income tax cut would be retroactive to January 1, 1994, a full eighteen days prior to the inauguration. "Four months ago, I said I would put $1.4 billion of your tax dollars back in your pocket by cutting taxes over the next three years, with the first cut coming in July. And I say, why wait until the next fiscal year starts in July? Let's not keep economic growth waiting another minute." The crowd of supporters, many of whom were with Whitman on the campaign trail or who devoted endless hours of their time to help her get elected, applauded, shouted, and gave her a standing ovation when she announced the retroactive tax cut.

On the campaign trail, she promised to give most New Jersey residents a 30 percent tax cut over three years. Her initial proposal called for the first 10 percent cut to take effect July 1, 1994. Instead of giving taxpayers a 10 percent tax cut for half of the calendar year, she would give them 5 percent over a full year. The tax savings would be the same, only the reduction would begin earlier. "If President Clinton and his Congress can reach backward into time and raise your taxes retroactively, your governor and your legislature can cut them retroactively." Whitman also asked the legislature to retroactively eliminate all income taxes for those earning less than $7,500 and to eliminate a surcharge on the corporate business tax. The total cost of these measures was $318 million in 1994.

Her overall goal was to spur the New Jersey economy into action and to recover the nearly three hundred thousand jobs lost during the four years that Jim Florio was in the governor's seat. "New Jersey should be the engine of economic growth that leads this nation into the twenty-first century," Whitman said. "It should be a powerful engine of prosperity that gives our children the same opportunity that our parents worked so hard to give us—the chance for a better life."

She had a special message to the good-old-boys network and the special interest groups already lining up to thwart her efforts: "To those who question whether I am serious about bucking the special interests who hold so much quiet power in this city [Trenton], let me be clear. I did not run for governor to conduct business as usual. It's going to be different around here."

Leaders of the Republican-controlled state legislature immediately pledged their support, even though Senate President Donald DiFrancesco, who would be a constant vexation to the Whitman administration, had been asking the governor-elect to hold off on her tax cuts until January 1995.

Consistent with her appearances on the campaign trail, Whitman's delivery of the well-written inaugural speech was rather dry, her soft-spoken style almost contradicting the powerful message of the text. When delivering the speech, she decided to delete one line that was in the printed text handed to reporters: "I'm not one of the boys." When asked later why she deleted the sentence, Whitman smiled and said, "I figured it was obvious I wasn't one of the boys, so I left it out." Whitman was correct. No one was missing that point. The state chapter of the National Organization for Women sold $3 pins touting Whitman as the first woman governor. As the appointments to administration posts were announced, it was clear that women would hold key positions in the administration. Whitman's chief of staff, her chief of policy and planning, her attorney general, her secretary of state, her personnel commissioner, and her community affairs commissioner would all be women. Positioned directly behind Whitman during the inaugural speech was Deborah Poritz, a five-foot-tall, fifty-seven-year-old woman with long gray hair tied back from her face, who would become the first woman attorney general in New Jersey. Seated to the left of Poritz was Lonna Hooks, a black attorney with her hair in dreadlocks, who had cochaired Whitman's campaign and would become her secretary of state.

Some men of unusually high caliber were brought into her administration as well. Len Fishman, the attorney for the state's nonprofit nursing home association—who, on occasion, would go into nursing homes to

empty bedpans in order to keep in touch with the needs of the patients—
was appointed health commissioner. Born in Puerto Rico and reared in the
city of Camden, Gualberto Medina, who has a law degree from Temple
University and is a certified public accountant, was named commerce
commissioner. Medina immediately spurned the idea of a state-funded
chauffeur, choosing to drive himself in his travels throughout the state.

Inauguration day was bitter cold and windy with icy, treacherous roads
throughout the state, forcing cancellation of the inaugural parade and making it difficult for people to travel to the ceremonies. A smiling, buoyant
Whitman wore a collarless, dark green suit, decorated with gold buttons.

Volunteers, many of them women, gathered at the Masonic Temple
adjacent to the War Memorial to listen to the speech coming from portable
speakers and to bask in their achievement: they had helped elect the state's
first woman governor. In interviews with the *Trentonian,* they expressed
their feelings. Maureen Morrison, a seventy-five-year-old Whitman volunteer from northern Bergen County, had been waiting for this day since
Whitman nearly upset Bill Bradley in the 1990 U.S. Senate race. "We are
very proud. We worked very hard. That's why we still have bumps on our
fingers—from sending out literature."

Betsy Holdworth of Morris County said Whitman had the courage of
her convictions: "It's not going to be easy, but she can do it." Peg Emberger
of Cape May County said Whitman had opened up opportunities for other
women: "We hope there are a lot of twelve- and thirteen-year-old girls who
realize that their options have opened up and the future is a little brighter
for them."

Outgoing Gov. Florio, seated just a few feet from the incoming governor during the inaugural ceremony, held his wife Lucinda's hand and
showed no emotion when Whitman described the state government he
had reigned over as riddled with "duplication, inept planning, and inade-
quate service." Sitting stiffly in his seat with a wooden grin, Florio withheld his applause when Whitman announced the tax cuts, while Democratic U.S. Sen. Frank Lautenberg squirmed uncomfortably and whispered
into a Florio cabinet member's ear before rising to his feet.

As Whitman signed her first executive order, creating an economic
master plan commission, she promised to "cut through the needless overregulation that drives businesses out of New Jersey and discourages new

firms from locating here." She called for the development of a core curriculum in the state's schools that would teach every student the basics of reading, writing, and arithmetic, and she asked the legislature to support a school voucher system that would provide students with taxpayer money to attend private schools in Jersey City, where the state had taken over the public education system.

As Whitman took office, New Jersey ranked first in the nation for the amount of money spent on each student ($9,522) and thirty-ninth in Scholastic Aptitude Test scores, even as the state supreme court continued to rule that the educational system violated the New Jersey Constitution by failing to provide city students with an adequate education. "We must make it our top priority to teach our children—all our children—to read in kindergarten, first grade, and second grade, when they are enthusiastic about learning," Whitman said.

Whitman also pledged to enact an anticrime program that would force criminals to serve 70 percent of their court sentence and would put three-time violent offenders in prison for life. As she brought her address to a close, Whitman asked New Jerseyans to look to the future. "It will take everyone's help to meet the challenge ahead. It won't always be easy, and we won't always agree. But we must not fear change."

As Whitman left the ceremony for the statehouse, she put on a pair of black boots. John Whitman, in a scene that must have made the hearts of feminists nationwide flutter, carried her high heels.

Meanwhile, the *Trentonian* reported that the local diner lunch bunch needed only one finger to wave goodbye to Gov. Florio. Those eating at local diners called the departing governor a bum, a liar, and a sneak. "I'd like to meet him on the street one time," said Richard Johannes, fifty-six, of Trenton, a truck repairman eating a turkey platter at Pat's Diner in Hamilton, the suburban township outside Trenton that helped Whitman gain her slim margin over Florio. "I'm sure there's not too many people who can say something nice about anybody that can come in and run the state the way he did and steal from hard-working people by giving cronies important jobs so he can reap the benefits."

"We can't like him," said Richard Korchman, owner of a thirty-two-year-old truck repair business that was nearly destroyed by Florio's tax on truck repair sales. "Some of our customers were going right over the river to avoid the taxes. Our business went down to nothing in the first three months after he [Florio] took office." However, Dorothy Tildon, also of Hamilton, had a warning for Whitman: "I voted for her with an open mind. But the first time she starts some of her shenanigans, she's on my list."

That evening, Whitman, dressed in a deep blue silk dress with an organza overlay, danced with John to the beat of 1960s music, as three thousand celebrated her victory at the inaugural ball in the Edison Exposition Hall. The decor was sophisticated with blue satin tablecloths and white orchids floating in fish bowls to replace the traditional flower centerpieces. The guests, many of them in chic black evening attire and stylish furs, braved the icy roads and a traffic jam to dine on Cornish game hens, wild rice, and chocolate mousse. The mood at the ball was euphoric. "She's got real guts, and she's leading with her chin," Jan Buck, a Princeton lawyer and businessman who was celebrating the Whitman win, told the *Trentonian*.

When the celebrating ended, the cold reality of the situation became clear. Whitman had two months to come up with a state budget plan that would allow her to keep the promise she made on inauguration day. She was proposing to cut revenues at a time when budget experts were already projecting a $1.7 billion deficit in the $15 billion state budget.

Working in Whitman's favor, as she prepared to cut taxes, was the enormous power at her disposal. New Jersey's governorship is considered one of the most powerful in the nation. The governor, who does not even have to share power with a lieutenant governor, has the ability both to impound budgeted funds and to remove items from the budget with a line-item veto. In addition, New Jersey's governor appoints all the state's judges, board and authority members, and top state officials, including the attorney general. The state senate must confirm cabinet appointments, judgeships, and some of the appointments to boards and authorities.

There also was precedent for what Whitman had pledged. Republican governors in Michigan, Massachusetts, and Arizona had already cut taxes and spending despite brutal battles with entrenched bureaucracies and powerful special interest groups. In Michigan, Gov. John Engler, who took office in 1991, cut spending to cure a $1.9 billion deficit and kept the growth of the general budget to under one percent. Welfare advocates and the teachers' union excoriated Engler and his supporters for cutting back on welfare payments and ending the property tax as a means for funding the state's schools, but he pushed the reforms through anyway. By late 1993, *U.S. News and World Report* had credited Michigan with having the tenth strongest economic recovery in the nation. By 1995, the state's unemployment reached an all-time low, and Michigan was number one in the nation in the creation of manufacturing jobs.

In Massachusetts, Gov. William Weld cut state spending, repealed the state sales tax on services, and cut income taxes. In Arizona, Gov. Fife Symington cut taxes and revamped government. In her own back yard, Whitman had another example, as Bret Schundler, the first Republican mayor of Jersey City in seventy-five years, had cut both property taxes and the city budget shortly after taking office. Unfortunately, after cutting taxes twice, Schundler was forced to raise property taxes ($50 million) to about their previous level. The city's budget was hurt by increasing costs for police, firefighters, and schools. In addition, Jersey City's overly high assessment of commercial properties in the 1980s came to roost, as the city was forced to lower tax payments for a number of key properties. Schundler is expected to have a difficult time when he seeks reelection in 1997. The people who had been through the tax-cutting process in other states advised Whitman to hire people for her top positions who were tough and who had a burning desire to implement her policies. "That resolve and fire in the belly has to be there," said Doug Cole, an aide to Symington, in an interview with the *Trentonian*. In addition, those who had been successful at cutting taxes and the size of government said Whitman would need to sell her point of view. Anne Mervenne, one of Engler's top aides, told the *Trentonian* that Engler's team of twenty competed against the voices of thousands when the budget cuts were made. "You need to have a coordinated effort in getting your message out to the people."

Whitman appeared to heed the advice. After putting together a small team of close aides to craft her first budget, she went on the road to sell her philosophy of a smaller, smarter government and to solicit public support. For two months, Whitman traveled throughout New Jersey making an almost daily round of public appearances. Her schedule varied from watching a soccer match at a Newark school, to visiting a boat yard along the shore, to giving the opening remarks at a state college conference. She used town meetings and call-in shows to sell her message that New Jersey must lower taxes and ease government overregulation in order to get the economy back on its feet.

She went on an urban tour through four of the state's cities. In Asbury Park, a deteriorating shore resort, she listened to members of a neighborhood crime watch tell how children in the community were sent to buy drugs for their parents. She watched Hispanic women use a computer program to learn how to read and write. She stopped on a street corner to shake the hand of a man who came from a drug rehabilitation program just to meet the governor. New Jersey residents were surprised by the governor's down-to-earth personality. With her endless energy she took the state by storm.

Whitman did all this while routinely holding one or two news conferences a day in Trenton. However, she could be seen purchasing a cup of tea at the newsstand in the basement of the statehouse or eating at Penny's corner restaurant with her junior staffers as often as she was seen at more formal political affairs. (Her favorite foods are tuna melts, sushi, and hot wings.) When she cast the first fishing line to open trout season in New Jersey that year, people couldn't believe that she stayed to fish for the entire morning.

The one-hundred-forty-five-pound, five-foot-eight governor, solidly built with casually coiffed hair, a large smile, and the Todd family nose, spends any free time she has mountain biking, hiking, playing tennis, golfing, riding, or whatever else she can find to do in the outdoors. (When she can't be outside she uses an exercise or rowing machine.) She lives in the estate-like Pontefract without air conditioning. If need be, like her mother, she can milk a cow, drive a tractor, mow a field, and bail hay.

The troopers on the New Jersey governor's security detail underwent the greatest adjustment. Many of them disliked Florio who, despite his blue-collar background, often was aloof with them. As soon as Whitman arrived, she insisted on sitting in the front seat of the car with the trooper chauffeur and playing her show tunes. "I always ride in the front. [Riding in the back] is too much like *Driving Miss Daisy.* I said, 'Forget it.' " For the troopers, the only drawback to Whitman's election is the show tunes. "I have two disk holders in the car, and the one that they hate is the one that is under the seat because that has all the show tunes on it. I try not to sing out loud because I know I can't carry a tune, but I can't resist whispering under my breath because I know almost all the words to every one of them."

After Whitman was sworn in as governor, the troopers learned that they were expected to join her for a variety of activities, including a quick pick-up game of basketball and miles of mountain biking. "I said very early on that I refused to be followed by a car when I was biking, so they had better learn how to mountain bike and toughen up certain parts of the anatomy that weren't so tough."

Whitman is known for her ability to slip away from the troopers. Her greatest escape was at Yale University in New Haven, Connecticut, in the fall of 1994. "The troopers thought they had gotten me because their room was right next to mine, and they were dorm-type rooms. There was no way I could get out of my door without them seeing. There was a moat around this building. There was no water in the moat, but it was a drop of about five feet and then a stone wall with a wrought-iron fence on top of it, which made the whole thing about eight feet. So they were pretty sure that I was safe."

The escape plan began before Whitman gave her speech at the university. "I had already had Jason [Volk, Whitman's twenty-four-year-old aide who sometimes has trouble keeping up with his forty-nine-year-old boss] move his casual clothes into my room. After I gave my speech, we claimed that I had a lot of calls that I had to make, so we shut the door and changed into [casual] clothes and let ourselves out the window and then pulled ourselves up over the stone wall and then over the wrought-iron fence."

Whitman selected a poster-size picture, used to advertise her visit, to leave a message for the troopers. "I had taken one of these pictures of me, and I tacked it to a chair and moved it in front of the window and did one of those [cartoon] bubbles and said, "Bye guys."

The escape, however, was almost foiled. "Jason and I got out over the fence. I was halfway over the wrought-iron when he said, 'Get back. Get back,' because the people from the dinner were starting to come down the street. So I thought, 'This is really going to be it. I am going to impale myself on this fence.' I had one leg over, one on one side and one on the other. I could envision the headline, 'Governor bled to death on wrought-iron fencing.' "

But she made it over the fence unharmed. "We jumped down, ran across the park, and found a sports bar, a place to shoot darts (the troopers taught her how to play) or play pool, and called them from there," she recounts. After the episode, Whitman says the troopers declared it a hopeless task to try to detain her.

The complex nature of New Jersey's governor is revealed by the people she holds in high esteem. She is wild about the famous dancer Fred Astaire because of his elegance and grace. Her hero is Abe Lincoln, whom she admires for his dignity, his innate understanding of people, and the humanity with which he treated the South. During one of the gubernatorial debates, she cited her parents as the people who had influenced her the most during her growing years. She is fascinated by Eleanor of Aquitaine, the wife of Louis VII of France and then of Henry II of England, and mother of Richard the Lion-Hearted. If she had the chance to go back in history, she would visit a mountain in Galilee in 30 A.D. "I would love to go back to the time of Christ and just be there for a sermon on the mount, or some of those moments, to get the impact and the feel."

When she has time to read, Whitman selects historical biographies. However, the practical, day-to-day tasks in Trenton leave her with little time to muse about history. In 1994, the newly elected governor spent most of her time focused on the billion-dollar state budget. Without saying exactly how she would pay for them, Whitman managed to convince the Republican-controlled legislature to pass her first round of income tax cuts in early March. Only hinting that the upcoming budget would be painful, she wounded some egos in the Republican-controlled senate and assembly by withholding budget details from the lawmakers.

The budget was developed under the direction of Treasurer Brian Clymer, a transportation chief under President George Bush who was brought in from Pennsylvania. Clymer was viewed as a tough guy who could wield the budget ax more easily because he had no political alliances to protect in New Jersey. Also key to the budget process were former Trenton lobbyist Judith Shaw, the first woman to serve as chief of staff to a New Jersey governor, and Peter Verniero, Whitman's personal and campaign lawyer who later replaced Shaw as chief of staff. Whitman also sought counsel on major budget decisions from John; friend and cochairperson of her campaign Hazel Gluck; Malcolm S. Forbes, Jr.; Wall Street economist Lawrence Kudlow; Jane Kenny, her chief of policy and planning; and Lyn Nofziger.

When some members of the Senate Appropriations Committee balked at approving the tax cuts before a budget was crafted to pay for them, Whitman invited the senators for a powwow in her office. Asserting their role as a coequal branch of government, the lawmakers were reluctant. They wanted Whitman to come to them. Whitman placated them by taking Clymer with her for a budget session on senate turf, but the session told the lawmakers little. Whitman merely acknowledged their concerns and told them that details of the budget plan would be revealed to them during later budget hearings. Much the same as on inauguration day, when Whitman finally unveiled her first budget on March 15, 1994, she surprised everyone by doing more than just funding the first round of tax cuts. The budget contained a financial maneuver that allowed her to avoid deep cuts to state government while at the same time enabling Whitman's administration to call for yet a second round of income tax cuts. She proposed an additional 10 percent cut in income taxes for middle-income taxpayers, effective January 1, 1995. The new round of cuts would bring the total reduction in income taxes for most New Jersey residents to 15 percent, half of the 30 percent she promised on the campaign trail in 1993.

The full tax cut would affect individuals earning less than $40,000 and families earning less than $80,000. For families earning more than $80,000, there would be a new tax cut of 2.5 percent; for those earning more than $150,000, there would be an additional tax cut of 1 percent.

Wearing a salmon-pink suit, a confident, poised Whitman, in a budget address delivered to a statewide television audience, promised still more: "Make no mistake: I will call for a third tax cut next year. For democracy to work, those who ask for your vote must keep their promises."

Yet Whitman's $15.3 billion budget called for a reduction in state spending of only $123 million, or less than 1 percent. The philosophy was: "You don't spend more money than you are taking in. Government shouldn't either." This was hardly the rhetoric of a big budget cutter, but the administration said there was too little time to come up with more dramatic cuts because Whitman was working with the system she had inherited from Gov. Florio.

Even though Whitman had criticized former Gov. Florio on the campaign trail for using "one-shot" revenue sources to balance his budgets, she had come up with one of her own. Instead of making significant cuts in state government, Whitman gained a significant portion of the nearly $2 billion needed to close a budget deficit and pay for $625 million in tax cuts by putting less money into the pension and benefit funds that state workers would draw on in future years, budget documents revealed. The plan, in addition to scaling back on the amount of money put aside for benefits in future years, would end a special 2 percent Social Security contribution by the state for each state employee. Whitman promised that the savings gained from reducing the state's contribution to the pension funds would not affect future benefits for retired workers.

The budget also would reduce the state work force of 65,000 by 1,700, mostly through attrition. The total number of workers who would be laid off was estimated at 606, and by June that estimate was further reduced to 400.

Whitman managed to divert attention away from the lack of substantive budget cuts by making some reductions in the state's bureaucracy. In a dramatic presentation, similar to the style used by Ronald Reagan, Whitman placed people in the audience who had made suggestions for savings and asked them to stand at the appropriate time. As she called for the elimination of the State Department of Higher Education, which she said would save $7.3 million, she mentioned Frank Merlo, the man who had made the suggestion. Merlo, a professor at Montclair State College, was one of thousands of people who had offered budget-cutting ideas through talk shows, town meetings, and letters in response to Whitman's Our Tax Dollars program. In a letter to Whitman, Merlo said that the Department of Higher Education had become a self-sustaining bureaucracy that performed make-work to justify its existence. Whitman agreed, saying the department was duplicating functions already being done by individual college administrations. (Ironically, Whitman's mother had served on the department's Board of Higher Education in the 1980s.) The cost-saving ideas of six people either had been acted upon or were under consideration by the State Treasury Department, including a suggestion to privatize two state marinas and six state daycare centers, with savings expected to total $20 million.

Whitman also announced that she would save taxpayers money by eliminating the Public Advocate, which she said was duplicated by other services. She called for a scaling back of the $2 million in state funds for New Jersey Network with a line that stunned some of her own aides: "Government control of the media went out with *Pravda*." Announcing the closing of seven of the state's thirty-nine National Guard armories, she quipped, "The Russians are not coming—except, hopefully, as tourists."

Rhetoric aside, as in past years, the budget was balanced not so much by tough actions and hard decisions as by fiscal maneuvering. During the Florio administration, the state rescued itself from dire financial straits by thinking up imaginative new fiscal schemes just in the nick of time: selling a segment of a state highway to one of its own authorities, recalculating the value of pension system assets, collecting utility taxes ahead of schedule, and refinancing the state debt. Whitman had resorted to the same budget magic by using the pension restructuring scheme. The state's official actuary, Buck Consultants, approved the plan by saying the state was adequately funding the pension system. The problem was that the pension-system restructuring, like the other maneuvers, was a short-term solution that did little to contain rising costs. Next year, it would have to be replaced with comparable budget cuts, or with new gimmicks.

The Whitman administration tried to justify the one-shot revenue source by saying it totaled only $800 million, half of the $1.5 billion in one-shots that Florio had used to balance his last budget. "With this budget, we reduce our reliance on one-shot revenues by nearly one half," Whitman explained.

When local government officials complained that Whitman's tax cuts and budget would increase property taxes, she threw the issue back at them by suggesting that if she could find ways to cut the fat out of a budget, so could they. "We are starting the process of bringing sanity to government spending here in the statehouse—and hopefully in your county courthouses, your town halls, and in your schools."

The Republican legislature immediately predicted smooth passage for Whitman's budget. The day Whitman unveiled it, Sen. Robert Littell, chairman of the Senate Budget Committee, said the framework of Whitman's budget proposals would ultimately be adopted.

Over the next two and a half months, the Republican-run legislature would hold twenty-five hearings and make countless deals and compromises that would only make minor changes in Whitman's spending plan.

The New Jersey Education Association (NJEA), the state's most powerful lobby with 144,500 members, including teachers and school workers across the state, challenged Whitman's budget and announced plans to increase its members' dues in order to launch a $10 million media blitz to ward off the budget cuts. Actuaries for the state employee unions said that the Whitman pension scheme would mean that in the future, the state would have to shell out huge sums of money to shore up retirement funds, or else cut benefits.

Even before Whitman unveiled her first budget, there was no love lost between the NJEA and the governor. The Education Association had spent $195,000 in the final days of the 1993 gubernatorial race trying to defeat Whitman, because she supported a publicly funded voucher program for Jersey City's private schools. The Whitman administration, although reluctant to strike back at the union's challenge to her first budget, eventually distributed 107,000 letters explaining her position to teachers across the state. She held firm on her budget proposal when more than a thousand chanting state workers and teachers, claiming she was raiding pension funds, rallied in front of the statehouse.

Whitman's other hurdle was the Republican-controlled senate where members always had to be stroked during the budget process. While the Republicans enjoyed a substantial margin in the state assembly, the GOP could only afford to have three of its senators defect on the budget plan before it died. Nervous senators added $70 million to the municipal-aid pot, and Whitman acceded to the more generous helping of money. While the senators were disquieted by the moaning of the multitude of labor unions representing state employees, the pension scheme's selling point was that it was politically easier to handle than other alternatives, such as massive spending cuts or a large number of state employee layoffs. "It comes down to, where are the alternatives?" Republican Sen. Peter Inverso of Hamilton told the *Trentonian.* "Are we talking about one billion in layoffs and reductions to state government? We have the unenviable position of being between a rock and a hard spot."

In the end, it was Whitman's popularity with the New Jersey electorate that pushed her first budget through the legislature and wielded the first blow in twenty years to the powerful teachers' union. In a statewide newspaper poll in May 1994, 78 percent of those questioned said Whitman was doing a good or excellent job. In another signal to lawmakers, taxpayers, who vote on school budgets in New Jersey, defeated nearly half of the proposed budgets that spring.

Polls showed that the public supported Whitman's policies and wanted government spending in New Jersey brought under control. The lawmakers knew they would fare better politically by siding with the enormously popular governor rather than with the powerful special interest of the unions. Whitman's plan to have the public weigh in on her side had succeeded. Senator Leonard Connors, a Republican from Ocean County, who is difficult to bring on board when budget votes are cast, said he didn't like the pension scheme. But with the public on Whitman's side, "She doesn't even have to listen to the legislature."

Senator Dick LaRossa, the first Republican to represent the traditionally Democratic Trenton district in fifty years, constantly challenged Whitman's taxing and spending cuts because eighteen thousand state workers resided in his district. The dispute between LaRossa and the governor brought to light her sense of humor when, during the heat of the budget process, they ran into one another at a golf tournament. LaRossa, trying to make friendly small talk, asked Whitman what she hoped to shoot that day. She quickly responded, "You." In the end, however, the senators, including LaRossa, fell into line, and Whitman's budget was approved by the state legislature on June 29, one day before the June 30, deadline mandated by the New Jersey constitution.

Before the ink was even dry on her signature on the first budget bill, speculation had begun about how Whitman's campaign promises would fare under her second budget. But with her popularity as high as any governor's since the 1980s, Whitman would spend a significant amount of time—both in and out of the state—building up her political capital before beginning to tackle the next fiscal year's spending plan.

By keeping her promise to cut income taxes, Whitman had gained national attention and was skyrocketed to political stardom. In August she was featured in *Esquire, Mirabella,* and *Vogue* magazines. *Vogue*'s five-page report, titled "The Liberation of Christie Whitman," included a picture of thirteen-year-old Christie at the Republican convention in Chicago, as well as a photograph of Whitman being kissed by a cow at Pontefract. In *Esquire,* George Will called her "a breath of fresh air." *Mirabella*'s piece, titled, "Favorite Daughter," contained a quote from Republican U.S. Senate Leader Bob Dole: "Christie Whitman is a rising star in the party, with virtually unlimited potential."

Whitman was being talked about as a vice-presidential candidate for 1996, and perhaps even a presidential contender. At the Political Americana, a Washington, D.C., store that sells presidential political memorabilia, buttons touting Whitman for president were selling well.

In the fall of 1994, Whitman toured the country campaigning on behalf of twenty-two Republican candidates running for major offices. With trips paid, in part, by the Republican State Committee, she traveled to New England, California, the Midwest, and the South, where she delivered a message of fiscal conservatism and social moderation. Whitman raised $3.5 million for the candidates she campaigned for and, along the way, gained political allies and IOUs from across the nation, with candidates going so far as to call themselves Whitman Republicans.

During a six-state swing that took her to the Midwest and South in late September, Christie Whitman stumped for Betty Montgomery, who was seven points down in her race to become Ohio's first woman attorney general. "[Whitman] brings a new kind of look to the Republican party, a new kind of feel on the issues," Montgomery told the *Trentonian.* "Many people view the Republican party as full of old, white, rich males."

On November 8, when the Republicans seized control of the U.S. Congress for the first time in four decades and captured governor's seats in more than half of the statehouses throughout the nation, newspapers were quick to note that eighteen of the candidates Whitman had campaigned for won, including George Pataki in New York and John Rowland in Connecticut. What was described in the *Record* of Hackensack as Whitman's "Midas touch" had enhanced her national clout and improved her potential as a vice-presidential candidate.

Governor-elect Pataki and Maryland gubernatorial hopeful Ellen Sauerbrey touted Whitman as the inspiration for the promises they made to cut taxes. GOP winners backed by Whitman included Gov. Pete Wilson of California, Tom Ridge of Pennsylvania, George W. Bush of Texas, and Betty Montgomery, who became Ohio's attorney general. Whitman also campaigned for Rick Santorum of Pennsylvania, Olympia Snowe of Maine, Spencer Abraham of Michigan, John Ashcroft of Missouri, and Fred Thompson and Bill Frist of Tennessee.

Whitman, who had campaigned only once or twice for most candidates, acknowledged that she had not been a deciding factor in any of the races. "The fiscal issue was the overriding issue in this campaign," she told the *Record.* "The message of cutting taxes, of controlling government spending was a very powerful message." At home, however, Whitman's "Midas touch" failed to help State Assembly Speaker Chuck Haytaian, who unsuccessfully challenged Democratic U.S. Sen. Frank Lautenberg. Haytaian was unable to overcome campaign problems and an antiabortion position, both of which hurt him with New Jersey voters.

The Haytaian race provided the one political ripple in Whitman's fall campaigning. Whitman was pressured by Lautenberg supporters to denounce New York talk-show host Bob Grant, whose show both Whitman and Haytaian had appeared on, for making statements that a group of black ministers considered racist. (Black leaders objected to Grant's characterization of black rioters in Los Angeles as "savages.") Whitman, at first, agreed and said she would not make another appearance on the Grant show, thereby leaving Haytaian, who refused to comply, in a political quandary. Whitman then angered the black ministers and confused the issue when she reversed herself. After receiving a flood of telephone calls and letters from Grant listeners, she changed her mind and decided to appear on the Grant show for a discussion on racism.

During the month following the GOP victory in Washington, Whitman stepped forward as a spokesperson for the party's moderate faction. Starting with a speech in Washington just three days after the election and continuing on NBC's "Meet the Press" and at Republican conferences, Whitman urged the victorious Republicans to focus on fiscal, not social, issues.

During her November 11 speech to the Washington Research Group, Whitman warned the party that it must keep its promises: "The rebellion has given Republicans what we have badly wished for: control of the Congress and a majority of governorships throughout the nation. With that control comes the obligation to produce policy that matches the rhetoric. The voters have shown they have little patience or forgiveness for politicians who don't keep their promises. Our party must prove that our word in campaigns is our bond in government. Otherwise, we'll find ourselves right back in the wilderness where we wandered for forty years. My advice to the new Republican majority in Congress is simply this: do what we're doing in New Jersey and what Republican governors and legislatures are doing all across the country. Focus on the fiscal issues that got you elected. Cut taxes, cut spending, and replace programs that fail with government that works. Above all, include everyone."

Whitman spoke out in favor of a balanced budget amendment for the federal government, a presidential line-item veto, and term limits. Becoming a spokesperson for the nation's Republican governors, she said that they would accept reduced federal funding to help limit the national deficit if there was a corresponding reduction in costly federal mandates. Appearing with California Gov. Pete Wilson and Massachusetts Gov. William Weld on "Meet the Press," Whitman called on the federal government to allow the states to manage Medicare and welfare programs.

A social moderate, Whitman is pro-choice on abortion and favors gay and lesbian rights. She is against school prayer (but favors a moment of silence) and is opposed to gutting the federal welfare system. She stung the conservative wing of the party by advising: "As the party of Lincoln, the Republican party ought to respect the personal as well as economic liberty of all people, regardless of race, religion, ethnic background, or sexual orientation. Intolerance of any group has no place. Discussions of issues of conscience do have a place—at the family dinner table, in churches and synagogues, and between doctor and patient. There is always something a little strange—to put it kindly—when politicians preach morality. I am not so sure we, or anyone else, for that matter, have the standing to be the arbiter of values for everyone."

At a governor's conference in Williamsburg, Virginia, where Whitman was drawing considerable attention from the media, Mississippi Gov. Kirk Fordice had this to say to a *Trenton Times* reporter about the conservatives' view of the governor from New Jersey: "She's the darling of the media, but she's a liberal. Anybody who thinks she can be the vice-presidential candidate is crazy. That's just bull."

Meanwhile, at home, New Jersey newspapers were doing their year-end assessments of the Whitman administration. There was little doubt that Whitman's popularity was still high, as public opinion polls showed 68 percent of the state's residents believed she was doing a good or excellent job. The newspaper stories noted, however, that while Whitman had kept her promise to cut income taxes, she had not made significant progress toward keeping the other promises she made while campaigning for governor. On the tax front, she had not yet kept her pledge to phase out the sales tax on telephone calls or to eliminate a fuel tax for out-of-state truckers. In addition, the governor had more promises to keep in the area of crime, including pledges to impose life sentences without parole for three-time felons and to require convicted criminals to serve at least 70 percent of their prison sentences. She also had promised to require juveniles convicted of a violent crime to spend some time in jail, to create a boot camp for nonviolent first-time juvenile offenders, and to appoint state supreme court justices who support the death penalty.

However, when tragedy struck a Trenton suburb in July, Whitman strengthened her anticrime record by supporting legislation requiring public notification when a sex offender moves into a New Jersey neighborhood. There was a public outcry for the law when seven-year-old Megan Kanka, of Hamilton, was brutally raped and murdered and the convicted sex offender who lived across the street from her was charged with the slaying. While the legislation initially received a lukewarm reception from the governor's office, once public sentiment for the law mushroomed, Whitman gave it her full support. After attending a public rally urging passage of the legislation, Whitman began wearing the small, pink ribbon that became the symbol of what is now known as Megan's Law. Megan's mother was on hand at the statehouse when Whitman signed the bill into law in October 1994, and the two women embraced after the signing in what proved to be a gripping public scene.

On the spending front, Whitman had kept her pledge to limit the state's annual growth to 3 percent and to leave the state's popular homestead rebate program, a tax break for property owners, in place. She had not yet kept her promises to institute $500 million in management reforms, to sell her helicopter, to privatize the New Jersey Sports and Exposition Authority, to establish a bond review board to review and consider the cumulative effects of borrowing on taxpayers, and to create a Sunset Commission to review and eliminate outdated programs and regulations. On education, Whitman had not yet fulfilled her pledges to create a pilot school-voucher program in Jersey City, to develop statewide core curriculum standards, to increase state monitoring of local schools, to divert 2 percent of the state's education aid to educational innovations, and to provide school aid incentives for school districts to regionalize services like busing to save taxpayers money.

But with the national focus on her tax cuts, Whitman wasn't fielding questions about unkept promises. Instead, as the year ended, she was answering queries about the likelihood that she would leave New Jersey in 1997 for national office. In December 1994, Whitman was among six

Republicans pictured in a *Newsweek* article on the "Republicans' New Deal," and *People* magazine listed her as one of the twenty-five most intriguing people of the year. Downplaying talk about a run for the vice presidency, Whitman said the national attention could disappear as quickly as it came. She pointed out that in *Esquire,* she had shared the page with Lassie, and in *People,* she followed spy Aldrich Ames on the list of the most intriguing.

When *Newsweek* asked her about her chances of becoming a vice-presidential candidate, she said that the idea was silly: "I want to do the best job I can for New Jersey." The magazine's response: "Spoken like a true candidate."

12

A Promise Kept

"Why wait to return as much money as we can to taxpayers? Why wait until next year to keep a promise we can keep now? Today, I am asking the legislature to complete the 30 percent tax cut in this budget—one full year ahead of schedule."

Gov. Christie Whitman (January 23, 1995)
from her second budget address.

In the midst of all the national attention, Whitman would now unveil her second budget. Political analysts and administration officials agreed that it would be the toughest of her term in office. Whitman's success—or lack of success—in handling a tough budget year was certain to have an impact on her role in national politics. "Her national reputation is at stake," said Democratic consultant Steve DeMicco. "If the promises of her policy come up short, then the bloom will be off the apple."

Whitman spokesman Carl Golden said that that wouldn't happen: "The second year was always seen by us as the really tough year. She is committed to continuing on course. She feels she has a binding contract with the people to whom she turned for support a year ago, and she intends to honor that contract."

According to newspaper reports and Whitman's own budget people,

251

she faced a $2 billion deficit. The tax cuts she already had in place would cost the state $625 million, and she was promising that more cuts were in the making. Meanwhile, a state takeover of the county courts would cost $105 million, and Florio's scheme to refinance the state debt would come to roost with debt payments jumping a whopping $360 million. Whitman's one-shot revenue scheme for her first budget automatically created an $800 million hole in the upcoming spending plan. And increased costs, including a federal mandate to put a multimillion-dollar car emissions testing program in place, would put an additional strain on the budget process.

Whitman administration officials appeared frantic. Sources inside the administration declared that Whitman would be forced to cut state government 15 to 20 percent. There were rumors that the layoff of state employees could reach as high as five thousand. "Massive, massive cuts" were predicted by highly placed state officials. Republicans, like Sen. Dick LaRossa, were urging Whitman to hold off on her next round of tax cuts. Undermining Whitman's income tax cuts, Republican Senate President Donald DiFrancesco came up with his own proposal to cut property taxes, thereby fueling the Democrats' contention that Whitman's policies were the cause of escalating taxes at the local level.

Throughout the fall of 1994 and into January 1995, the Whitman administration carefully orchestrated the budget process. Officials painted a dire fiscal picture for reporters and the public. In year-end interviews, Whitman warned that there would be layoffs, although she wouldn't say how many, and cutbacks in departments and services.

There was speculation that Whitman would call for another 5 percent income tax cut, bringing the total tax cut to 20 percent for most New Jersey residents.

Carefully planned press conferences began to reveal pieces of the budget plan. The Human Services Department announced that Medicaid payments to New Jersey hospitals would be cut 20 percent, and the payments to nursing homes would be trimmed by 3.6 percent. While some were snickering, Whitman announced that she was going to save money by having state employees outside the Department of Transportation volunteer as drivers for the state's snowplows. To prove she was serious, Whitman completed the test for a commercial driver's license, and wearing blue jeans, sneakers, and a hard hat, she climbed behind the controls of a salt loader and drove it a few feet.

Complicating the budget process was the state's need to negotiate contracts with six state-worker unions, representing 82 percent of the state work force—59,000 workers. All of the union contracts would come up for renewal on June 30, 1995, the same date the New Jersey constitution mandated the passage of a balanced state budget for the budget year beginning July 1. Bob Pursell of the Communications Workers of America (CWA), representing 34,000 state employees, was calling it "fiscally irresponsible for the governor to proceed with another tax cut."

Working in Whitman's favor, however, was the fact that early predictions of 600 layoffs in her first budget had never materialized; only 250 workers has been laid off during her first year in office.

On December 20, a story in the *Star-Ledger* gave the first hint that the budget crisis had eased. The newspaper, citing statehouse sources, reported that Whitman's budget woes for the upcoming year were expected to ease dramatically because of surging revenues and an unexpected budget surplus. Carl Golden and Treasurer Brian Clymer debunked the story, saying they had no idea what revenue numbers the *Star-Ledger* was referring to when it wrote that the budget deficit was likely to be closer to $1 billion than the expected $2 billion. In reality, top legislative leaders and some people inside the governor's office knew that things were looking far better than expected.

On January 3, the Governor's Council of Economic Advisors reported that 1994 was New Jersey's best economic year since 1988, with 65,500 new jobs created. Whitman attributed the upswing in the state's economy to an overall improvement in the national economy, as well as her own economic policies. Democrats, however, immediately attacked the number of new jobs by saying Whitman would still fall far short of the 450,000 jobs she had promised on the campaign trail.

Surprisingly, Whitman denied that 450,000 jobs was ever a hard-and-fast campaign promise. She said that the number had only been used to refer to the number of jobs lost during Florio's term in office. Nevertheless, newspapers, in stories the following day, quoted transcripts of Whitman at a September 21, 1993, press conference: "If our policies move the state's economy back to its historical trend line, it means the creation of 450,000 jobs."

Continuing to set the stage for her budget message, Whitman's chief of staff, Judith Shaw, told the labor unions on January 5 that pending budget cuts could result in the loss of 2,437 state jobs, many of them through the privatization of state services, such as veterans' nursing homes and motor-vehicle inspection stations.

Meanwhile, in her first State of the State address on January 10, 1995, Whitman, dressed in a teal suit and white blouse with a scarf-like collar, renewed her pledge to cut taxes, streamline state government, and improve the New Jersey economy. The pressure of the national attention was being felt inside the administration. The atmosphere before the speech was tense as Whitman walked the short distance from her office to the assembly chambers. "Make no mistake about it, the budget I present on January 23 will continue the income tax cuts and business tax reductions that are fueling our economic recovery. We keep our promises. And it's paying off."

Coming one day after a *New York Times* story described Whitman as a rising star on the national political scene, where she was viewed as a potential vice-presidential candidate, the tone of Whitman's State of the State speech left more than a few people thinking that Whitman showed a tendency to take too much credit for her accomplishments and for an improving economy. The *New York Times* referred to the speech as "buoyant to the point of braggadocio." The *Trentonian* reported that it was delivered in a cockier manner than Whitman previously had exhibited. "Where America is going, New Jersey is going first," Whitman bragged. The question people were asking was whether Whitman was beginning to pat herself on the back too much and whether national attention had pushed her ego to new heights. The *New York Times* was quick to note that she took a potshot at former New York Gov. Mario Cuomo: "A year ago, the governor of New York looked at New Jersey and laughed. He said our plan to cut taxes and stimulate economic growth would never work. Well, today New York has a new governor, George Pataki, and he has a copy of our plan on his desk. And nobody's laughing at New Jersey any more." Union officials joined those who saw the speech as a little too self-assured and as inaccurately portraying the unions' relationship with the Whitman administration. Whitman, citing an unprecedented meeting with union officials on the budget, said, "We are getting so good at bringing everyone to the table that I'm thinking about offering our services to [strike-plagued] Major League Baseball."

True, the administration had held two informational sessions with the unions and sponsored one labor-management conference, but Whitman's statements went "beyond the reality of the situation in New Jersey," said John Loos of the Communications Workers of America.

Cliff Zukin was among those who said that Whitman's speech was a bit too euphoric for a governor whose accomplishment to date had been cutting income taxes. In light of the national and regional upturn in the economy, Zukin said, "This is not Christie Whitman magic in New Jersey."

After the speech, Whitman drew praise from the business community by calling for a streamlining of the application process for environmental permits, but even Republican lawmakers withheld their applause when she announced that she planned to fund transportation projects by continuing a surcharge on motor vehicle registrations. And Whitman's administration drew unexpectedly harsh criticism from Jersey City Mayor Bret Schundler when she announced a delay in implementing Jersey City's school voucher program. Acknowledging that the proposal for vouchers would not pass in the state legislature, Whitman appointed a commission to study the concept, thus delaying its start until at least September 1996.

Those close to Whitman blamed the less-than-modest tenor of the speech on the chaotic committee process that had been used to write it and last-minute changes in the text that left the governor somewhat uncomfortable. The State of the State speech faded into the background, however, when on January 20, 1995, three days before Whitman was to deliver her second budget message, word arrived in New Jersey and across the country that Whitman had been chosen to deliver the Republican response to President Clinton's State of the Union Address.

Whitman would be the first woman and the first governor given the coveted nationally televised spot normally reserved for members of Congress. Party leaders said she was picked because her tax and spending cuts in New Jersey reflected what Republicans were trying to do on a national level. Whitman's selection did two other things: it was a sign that the party wanted to show its diversity by choosing someone with moderate social views, and it demonstrated the important role state government would assume under the Republican leadership in Washington. The speech would further elevate Whitman's rising-star status by showcasing her to a national audience. If she did well, it would boost her chances for higher political office. "She's in the big leagues," Stephen Salmore, Republican consultant and professor at Rutgers' Eagleton Institute of Politics told the *Trentonian*. "This is an opportunity to be seen as a national figure."

New Jersey Democrats predictably grumbled that Whitman was spending more time worrying about her national image than about New Jersey business. "She's playing to the national stage," charged Democratic Assemblywoman Shirley Turner in a *Trentonian* interview. "If you're playing to the national stage, you're going to be more interested in appearance, and not much in the way of substance. It's all sizzle and no steak." Carl Golden said Whitman was flattered by the invitation, but he insisted that she had no interest in the national ticket: "She's been clear. She has no aspirations in that direction."

As Whitman presented her second budget to a joint session of the legislature at the statehouse in Trenton on January 23, 1995, she once again managed to surprised everyone, including New Jersey Republican leaders, by announcing that she would cut income taxes for most New Jersey residents by another 15 percent, thereby keeping her 1993 campaign promise to reduce the tax by a total of 30 percent. It would be a promise kept—a year early.

Whitman said the first two income tax cuts had spurred the state's economy enough to fund the final round of cuts: "So why wait to reinvest in New Jersey's future? Why wait to return as much money as we can to taxpayers? Why wait until next year to keep a promise we can keep now?"

The tax plan, costing $247 million for the upcoming budget year, would cut income taxes by 15 percent for families earning up to $80,000 a year and individuals earning up to $40,000, beginning January 1, 1996. Whitman had already reduced those residents' income tax bills by 15 percent. In the higher income brackets, the total income tax reduction would be 23 percent for individuals making more than $40,000 and families making more than $80,000; and 10 percent for individuals earning more than $75,000 and families earning more than $150,000. In a press conference after the budget address, Whitman said she had fully met her 1993 campaign promise. Even her aides, however, agreed that she had not quite reached the tax cut promised for the upper income brackets. She fell 2 percent short in the middle-income bracket and 10 percent short of her promise in the highest bracket.

In addition to the tax cuts, Whitman announced that her new $15.9 billion budget would increase state spending by $483 million, or 3 percent. In another surprise, she said cost savings and tax collections, flowing into the state coffers at higher-than-expected levels, had virtually wiped away the state's $2 billion deficit.

Even with the tax cuts, state government would be raking in more taxes and fees than ever. During the budget year beginning July 1, 1995, the state, because of an upswing in the economy, was now expected to bring in $532 million more in several types of taxes—income, corporate, and sales—than originally projected.

While not containing any sweeping reductions or reforms to state government, the budget did call for a $219 million reduction in the money spent by state departments and a 3,400 reduction in the state work force. A large majority of the job reduction (2,199) would result from turning government services over to the private sector. Playing hardball with the state unions as contract talks were about to start, Whitman did not put any money in the budget for pay raises, a typical negotiating strategy.

While some members of the press speculated that Whitman made the decision to announce the 15 percent tax cut after being invited to give the national response to Clinton's speech, the governor and her top aides said the decision was made before the invitation. In addition to cutting income taxes, the budget called for three tax breaks for businesses. Whitman proposed a tax cut for national companies that open a branch office in New Jersey. She called for a repeal of the state's sales tax on advertising in the yellow pages. And she proposed reducing the corporate income-tax rate from 9 percent to 7.5 percent for twenty thousand small corporations.

While trimming the state budget in some areas, Whitman increased and maintained spending levels in others. Her budget called for spending an additional $3.5 billion over the next four years on road projects. It funneled an additional $181 million to schools, retained a property-tax relief program for homeowners, and kept aid to municipalities at its current level. The budget called for saving state money by turning state operations, such as state-run daycare centers and motor vehicle inspection stations, over to private companies. It dipped into the pocketbooks of consumers by applying the 6 percent sales tax to the full price of items purchased with store coupons instead of using the discounted price to calculate the tax. It called for a $5 surcharge for people who do business with the Department of

Motor Vehicles in person, rather than by mail. Whitman also included an increase in a variety of occupational fees, including dairy licenses, teacher certifications, and professional board memberships.

Whitman's budget address tried to preempt charges by Democrats that her third round of income tax cuts would result in higher property taxes. "The state does not collect a penny of property tax. The state does not spend a penny of property tax. Those functions are the exclusive domain of the counties, the municipalities, and the school districts." Whitman's opponents immediately decried the budget. Robert Pursell of the CWA declared that it exposed the "darker side of Gov. Whitman." Democratic Sen. Bernard Kenny charged that the budget was balanced on "uncertain revenue projections and taxes on the savings of supermarket coupon clippers."

At first, senate budget chief Sen. Robert Littell called Whitman's budget an "easy sell" in the senate. "They will analyze and debate it, but in the final analysis, the budget will be passed essentially intact," Littell predicted. (Later, however, after Whitman tried to remove Littell's wife, Virginia, as head of the state GOP to replace her with Assembly Speaker Chuck Haytaian and after the legislature's own accountants raised questions about the accuracy of Whitman's revenue projections, Littell and several other Republican senators began to balk at the new tax cuts.)

Whitman used the income-tax cuts as the major selling point in her response to the State of the Union Address on January 24, 1995. Responding to President Clinton's attempts to win back disenchanted middle-class voters with a tax-relief plan, Whitman said a Republican revolution was sweeping the nation, and New Jersey was a prime example of what it could achieve. Low-keyed but poised and relaxed, Whitman addressed the nation from the ornate assembly chambers in the statehouse. She waited far longer than expected to deliver the response because Clinton talked for an unusually long eighty minutes. When she did appear, dressed in an electric blue suit, she broke the ice and set a comfortable tone for her speech by joking with national viewers about not demanding equal time. In a careful rather than dramatic delivery, she talked about taxes: "Here in New Jersey, like so many other governors, I was told my tax-cutting policies were a gimmick. I heard we couldn't do it, that it was impossible, that it would hurt the economy. But I had given my word to the people of New Jersey that we would cut their taxes. And we did."

She outlined, on behalf of the national party, the agenda of change:

We're committed to reforming welfare: to encourage people to work and to stop children from having children. We want to force the government to live within its means by stopping runaway spending and balancing the federal budget. We want to lower taxes for families and make it easier to achieve the American Dream—to save money, buy a home, and send the kids to college. We're going to stop violent criminals in their tracks, with real prison time for repeat offenders and a workable death penalty. We must send a message to our young people that crime doesn't pay. And we're going to slash those unnecessary regulations that strangle small business in America to make it easier to create more jobs and pay better wages and become more competitive in the global marketplace.

Using head movements and eye direction rather than hand gestures to communicate, Whitman came across as sincere. She licked her lips when she charged that while Clinton sounded "pretty Republican," he had been responsible for record tax increases. "There's nothing virtuous about raising taxes. There's nothing heroic about preserving a welfare system that entraps people. And there's nothing high-minded about wasting other people's money on big-government spending sprees."

On behalf of the Republican party, Whitman made the same pledge to the American people that she had made in her State of the State Address to the people of New Jersey: "By the time President Clinton makes his next State of the Union Address, we will have lower taxes. We will have more efficient government. We will have a stronger America. We will have more faith in our politics, more pride in our states and communities, and more confidence in ourselves."

Whitman's performance got high marks. House Speaker Newt Gingrich, who selected Whitman for the response, said at a Washington, D.C., news conference that she had done a brilliant job. "She is clearly just a very articulate and attractive advocate of our cause."

Others said she was far more than that. Washington-based Republican political strategist Roger Stone told the *Trentonian* that Whitman was no longer just on everyone's short list for the vice presidency. She was the frontrunner. Not since 1951, when Richard Nixon came on the scene as a vice-presidential candidate and Dwight Eisenhower selected him as his 1952 running mate, had someone emerged as the frontrunner for the vice presidency so early in the political season. (In 1951, Christie Todd was five years old, and her father, Webster Todd, was heavily involved in the party's selection of both Eisenhower and Nixon.)

While it is unseemly to actually run for vice president since that choice belongs to the presidential candidate, hopefuls position themselves. "She is positioning herself the way any smart politician would," said Gary Nordlinger, a Washington, D.C.-based consultant to Democratic candidates for more than twenty years. "She has now entered a small arena of Republican candidates," Republican consultant David Welch said in January 1995. "It has become common for people to discuss her name. In Wisconsin, Nebraska, and Oklahoma, when Republicans are talking about possible presidential and vice-presidential candidates, she is now mentioned in the average conversation."

In January 1995, the *Washington Post* asked Senate Majority Leader and presidential contender Robert Dole if he would consider Whitman as a running mate: "She'd certainly be on anybody's short list," he said. Then he added, "Maybe it'll be a woman running with a man. Maybe Christie will pick some man. Who knows what's going to happen this early?" But political analysts—and Whitman's close advisers—dismissed the notion that she might be a presidential candidate. "I don't think they even considered the possibility," said Malcolm S. Forbes, Jr., who himself became a presidential contender. It was a matter of economics. A presidential race was expected to cost more than $20 million, and Whitman was in no position to raise that kind of money.

After making her nationally televised speech, Whitman moved quickly to keep two more campaign promises. The day after the national address, she surprised a number of people by keeping her campaign promise to dedicate a New Jersey rest stop to New York radio talk-show host, shock-jock Howard Stern. Whitman telephoned Stern's show to tell him that a plaque, with a drawing of the talk show host opening the door to an outhouse, would be placed on a two-foot high stone at a rest stop on Interstate 295. During the 1993 race for governor, Stern had offered to endorse the first gubernatorial candidate who called into his show, but he wanted something in exchange: a New Jersey Turnpike rest stop named in his honor. Whitman had called first and struck the bargain. Now she was keeping the promise, just on a different New Jersey roadway. The Whitman administration, however, misgauged the public's reaction to naming the rest stop after Stern, who is known for his lewd humor, vulgar characterizations of women, and degrading remarks about minorities. Editorial writers at a number of newspapers attacked the dedication, and it was criticized by blacks and women.

The president of the state chapter of the National Organization for Women, Myra Terry, was livid. "To Howard Stern, women are sex objects for his own amusement. He promulgates stereotypes that label women as whores, lesbians, or bitches." Whitman spokesman Carl Golden replied, "Where the hell is everyone's sense of humor?" But the national implications became apparent when the April 3, 1995 edition of *Time* magazine listed Whitman in its "Losers" column for the stunt. After the plaque was stolen and sent to Stern, the Whitman administration said it would not be returned to the rest stop. Whitman kept a less controversial campaign promise early in 1995 when she announced that the governor's helicopter had been converted into an emergency medical aircraft. Using the helicopter as a symbol of government waste during her 1993 campaign for governor, Whitman had originally promised to sell it.

During her second year in office, Whitman's outspoken comments continued to generate media attention. In April, Whitman stirred another controversy when in an interview with a British journalist, she said a game involving young black males, called "Jewels in the Crown," was responsible, in part, for unwed teenage pregnancies. Whitman made the remarks while explaining why she was opposed to Republican proposals to deny welfare payments to unwed mothers. "As regards to unwed mothers, there's a game called 'Jewels in the Crown' that young black males have, and it's how many children you can sire outside of wedlock. You can't legislate against that."

The comments appeared in the *Independent of London* just as Whitman was leaving on a trade mission to the city, and she apologized at a statehouse news conference. She said she never intended to suggest that black males were the single cause of unwed teenage mothers. "I would certainly apologize if anyone were to presume that I was implying that it was only one community that suffered from the problem. That is certainly not the case, and I know better than that. The problem of unwed mothers is not relegated to the African-American community by any stretch of the imagination."

Whitman, however, never backed away from the accuracy of the comment. She said that she had been told about the game by black parents at a home for children with AIDS, and a social worker had confirmed the information. Nevertheless, Walter Fields, political director of the New Jersey branch of the National Association for the Advancement of Colored People, called Whitman's remarks racist and made reference to her wealthy upbringing. "I think there clearly is a racist streak in the governor, and I don't feel bashful about saying it," Fields told the *Philadelphia Inquirer.* "Her whole upbringing, her whole background does not suggest having had a prior constructive relationship with black people."

However, the prominent black leader who stood by Whitman during the Rollins crisis, the Rev. Reginald Jackson of the St. Matthew A.M.E. Church in Orange, said Whitman was merely repeating what she had been told by black women. "I don't think she intended to malign the African-American community," Jackson told the *Inquirer.* "If we are going to move beyond the issue of who is racist, we have to be genuine and frank and communicate with one another." The incident gave Whitman's opponents the chance to recap the Rollins incident and to make reference to Whitman's association with Howard Stern and Bob Grant, who have both been accused of racist remarks. Assembly Democrats sent the statehouse press corps a cartoon of Whitman, dressed in a coat with a fur collar and wearing a jester's cap with three "Jewels in the Crown"—Ed Rollins, Bob Grant, and Howard Stern.

In April, Whitman also jumped into the fray when a Trenton city councilman made a sexist remark about two women who had been appointed to top positions in the city administration. The councilman told the *Trentonian:* "You might have a problem, because you know how women get at that time of the month." Whitman shot back: "That's incredibly ignorant. I've known men to have the same kind of problems, not just monthly, but weekly."

Whitman also chided presidential hopeful Sen. Phil Gramm (R-Texas) for the response he gave on national television when asked if he would be interested in having a woman for a running mate. Gramm said that he would, except that Sophia Loren is not a United States citizen. Whitman termed the remark gratuitous and an insult. Whitman again showed some spunk by making a decision in April 1995 that three previous governors had passed the buck on. She acted quickly to kill a proposal that had been alive since 1977 to build a golf course at Liberty State Park, located along the New Jersey shoreline behind the Statue of Liberty and Ellis Island. Proposed under Gov. Brendan Byrne, supported by Gov. Tom Kean, and ignored by Gov. Jim Florio, the plan was keeping the state acreage from public use. Yet no governor had possessed the courage to nix it. In a closed session with her staff, Whitman was advised to stay away from the controversy. Angry at the state's inability to make a decision, Whitman slammed her hand down on the conference-room table and declared, "Damn it, we have to do this." Ending the plans for the golf course, Whitman directed state officials to tap New Jersey's Green Acres fund to build walkways along the waterfront, opening a greater portion of the park for visitors to enjoy. Sam Pesin, whose late father had founded the park, told the *Record* that Whitman had "listened to the voice of the people."

As June of her second year in office approached, Whitman had more to worry about than golf courses. She came under fire when lawmakers discovered that she had diverted $50 million, earmarked for health benefits for the working poor, to help balance the 1994–1995 budget and pay for her income tax cuts. And school officials began screaming when she threatened to cut payments to seventy school districts by a total of $11 million to penalize them for spending too much money on nonteaching jobs.

At the same time, city and county officials from the Trenton area were openly criticizing the Whitman administration for its failure to take a more active role in keeping companies from leaving New Jersey and migrating to the South. Despite the announcement that the Mercer County area surrounding Trenton could lose 3,300 private-sector jobs in less than a year, as firms decided to move elsewhere, Whitman remained cool to the idea of offering firms cash incentives to stay or locate in New Jersey.

On the budget front, the Whitman administration was locked in a dispute with the legislature over the amount of revenue the state's taxes would generate during the budget year beginning July 1, 1995. According to budget experts at the Office of Legislative Services, the administration's calculations were so inaccurate that the state was likely to come up $680 million short of its needed funding by the end of the budget year. Treasurer Brian Clymer denied the charge.

Even Republican senators were complaining that Whitman had provided no specifics on how turning state services over to private companies would save money. There was concern about the outcome of pending contract talks with the state unions and about the amount of additional debt the state was incurring by increasing funding for the transportation trust fund. In addition, budget chief Sen. Robert Littell argued that the state could be hard hit when the Republican Congress began to slice funding to the states.

However, with Whitman's popularity holding strong with the New Jersey electorate, the senators had little leverage against the governor. A *Star-Ledger*/Eagleton poll in June showed that more than half of the New Jersey residents (53 percent) believed Whitman was doing a good or excellent job as governor. Only 11 percent gave her a "poor" rating. Echoing his comments from the previous year, Sen. Len Connors, who expressed serious concerns about the budget, said: "She is going to get anything she wants. She is a very popular governor."

Whitman expected little trouble for her budget in the assembly where the Republicans held fifty-two of the eighty seats and where Assembly Speaker Chuck Haytaian (whom Whitman would name as the new chief of the Republican party in New Jersey to replace Mrs. Littell) maintained tight control of his members. In the senate, where the budget would fail if more than three of the Republican senators balked, Senate President Donald DiFrancesco was now firmly in Whitman's corner. (Some were whispering that DiFrancesco had his own personal reasons for helping Whitman. If she vacates her office early for a federal post, the state constitution mandates that DiFrancesco take over as acting governor until the next election.)

The Republican senators who were still balking at the budget plan were Littell and Sen. Dick LaRossa and Sen. Peter Inverso from Trenton, whose districts include a large percentage of the state's employees. Other Republican conservatives in the senate, like Connors and Sen. Henry McNamara, were grumbling that Whitman's budget failed to call for any sweeping reforms or reductions in state government.

However, as the budget deadline of June 30 approached, the governor's office and the legislature narrowed their dispute over revenue projections to $383 million. On June 27, three days before the deadline, the state legislature approved both Whitman's budget and the tax cuts. Yielding to the wishes of the state employees within their districts, Inverso and LaRossa, abstained on the tax cut, but enough Democrats joined the vote so that it passed easily in both houses.

The Republican lawmakers tinkered with the state budget before passing it, deleting some of the items Whitman wanted, but adding $65 million in spending, including $20 million for pet projects in the districts of influential lawmakers. In an effort to thwart Whitman's plans to turn the state's motor vehicle inspection stations over to private companies, the legislature added $2.4 million to the budget to keep the inspections workers on the state payroll.

The budget easily passed in the assembly by a fifty-four-to-twenty-three vote, but ran into problems in the senate, where it passed along party lines with just one more vote than needed, twenty-two to seventeen. Republican conservative Sen. Henry McNamara refused to vote for the budget because it failed to make enough cuts in state government. For a time, Sens. LaRossa and Inverso withheld their votes, and then relented. In her second year in office, Whitman had shown a new ability to persuade recalcitrant senators to vote her way. She polished the talent when she convinced staunch Republican opponents of the state's new emissions standards to vote for the plan.

As expected, the opposing party attacked the budget plan. Senate Democratic leader John Lynch charged that Whitman had resorted to rosy revenue estimates and additional debt to fund the tax cuts. The Democrats were able to bolster their argument with statistics from the Office of Legislative Services, the research arm of the legislature. Because Whitman had added billions of dollars in new debt to the state's Transportation Trust Fund for road projects, OLS estimated that debt payments by the state would quadruple over five years, jumping from $255 million to just short of $1.2 billion. However, Whitman argued that the construction projects would mean 250,000 jobs for the state. Even though the Whitman budget kept aid to municipalities basically even, the opposition party continued to argue that Whitman's policies would drive up local property taxes.

On June 30, Whitman signed what was now a $16 billion budget into law. "This budget keeps promises. It cuts taxes, reduces the historical growth of state government, maintains a healthy surplus, and invests in important programs." The new plan increased state spending by about $491 million (3 percent) over the previous year's budget and provided the state with a $541 million surplus.

In its final form, the budget called for 481 layoffs, 715 jobs eliminated by privatized services, and 1,673 jobs cut back to thirty-five-hour work weeks. (Whitman's privatization program will ultimately force 2,000 from the state payroll.) Whitman left most of $20 million in local "pork" in the budget. "I have respect for the areas where they felt there was a specific need that could not be met without some help from state government."

Whitman angered the state unions by axing the $2.4 million the legislature had added to keep employees at the state's motor vehicle inspection stations on the state payroll. Angry union officials harshly criticized Whitman and her budget: "The woman's never been denied anything in her life," Katherine Black, an official with the Communications Workers of America, told the *Asbury Park Press*. "She doesn't know what it's like to struggle for a paycheck. . . . She has no idea what she's doing to people's lives."

Four days later, at an old-fashioned July 4 celebration and parade in Milltown, New Jersey, marked with American flags, hot dogs, and beer, Gov. Whitman signed the final phase of her promised income-tax cuts. Children, seated on the risers behind Whitman, carried signs, saying, "30 percent" and "Promises made. Promises kept."

"As you know, I believe in lower taxes," Whitman told the cheering crowd. "I believe in keeping New Jersey open for business, and I believe in promises. That's why I'm giving New Jersey the full tax cut that I promised less than two years ago. Our tax cuts return your money, not the government's money. It doesn't belong to the government. It belongs to you, and you've earned it." The crowd burst into applause. And as the governor signed the tax cut, fireworks filled the daytime sky.

At a total cost of $1.2 billion to the state's coffers, most New Jersey residents would see their income taxes cut by 30 percent. According to the state treasurer, it would mean: A family earning $25,000 would save $120; a family earning $75,000 would save $555; a family earning $200,000 would save $1,671 (16.6 percent). "Not only will this tax cut give families more control over the money that they earn, it will produce a stronger New Jersey. That means jobs for everyone. That's what we're after. From the working poor to the highly skilled professional, these tax cuts will work for New Jersey."

Critics were quick to point out that Milltown was one of the municipalities where property taxes had increased, but Whitman, once again, responded that local government needed to control its own spending. Newspaper accounts also noted that Whitman had yet to keep her campaign promise to remove the sales tax on telephone services and (because the lawmakers had balked) and had not offered tax cuts for businesses.

After she signed the tax cut, a crowd of people immediately swarmed around Whitman, all of them wanting her autograph. All day long, those attending the event had been pressing her, seeking to shake her hand, asking for autographs, and trying to take pictures with her. Whitman's media man, Mike Murphy, was there with a video crew to record the reaction. "She kept her word," Chris Palmer of East Brunswick told the *Record.* "I think it's a great day."

There were a few signs of protest during the celebration. All day long, people wanted to know what Whitman was doing to keep the New Jersey Devils, the Stanley-Cup-winning ice hockey team, from moving south. A fire truck from East Brunswick was plastered with signs, saying, "No Devils. No Whitman." (The Devils eventually agreed to stay for at least a year.) And a small plane crisscrossed the sky with a banner that said, "Christie—Don't privatize the DMV." As soon as Whitman had signed her budget, angry DMV workers who were about to lose their jobs, walked off the job in Trenton. Almost immediately, Whitman began talking tough in an appeal to keep the public on her side.

"You can't expect state government to continue to support jobs that it can't justify," Whitman told the *New York Times.* "That's unfair to taxpayers, and it's bad for government. It leads to the kind of government where each year's job level is the basis for the next year, and you just see it increasingly expanding, and the only place you get the money for that is from the taxpayers."

It is illegal in New Jersey for state workers to strike, and it was clear that Whitman wasn't afraid of a showdown with the state unions. She warned state workers that strikers would face a loss of pay and possible dismissal, and she said that in the event of a strike, she would keep the state operating with nonunion personnel if necessary. The Whitman administration was counting on the public being on its side, reaping the same political benefits that President Reagan enjoyed during the air controllers' strike at the start of his first term. "My gut reaction is that the governor has nothing to lose by a strike," Rider University political scientist David Rebovich told the *Courier-Post* of Camden. "People think state workers are overpaid for jobs where they sit around and drink coffee all day." When the toll collectors on the Garden State Parkway and the New Jersey Turnpike walked off their jobs at the start of the holiday weekend, state workers got an indication of just how hard-nosed the administration would be. At a cost of about $500,000 to the state in lost revenue, motorists were waved through the booths for sixteen hours, then temporary workers and management employees began taking the tolls. After a judge ordered the striking workers back and they saw that the toll booths were operating without them, the strikers returned to work.

The maneuver was a public-relations coup for Whitman. During the walkout, Whitman issued a statement saying that public employees cost the taxpayers of New Jersey too much money. She said the average salary for a New Jersey state worker is about $39,000, plus $12,000 in retirement and health benefits—7.5 percent higher than equivalent private-sector jobs. In addition, state workers get ten weeks of paid time off each year, including vacations, holidays, sick days, and personal days. "We should not ask tax-payers to subsidize public wages and benefits that are so much greater than what they themselves receive."

By early July, the administration had reached a contract agreement with the first of the state labor unions in what was seen as a victory for Whitman. The American Federation of State, County, and Municipal Employees agreed to no salary increases for the first two years of the contract and a flat $1,000 bonus for each of the two final years of the agreement. In addition, for the first time in twenty years, state workers would make copayments on their health-insurance coverage if they chose anything other than the state-approved HMO.

In an analysis on July 5, the *New York Times* wrote: "Although Mrs. Whitman's philosophy verges on the liberal on social issues like abortion rights and welfare, when she deals with the direct heirs to the progressive movement in America in organized labor, she sits squarely with the most conservative of her fellow Republicans."

Whitman continued to build her political capital in 1995 by keeping a campaign promise to get tough on crime. At a ceremony inside the barbed-wire of the Yardville Correctional Center for juveniles, Whitman signed a "three strikes and you're in" bill. Under the new law, criminals convicted of a third serious violent crime would face life imprisonment with no eli-gibility for parole until they serve at least thirty-five years and are at least seventy years old. "Government has a fundamental responsibility to make our streets safe," Whitman declared. Sounding like a tough county prosecutor, she put what she termed a "small group of predators" on notice: "You may think you're going to spend the rest of your life doing crime. We say you're going to spend the rest of your life doing time."

The legislation was expected to cost the state's Department of Corrections $1 billion over thirty years. Whitman had conditionally vetoed the original version of the law, deleting the three-strikes penalty for lesser crimes. As originally written, the bill would have cost the state $2 billion. "We have avoided the pitfalls that other states have fallen into, where someone who steals a pizza can face life imprisonment."

Further boosting her national exposure, Whitman appeared as the guest host on CNN's "Larry King Live," one of the nation's most influential interview programs, in July 1995. CNN producers said Whitman was selected because she was of national interest and because of the "television charisma" she showed during her response to the State of the Union Address in January.

Appearing with three panelists, CBS's Lesley Stahl, NBC's Lisa Meyers, and ABC's Jeff Greenfield, Whitman behaved like a pro while one million viewers watched. Dressed in a bright blue suit, she began the show with the good-natured grousing that comes naturally to her and then grabbed firm control of the show's agenda. When sticky questions were posed about New Jersey's state-run television station and the state's unemployment rate, Whitman deftly signaled for a station break or quickly moved to another issue.

When one caller told her he had left New Jersey because he had lost his job, Whitman responded: "Well, we're creating more."

While New Jersey Democrats, charging that Whitman was driven by her ambition for national office, continued to lambaste her policies, there was little doubt that her 30 percent tax cut had enhanced her popularity at home and her national reputation. "With a recently enacted $16 billion budget, she has cut income taxes as promised in two years instead of three, without shredding local aid or social programs," a July 1995 editorial in the *New York Times* stated. "Small wonder that she is being talked about for the national Republican ticket."

By the fall of 1995, observers in Trenton had begun to call Whitman "the Teflon governor." She was on a roll, and it appeared that nothing could touch her. Even though she had slipped slightly in the public-opinion polls, the state GOP, which traditionally would suffer some setbacks during a Republican governor's second year in office when the bloom of the first year vanishes, instead was looking forward to gaining some seats in the state assembly. While some speculated that Whitman would choose to just rest on her laurels, spokesman Carl Golden said the governor was about to tackle the state's educational funding system, which the New Jersey Supreme Court has ruled unfair to city students. Earlier in the year when the state took over the Newark schools, horrendous conditions for students were uncovered in a system where money was lavishly spent on administration. While Whitman may be hesitant to waste any political capital, the governor who solves the state's educational woes would no doubt be considered a hero.

If Whitman does not seek national office, it is certain that she will run for reelection in 1997. Two years out from the race, with the Democratic party in New Jersey in near shambles, her chances of winning appeared very good. Meanwhile, some political observers were saying her chances were slim of being on the 1996 presidential ticket. Others were saying it was a certainty. Whitman maintained that she was not actively interested in the vice presidency but avoided saying that she would turn it down if it were offered. Political watchers, however, were saying that Whitman could face some problems as a potential vice-presidential candidate if her tax cuts created budget problems for New Jersey. Early in the year, the "Washingtoon" in *Time* magazine showed Whitman on stage in a ballet costume with budget-cutting scissors in her hands. "New Jersey Gov. Whitman danced across the political stage to instant stardom," the cartoon states. "And, oh, those Republicans nationwide fell in love!" One elephant in the crowd said, "A woman VP in '96." Another said, "Let's nominate her quick before there's time to find out if her policies work."

In his newspaper column, William Rusher warned conservatives that Whitman did not even qualify as a moderate Republican, but was "a direct political descendant of Nelson Rockefeller, whose influence had to be extinguished before the Republican party could go on to conservatism." The *New York Times* editorial sounded this note of caution:

> Looked at closely, Mrs. Whitman's fiscal practices reflect less of a
> Republican revolution in downsized government than the same old game

of spending now and paying the price later. . . . A multibillion-dollar transportation program is being funded by new and newly refinanced bonds that are going to drive up the cost of debt service. . . . The governor also "paid" for the tax cut by inflating tax revenue projections and by optimistically assuming that there will be savings from her privatization programs. . . . Those looking for Mrs. Whitman to have a national impact should be watching the economic indicators carefully to see whether the gambles she is taking on taxes and budgeting end up costing taxpayers more money and hurting the state's future financial health.

An even more serious obstacle to the vice presidency could be Whitman's prochoice position on abortion, as antiabortion forces within the Republican party were threatening to boycott any candidate who is prochoice. As early as February 1995, Christian Coalition Executive Director Ralph Reed was saying that religious-conservative voters would not support the Republican ticket in 1996 if either candidate favored abortion rights. According to Phyllis Schlafly, candidates will not qualify even for the vice-presidential slot unless they denounce abortion.

Meanwhile, moderates within the party were warning that if the Republicans put two antiabortion candidates on the ticket, GOP women would be the first to leave the fold, and Republicans could destroy their chance to reclaim the White House. Presidential hopeful U.S. Sen. Arlen Specter (R-Pennsylvania), a prochoice candidate, said 43 percent of the nation's Republicans support abortion rights. He told the Associated Press, "If we insist on excluding about half the party, it will give Bill Clinton his best chance, perhaps his only chance, to win."

In the eyes of a number of national political operatives, Whitman is seen as the ideal candidate to balance the 1996 Republican ticket. She is a woman, a governor from the Northeast, a fiscal conservative with a record for cutting taxes, and a social moderate. "She would balance virtually any of the presidential contenders," said U.S. Rep. Dick Zimmer (R-New Jersey), who served as cochairperson of Whitman's gubernatorial campaign.

Whitman's rise to the governorship and her potential as a vice-presidential candidate, together, are a promise kept in a larger sense of the words. In a personal way, what Whitman has accomplished goes beyond cutting taxes in New Jersey. The little girl who pondered pranks in the sycamore tree at Pontefract has fulfilled her own personal potential, or promise. Even if she were to serve only one term as governor, and never go on to higher office, she has kept the promise that her parents had asked her to keep, to return something to society, to give of herself for all that she has received.

In a sometimes less-than-serious way, the governor who loves to grouse with her children and husband, who likes to sneak away from the state troopers, and who has learned to twist lawmakers' arms like a North Jersey ward boss has dedicated a significant portion of her life "for the people."

On a hot June day in 1995, with no television cameras rolling, the governor, carrying a plastic water bottle in her hand, left her statehouse office to watch professional bikers weave their way through the Trenton streets. A nine-year-old girl from the city approached her on the sidewalk and asked if she would pose for a picture. Whitman walked along the sidewalk, arm-in-arm with the girl, to the location where four other city children were waiting. While Whitman posed for a home-camera shot with the youngsters, no one, except the security troopers and a few passersby, watched. In the true sense of the words, it was a promise kept.

Those close to Christie Whitman believe that she will hold true to the principles that she espoused as a young Republican. She will remain a fiscal conservative, even if that just means cutting taxes. Yet, in the eyes of some, she has fallen short as a true conservative, willing to hack away at big government. On social issues, she appears willing to give up any aspirations for higher office in order to stand by her more liberal positions on abortion and welfare reform. She is a voice of caution to the Republicans, reminding them that people matter. Christie Whitman has hop-skipped to the top of New Jersey politics—jumping from freeholder to utilities president, to senatorial candidate, to governor: an unheard-of leap.

But it is not as if she were ill-prepared. Reared in the Todd household where she dodged the vacuum cleaner on Sunday mornings when her father was angry, argued with her parents over politics, and thrust a hand-sewn golf-tee holder into Eisenhower's palm, Christie Whitman has been taught the lessons of politics. She served in the federal bureaucracy at a time when young Republicans put on work gloves and went into the slums of Washington, D.C., to clean out debris; she donned a hard hat to inspect the construction of a county courthouse; she challenged New Jersey's most popular senator, and almost won; and she sparred with Jim Florio—knocking him out with a razor-thin victory.

Stumbling through her campaign for governor, Whitman managed to keep going at a time when no one thought she could win. When she was down by twenty-one points in the polls and every analyst in the state speculated that she was finished with a month to go in the race, her own Washington adviser said ninety-nine candidates out of one hundred would have hidden under the bed. Instead, Whitman put on her blue jeans and went out to meet the people of New Jersey. Because enough of the people liked what they saw, she became New Jersey's governor. The illegal alien issue tainted the campaign in a larger sense for Whitman, who still feels the shame that her parents would share if they were alive. However, in other ways she has been true to her heritage. She did not flinch when reporters attacked her for vacationing with her family in the middle of a brutal campaign; she went into a conference room with an angry Jesse Jackson and Al Sharpton and emerged as their friend; she stood toe-to-toe with labor leaders and watched them back away.

She has accomplished more than becoming the state's first woman governor, and more than cutting New Jersey's income tax by 30 percent. Christie Whitman's hero is Abraham Lincoln, who in his Gettysburg address talked about the importance of preserving a nation "of the people, by the people, for the people." Christine Todd Whitman has fulfilled her own "for the people" promise.

Name Index

275